Financial Management

Fourth Edition

GEOFFREY KNOTT

palgrave
macmillan

First edition 1985
Second edition 1991
Third edition 1998
Fourth edition 2004

Published by
PALGRAVE MACMILLAN
Houndmills, Basingstoke, Hampshire RG21 6XS and
175 Fifth Avenue, New York, N.Y. 10010
Companies and representatives throughout the world

PALGRAVE MACMILLAN is the global academic imprint of the Palgrave Macmillan division of St. Martin's Press, LLC and of Palgrave Macmillan Ltd. Macmillan® is a registered trademark in the United States, United Kingdom and other countries. Palgrave is a registered trademark in the European Union and other countries.

ISBN-10: 1–4039–0382–4
ISBN-13: 978-1–4039–0382–2

This book is printed on paper suitable for recycling and made from fully managed and sustained forest sources.

A catalogue record for this book is available from the British Library.

10	9	8	7	6	5	4	3	2
13	12	11	10	09	08	07	06	

Printed and bound in China

Contents

List of figures

Introduction

Sound management of the financial resources of a business is essential to its success. The financial manager must therefore have a thorough knowledge and experience of financial principles and practice, while other functional managers will operate more effectively if they have a basic knowledge of the subject.

This easy-to-read book is written at a level appropriate to:

- first-/second-year finance undergraduates and professional accountancy students as an introduction to financial management prior to taking their studies to a higher level, e.g. BA in accounting and finance; ACA, ACCA, CIMA.
- university and college undergraduate and postgraduate courses that require a basic knowledge of financial management, e.g. degrees in information technology and economics, MBAs, diplomas in management studies, and ACCA Diploma in Accounting and Finance.
- managers wishing to enhance their financial knowledge.

The book is structured so as to present a logical sequencing of material, comprehensively updated in this fourth edition. In particular, the chapters on investment appraisal and financial markets have been enlarged, with more questions added to the former.

Each chapter contains exercises and progress questions aimed at dissuading the reader from adopting a passive role, and readers will obviously benefit if they do not refer to the answers before attempting the questions.

For those readers who wish to take their studies of any particular topic further, a 'Further Reading' list has been added at the end of each chapter.

GEOFFREY KNOTT

Introducing Financial Management

The business objective and financial management

INTRODUCTION

■ In this first chapter we recognise the need for all organisations to set objectives – both for the long and the short term.

■ In particular, we discuss the main objective of a business organisation, and then consider the role of the financial manager in planning to achieve this objective.

LEARNING OBJECTIVES

When you have completed this chapter you should be able to:

1 Explain why the overriding, long-term objective of a business organisation is to maximise the wealth of its owners.

2 Describe the role of the financial manager in planning to achieve this objective.

1.1 The business objective

When individuals or organisations elect to use their expertise, time and money in a particular way, they have an objective in mind. The objective governs the decisions to be made.

For example, the management of a football team newly promoted to the Premier League would have the *long-term* objective of becoming top of the league. Improved spectator facilities and planned development of junior players would help in achieving this objective. In the *short-term*, however, the main objective would be to survive in the Premiership. Improved training and the immediate purchase of experienced players would help here.

Andrew Wilson has decided to leave his relatively safe job with a large insurance company to set up on his own as an insurance broker. He will operate from home, and will therefore need only a small amount of 'start-up' money to purchase office equipment.

What do you think will be Andrew's main objective in becoming self-employed?

If we ignore the value that he would probably place upon being independent of employers, Andrew would obviously hope to be better off financially than he was with his previous employer. He would expect to receive a net income, after paying his business expenses, of more than the total of his previous salary plus the interest that he would have earned on the capital invested in office equipment.

The figures for his first year's operations might be as follows:

	£	£
Net earnings from broking business		20,000
less Previous salary	16,000	
Interest on capital invested in office equipment	200	16,200
Net surplus for the year		£ 3,800

Note that Andrew has exchanged a relatively 'safe' income of £16,200 for a more *risky* business income of £20,000. Competition, or a downturn in business, might well reduce his future business income below its present level, and he will then have to decide whether the probability of his future business income being more than £20,000 is greater than the risk of it being less than £16,200. Andrew's attitude to risk will be the deciding factor in the continuance or otherwise of his business.

Andrew's sister Jane, who is the production manager of an electronics firm at a salary of £15,000 per year, has also become restless; particularly so since her recent large win on the football pools. She is considering starting her own business in the manufacture of electronic educational aids.

Premises for the venture could be rented but an amount of £100,000 would be required to invest in machinery and other equipment. Jane estimates that, in the first year, there is a 50 per cent chance of net earnings being as low as £20,000, but a 50 per cent chance of them being as high as £35,000.

Prepare some figures to show how Jane might fare, at worst, at best, and on average, during her first year in business.

Jane's expected average earnings are

$$(50\% \times £20,000) + (50\% \times £35,000) = £10,000 + 17,500 = £27,500$$

	At worst	£ Average	At best
Expected net earnings after providing for all expenses, including the future replacement of her machinery and equipment	20,000	27,500	35,000
less Management salary in previous job	15,000	15,000	15,000
Net earnings	5,000	12,500	20,000
Capital invested – machinery, etc.	100,000	100,000	100,000
Percentage rate of return on capital invested	5	12.5	20

Although Jane will make an economic profit at each level of activity, she must be convinced that the risk she is taking, of giving up a salary of £15,000 plus the return she could expect from an equivalent investment, is worth it. If the comparison is not favourable, after examining her current and future forecasts, she ought not take the risk.

From this last example, we see that a lonely, unrelated figure of *profit* is an inadequate business objective. Profit must, first, be related to the *capital invested* to ascertain the yield on that investment, then the yield compared with that obtainable from an investment of equivalent *risk*. Ultimately, the objective should be to maximise the wealth of the business owner consistent with the risks involved.

If Jane Wilson went ahead with her electronics venture, she would probably reach a point at which further growth in business was beyond her financial capacity. She would invite other people to join her in shared ownership of the business by forming a *limited company*, the term 'limited' meaning that the liability of each shareholder for the debts of the company is limited to the amount of money they have subscribed or agreed to subscribe to the business. These shareholders would not necessarily help in the day-to-day running of the company – they appoint *directors* to do that; but they do expect to receive a share of the profits each year in the form of *dividends*.

Shareholders' expectations do not stop at dividends, however; for they also anticipate that the value of their shares will grow as that part of the profit retained in the business is put to work, together with additional funds borrowed from other people. If these dividend and growth expectations are not realised, the market value of their shares will diminish, for prospective investors in the company will not pay a high price for inadequate returns.

In a free market economy, the main aim of company management is, therefore, to maximise the flow of cash dividends to shareholders, while keeping risk at an acceptable level. Success in doing this will maximise shareholders' wealth – reflected in the market price of their shares.

There are, however, certain constraints upon the objective of maximising wealth, and because of these perhaps 'optimising' is more appropriate. For example, government legislation which curbs the power of monopolies tends to keep prices, and thus profits, lower than they might otherwise be.

EXERCISE 1.3

List other factors that you consider act as constraints upon the maximisation of wealth.

Your list should include:

- Recognition by business of their *corporate social responsibilities*.
- *Government regulation* in the form of price controls (e.g. in privatised utilities), and taxation.
- Investors' objections to what they consider to be *unethical investments*, e.g. the sale of arms to unstable regimes.
- A moral obligation to pay *fair wages* to overseas' employees.
- *Health and safety regulations* in the operational environment, and also applying to the product.
- Support of *local community* sport and cultural activities.
- Adequate provision for employees' *healthcare and pensions*.
- Pressure for more *employee participation* in both management and profit.
- The possibility that company managements, being distant from shareholders, and acting in their own self-interest, may settle for *'satisfactory' rather than maximum profit*; for example, they may prefer to play safe and ignore risky, but apparently highly profitable projects, to protect their jobs.

How can the wealth maximisation objective be applied to services such as health, care for the elderly, and education, given that they all consume scarce resources? The short answer is that it cannot – except where commercially motivated organisations provide these services for people willing and able to pay for them.

In the United Kingdom at the present time, however, the majority of people rely on 'free' public provision, the cost of which is eventually met out of taxation, even though some capital expenditure may initially be financed by commercial organisation by way of government Private Finance Initiative (PFI) schemes.

The allocation of resources to those services is therefore largely the result of political fiscal decisions, which in the medium term are clearly dependent upon the state of the national economy.

While the discipline of a competitive free-market economy may not apply to public sector services, 'value for money' criteria can still be applied to their expenditure by central government. The application of *investment appraisal techniques* to capital expenditure, and strict systems of budgetary control, can help to ensure that overall expenditure is kept within the cash limits set by government.

However, because their outputs are essentially qualitative and not revenue raising, their success is more appropriately measured by performance indicators such as reduced hospital waiting lists and waiting times, and improvements in educational standards.

QUESTIONS 1.1

1 State which of the following is the main objective of a business:
    a increase its market share;
    b maximise its sales;
    c produce the greatest possible range of products;
    d maximise the wealth of its owners – in the long term;
    e survive.

2 What do you consider to be the main objective of the committee who run your local swimming pool?

(Answers in Appendix E)

1.2 The role of financial management

Any enterprise, whether run by one person or many, having a profit objective or not, needs money to acquire resources to operate. Resources include the skills and expertise of people, raw materials and land, each of which is limited by ownership and supply, and therefore commands a price. By this definition money for investment is also a resource – being limited in supply and certainly commanding a price.

Money for investment is referred to as *finance*, and it is available only because it has been withheld from consumption. Finance may have been accumulated and contributed by the owners of an enterprise, or it may have been borrowed from outsiders. Whatever its source, the responsibility for its acquisition, allocation and conservation is largely the province of financial management. Figure 1.1 shows the business planning and control cycle of a limited company, drawn to highlight the part played by financial management to achieve the business objective of optimising the wealth of its shareholders.

Strategic planning concerns decisions about what product or service is to be supplied, and to what group of customers. The resources required to achieve these plans will involve further decisions regarding *investment* and *financing*, followed by an efficient monitoring process to ensure that the acquired resources are being used as planned.

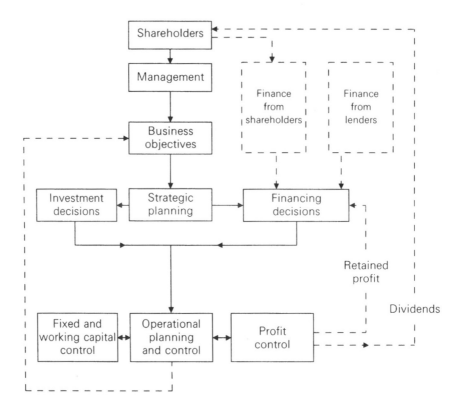

Figure 1.1
Financial
management in the
business planning
and control cycle

The role of financial management therefore embraces:

- *investment decisions* (allocating finance);
- *financing decisions* (acquiring finance);
- *controlling resources* (conserving finance).

QUESTIONS 1.2

The following nine items are on the agenda of a meeting of the management committee of a sports club. Indicate which of them will be of particular interest to the financial manager, stating in each case whether the decision to be made is concerned with financing (*F*), investment (*I*), or resource control (*C*):

1 A proposed increase in subscriptions.

2 Building an additional squash court.

3 Suspending a member of the club.

4 Providing a lock for the door of the equipment store.

5 Applying to the Sports Council for a grant.

6 Purchasing a minivan to transport teams to events.

▶

7 Writing letters to members who are in arrears with their subscriptions.

8 Choosing the players to represent the club in a darts match.

9 Deciding the date of the next meeting.

(Answers in Appendix E)

Investment decisions

To many people, the word *investment* suggests matters worlds apart from their daily lives. Stocks and shares, takeover bids, the *Financial Times* index – this is the stuff from which only the lives of people who are 'something in the City' are made! If we look more closely at the ways in which we dispose of our incomes, however, we find we are all investors to a varying degree.

Most people take out some form of insurance policy to cover risks to life or property. The premiums we pay are then invested by insurance companies in government and industrial securities to ensure that the fund out of which they will ultimately have to pay claims is maintained. Indirectly, therefore, most of us are investors in stocks and shares through our insurance policies.

EXERCISE 1.4

1 List other investment decisions which might be made by the average family.

Some of the following will probably be in your list:

1 Savings in National Savings, commercial savings banks and building societies.

2 Savings invested in the shares of limited companies.

3 Unit and investment trust investments.

4 Contributions to a pension fund.

5 Purchase of a dwelling house and land.

6 Purchase of antiques, precious metals, jewels, works of art and rare postage stamps.

Note that investments can be made in one of two ways; either by:

■ entrusting money into *someone else's management*; or by
■ purchasing assets that *we manage ourselves*.

Insurance policies and items **1–4** above are in the first category, items **5** and **6** in the second.

Whichever way we choose to invest, we expect the original sum invested to be recovered after a period of time, together with an additional sum, in the form of interest, rent or profit, to compensate for the risk and waiting involved. The element of risk in losing our original investment, or in receiving high or low incomes from our investment, will govern whether we put our money into, say, relatively risky shares or into 'safe' National Savings. Individuals with limited resources will, therefore, appraise alternative investments very carefully, with the aim of maximising their potential wealth, whilst keeping risk at the level acceptable to them. Higher risk will only be traded for higher returns.

Business firms behave in much the same way. Whether considering expanding or replacing production facilities, the purchase of another business or investment in the shares of other concerns, the trade-off between risk and rate of return is paramount in the decision-making process, and calls for the application of the most sophisticated investment appraisal techniques.

Financing decisions

Baden Alan, leader of a Norwich venture scout group, was anxious to know whether it would be possible to take twenty of his young charges to the Austrian Alps next year. Most of the boys' parents could afford to pay only half of the anticipated cost of £400 each.

His young assistant Clive, who worked in an accountant's office, offered to help Baden by drawing up a cash forecast for the next twelve months. The statement appeared as follows:

	£	£
Cash held at present		2,000
Expected receipts:		
Parents' subscriptions and donations	500	
Parents' and friends' bingo receipts	7,000	
Parents' and boys' fundraising	3,000	
County council grant for new hut	7,500	
Three-year loan from bank for van	7,000	
Sale of old minivan	2,000	27,000
		29,000
Expected payments:		
New scout hut	10,000	
Replacement minivan	7,000	
Bank loan repayment (minivan)	2,500	
Running expenses – minivan	2,000	
Travelling expenses	500	22,000
Forecast cash available		7,000
less Austrian trip subsidy 20 × £200		4,000
Forecast ending cash balance		£ 3,000

Baden was greatly cheered by this information. It looked as through his trip could go ahead. However, Clive cautioned him. 'Although the grant and loan assist our plan,' he explained, 'the eventual availability of cash depends mainly upon our making the bingo and fundraising successful.'

'Never fear,' assured Baden, 'now we know clearly what our financial position is likely to be, we can concentrate efforts on achieving the forecast cash target.'

From the above we see that financing concerns the acquisition of money necessary to help achieve objectives, and that the approach to financing decisions is, in essence, the same for everyone. Individuals, scout groups and limited companies must:

- assess how much finance they need for long- and short-term purposes;
- have knowledge of, and make efficient choices from, the various sources of finance available.

1 From Clive's cash forecast given above, can you summarise the two main sources of finance, and then divide each of them into two further subgroups?

You should have listed:

- *Internal sources*: (a) arising from the efforts and resources of parents and boys; (b) sale of existing surplus assets.
- *External sources*: (a) loan from the bank; (b) grant from the country council.

To sum up: we finance activities by using either our own money or someone else's. The shareholders of a limited company will either agree to a restrained dividend policy which provides for the reinvestment of profit, or they will subscribe further cash themselves.

Funds from *external* sources come essentially from new shareholders, lenders and government grants, and the financial manager will consult outside advisers regarding the most suitable types and sources of finance. The small businessman would probably approach his local bank manager, whilst the corporate Treasurer would deal with a merchant bank conversant with the wider capital markets. In both cases the package of finance ultimately agreed will be tailored to the requirement: short-term funds for short-term needs, e.g. an overdraft to cover a temporary shortage of funds; or long-term finance for long-term needs, e.g. an issue of shares to purchase another company.

Timing an approach to the market for finance is important both to reduce its cost, and to ensure that it is available when required.

QUESTIONS 1.3

Indicate which of the following statements describes the essentials of financing decisions:

1 Ensuring that the accounts present a true and fair financial view.

2 Assessing the profitability of an investment.

3 Assessing how much money is required, and the sources from which it can be obtained.

4 Comparing the financing arrangements of different companies.

(Answers in Appendix E)

Effective control of resources

Having set his sights firmly on the Austrian Alps, Baden will be highly motivated to achieve the financial targets set for the coming year. He will ensure that investment in the new hut, together with helpful parents and scouts, will yield the expected cash surplus from bingo and other efforts. Running expenses on the new minivan will be tightly controlled; it will be kept in good condition to maintain its secondhand value.

The hut and the vehicle are both relatively long-lasting (fixed) assets, but other resources, such as stores, amounts receivable from subscriptions (debtors) and cash, warrant the same attention. Slack control of stores can cost a fortune. Failure to collect subscriptions will upset cash flow projections, as will excessive expenses – perhaps affected by unforeseen inflation.

These control problems apply no less to business organisations, any differences being ones of scale and environment. It is not enough to acquire finance and convert it into the resources necessary to carry out investment plans. Control is a continuing process.

For example, effective control of resources by a manufacturing company would include:

- Checks to discover whether the *forecast benefits* of past investment decisions have actually materialised.
- Assessing whether *continuing investment projects* should be phased out and replaced by more profitable new ones.
- Maintaining debtors, stocks, cash and creditors at their most *efficient levels*, including provision for inflation.
- Ensuring that *foreign currency dealings* are protected by available market operations, and *overseas investments* managed efficiently.

TO SUM UP

- This chapter has illustrated the need for organisations to be clear as to their objectives, and that the main objective of a business is to maximise the wealth of its shareholders – subject to certain constraints.

- The role of the financial manager in the attainment of this objective is to provide information to facilitate optimal investment and financing decisions, and to ensure that the resources of the business are controlled effectively.

QUESTIONS 1.4

1 Explain whether you agree with the following statement by a business manager:

   'As long as investment appraisal is carried out efficiently, and finance obtained at cheapest cost, we should attain our objective of maximising profit.'

2 It is sometimes claimed that the main objective of a business is to increase its total sales: the more sales – the more profit! Do you agree?

3 State which of the following are the main functions of financial management, and briefly explain the nature of each:
   a Issuing shares
   b Financing decisions
   c Compiling cost statements
   d Keeping a record of shareholders
   e Producing the annual accounts
   f Paying dividends
   g Controlling the resources of the organisation
   h Internal auditing
   i Investment decisions.

(Answers in Appendix E)

FURTHER READING

Arnold, G. (2002) *Corporate Financial Management*, Financial Times Pitman, chapter 1.

Lumby, S. and C. Jones (1999), *Investment Appraisal and Financial Decisions*, Chapman & Hall, chapters 1 and 2.

McLaney, E.J. (2000) *Business Finance: Theory and Practice*, Prentice Hall, chapters 1 and 2.

Pike, R. and B. Neale (2003) *Corporate Finance and Investment*, Prentice Hall, chapter 1.

Samuels, R., F. Wilkes and R. Brayshaw (1999) *Management of Company Finance*, Chapman & Hall, chapter 1.

2 Financial analysis

- In Chapter 1 you saw how financing and investment decisions are vital elements in planning to achieve the objectives of an organisation. These will be quantified as sales, costs and profit goals covering the planning period, and supported by targeted values of fixed and working capital resources essential for the attainment of the plan.

- In this chapter we see how financial ratios used in the planning and monitoring processes are calculated.

LEARNING OBJECTIVES

When you have completed this chapter you should be able to:

1 Specify the five main categories of financial ratios used.

2 Calculate and evaluate individual ratios.

3 Explain the limitations of ratio analysis.

2.1 The need for financial analysis

It is the responsibility of the financial manager to monitor actual performance against planned goals and targets, and for this purpose he or she will rely on the information revealed by periodic financial reports produced by the accounting system.

EXERCISE 2.1

If a company's sales are £2 million more than planned, is this necessarily a good trading result?

Not necessarily; for if the additional sales cost £2 million to produce, no profit will result. Further, even if there is a margin of profit, it might not be sufficient to justify the additional investment in machinery, buildings and stocks of materials needed to support the increase in sales. The profit, as a percentage of capital invested, has to be acceptable.

There must be at least two related figures to yield meaningful information, with the result presented as a ratio, index or percentage as appropriate. Profit, as a percentage of sales, tells far more than separate profit and sales figures.

What range of information is required and can be deduced from a study of financial statements? Given that the three main functions of financial management concern investing, financing and controlling resources, we ought to ask questions to discover whether these functions are being effectively carried out. Four main questions may be asked, shown in Figure 2.1, linked with their respective function.

We now search out interrelated figures in the financial statements, which, when combined and presented as ratios or indices, help most to answer these questions.

The financial information available to interested people *outside* a business (e.g. bankers, stockbrokers and investment analysts) is very sparse. Limited companies are compelled by the Companies Act to publish a profit and loss account and a balance sheet once every year, and disclosure requirements are specified in the Acts. Most companies do no more than comply with the law, but this does not prevent the extraction of some very useful information from these statements. Indeed, since the passing of the Companies Act 1985, most of the ratios discussed in this chapter can be gleaned from published figures.

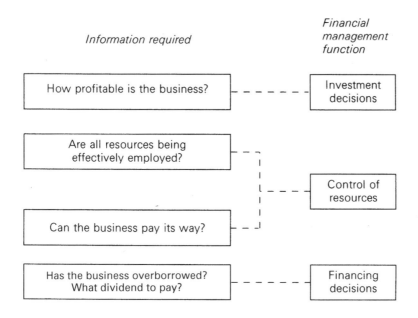

Figure 2.1
Information needed for financial management

2.2 Finance and the limited company

Ten years ago Mary Pike gained a university degree in computer engineering. Then, with financial assistance from her family, and factory accommodation provided by her local authority, she set up in business manufacturing personal computers and other computer equipment. Her success was phenomenal, and continued expansion pushed her total sales to their current year's figure of £2 million. The finance for this expansion came mainly from reinvested profit, some additional help from her family and a recently negotiated bank overdraft.

Mary's friend at university, Richard Newton, had started up a similar business at the same time, but in another part of the country. He also prospered but, because he did not have the advantage of family backing, he had borrowed very heavily during the last year.

Both businesses are now limited companies, but not *public limited companies* (plc), because they are not authorised to seek *public* subscription for their shares.

Their most recent profit and loss accounts and balance sheets are shown on page 17.

2.3 How profitable is the business?

Return on owner's capital

People who deposit money in a building society or savings bank account look for relative safety and ease of withdrawal, and therefore expect to receive only a modest interest rate. On the other hand, owners of business enterprises expect a higher return on their investment because there is a greater risk that they will lose their money. In a limited company this return can be measured by expressing profit, after corporation tax, as a percentage of shareholders' capital.

EXERCISE 2.2

Calculate the shareholders' rates of return from the accounts of Pike and Newton.

Pike: $172 \div 1,000 = 17.2\%$; *Newton*: $125 \div 600 = 20.8\%$.

Newton is yielding a higher return on shareholder's investment than Pike, but three very important comments are pertinent here:

Trading and profit and loss accounts for the year to 31 December 20XX

	Pike Electronics £000	Newton Computers £000
Sales	2,000	2,000
Cost of sales	1,400	1,500
Gross profit	600	500
less:		
Administration expenses	80	60
Selling and distribution expenses	130	115
Directors' fees and salaries	40	30
Interest on overdrafts and loans	6	45
	256	250
Net trading profit	344	250
Corporation tax	172	125
Shareholders' profit	172	125
Dividend paid	10	5
Profit for the year retained	162	120
Balance sheets at 31 December 20XX		
Fixed assets (*at cost*)	1,000	1,150
less:		
depreciation	450	500
	550	650
Current assets:		
Stock	600	350
Debtors	400	250
Bank	–	50
	1,000	650
less:		
Current liabilities:		
Trade creditors	250	150
Tax payable	250	250
Bank overdraft	50	–
	550	400
Working capital	450	250
Total assets	£1,000	£900
Shareholders' capital and reserves:		
Called-up share capital	500	100
Profit and loss account	500	500
	1,000	600
Creditors falling due after more than one year		
15% loan (repayable in 10 years)	–	300
	£1,000	£900

1 Although Newton has borrowed more and has paid more interest on those borrowings, this has been beneficial. The borrowed money has earned more than the net interest (after tax) paid, and the surplus benefits shareholders without any apparent sacrifice on their part.

2 Balance sheet values may be based upon original cost, and profit may not take account of the cost of replacing assets at ever-increasing prices. It is now standard accounting practice for some companies to show separate inflation-adjusted statements, but because this is not universal, published figures must be read with some caution.

3 If Pike and Newton were public limited companies, and their shares were quoted on the Stock Exchange, that quotation would normally represent the true market value of the shares. Theoretically, this should not differ from balance sheet values, but for the reason stated in 2 above, and others to be discussed in the chapter on valuation of shares, it probably will.

Other financial information of interest to shareholders includes earnings per share (EPS), and dividend as a percentage of share value. These are dealt with in Chapter 16, 'The Investor and Share Valuation'.

Return on management's capital employed

To compare how *managers* have performed against planned activity, or with another company of similar size and operations, we have to take a view different from that of shareholders, for four reasons:

▪ Taxation liability is not necessarily a direct proportion of profit. Among various adjustments made in the computation of tax, for example, are allowances for investment in industrial machinery and plant. *Profit before tax* is therefore a more stable comparative.

▪ Capital employed includes not only shareholders' funds but also *money borrowed*. This could include bank overdrafts that are constantly renewed and therefore a permanent feature of the way the business is financed.

▪ Interest paid on loans is not an expense of operating; it arises because of the way a business is *financed*, and should therefore be added back to profit before tax, to smooth out differences in financing arrangements.

▪ Some capital may be invested *outside* the business in long-term investments not connected with its main activity. Interest or dividends received from these investments should not count as *operating* profit, and the capital so invested should be deducted from the total capital employed.

After adjustment for the four aspects noted above, the ratio of management's return on capital employed is calculated as:

$$\frac{\text{profit before tax, interest and investment income}}{\text{total assets}} \times 100\%$$

Calculate the return on management's capital for Pike and Newton. Note that neither company has capital invested outside its business. Also, assume that Pike's overdraft will be constantly renewed long-term borrowing.

	Pike	*Newton*

$$\frac{344 + 6}{1,000 + 50} \times 100 = 33\% \qquad \frac{250 + 45}{600 + 300} \times 100 = 32.8\%$$

Note that Pike has performed slightly better than Newton. This is contrary to the shareholders' ratio which showed Newton coming out on top. The reasons for this can be seen by breaking down this ratio into its components as explained below.

Profit to sales; sales to capital employed

Net profit equals sales *less* cost of sales. It follows that if capital invested in a business is expected to produce a certain level of profit, this can be accomplished only if that capital generates an associated level of sales, for without sales there would be no profit.

By maximising the ratios of profit to sales and sales to capital invested, the ratio of profit to capital invested will be maximised. This can be expressed as follows:

$$\frac{\text{profit}}{\text{capital employed}} = \frac{\text{profit}}{\text{sales}} \times \frac{\text{sales}}{\text{capital employed}}$$

Note that sales cancel out on the right-hand side of the equation.

Calculate the *net profit to sales* and *sales to capital employed* ratios for Pike and Newton, showing them in the form of the equation given above to prove them correct.

Hint: the profit and capital employed figures should be those already used in the calculation of the return on management's capital employed ratio.

$$\frac{350}{1,050} = \frac{350}{2,000} \times \frac{2,000}{1,050} \qquad \frac{295}{900} = \frac{295}{2,000} \times \frac{2,000}{900}$$

$$33.3\% = 17.5\% \times 1.905 \qquad 32.8\% = 14.75\% \times 2.222$$

The two companies make an interesting comparison. Pike has earned a higher profit on each £1 of sales than Newton, but the latter has generated a greater number of £s sales for each £1 of capital invested. Even though their profit to capital employed ratios are almost the same, strengths and weaknesses are more tellingly revealed by breaking the primary ratio discussed in the previous section into its two subsidiary components.

Cost to sales

By digging a little more deeply, and calculating the ratio of each expense held in the profit and loss account to sales, further insight is given into the composition of the profit ratios already discussed.

EXERCISE 2.5

Calculate each cost in the profit and loss accounts of Pike and Newton as a percentage of sales. What do the ratios tell you of the operating performances of each company. and how do they compare? *Reminder:* leave interest out of your calculations.

	Pike		Newton	
	£000	**%**	**£000**	**%**
Sales	2,000	100	2,000	100
Cost of sales	1,400	70	1,500	75
Gross profit	600	30	500	25
Expenses:				
Administration	80	4.0	60	3.0
Selling	130	6.5	115	5.8
Directors' fees, etc.	40	2.0	30	1.5
Total expenses	250	12.5	205	10.3
Net profit	350	17.5	295	14.7

Comments

▪ Although the total sales are the same for each company, Newton has the higher production cost of sales, and consequently a lower gross profit than Pike. This might be because:

a each of the companies sells a different mix of products, some with higher production costs than others, or higher selling prices, resulting in different margins of profit;

b Pike is more efficient in production, leading to lower unit costs, or pays less for its materials and services;

c Newton has not increased its prices in line with costs;

d stock has been valued or counted incorrectly.

▪ The position between the two companies is reversed when expense ratios are compared. Pike is less efficient here and loses some of the advantage gained in production and/or selling.

1 The ratios of profit to sales and profit to capital employed of the Acme Company are 12% and 18% respectively. What is the sales to capital employed ratio?

2 Which of the following statements is **a** correct or **b** incorrect in connection with the calculation of the return on management's capital employed?
  i   Dividends paid to shareholders are deducted from profit;
  ii   Taxation is added back to profit;
  iii Capital invested outside the business, not connected with main activities, is disregarded;
  iv   Interest paid on loans is added back in arriving at profit;
  v   Management salaries are added back in calculating profit;
  vi   Long-term borrowed capital is ignored;
  vii Dividends received on investments *outside* the business are included in profit.

3 The Acme Company reports a gross profit to sales ratio lower than expected. What could be the reasons for this?

(Answers in Appendix E)

2.4 Are all resources being effectively employed?

You saw in section 2.3 that the sales to capital employed ratio measures the effectiveness of *total* asset usage. As total assets include fixed assets and working capital, a further analysis of each of these groups related to sales can help to pinpoint why the overall ratio is better or worse than expected.

What are the sales to fixed assets and working capital ratios of Pike and Newton? *Reminder:* Pike's overdraft is treated as a long-term loan and not a current liability.
  What do the ratios tell you?

	Pike	*Newton*
$\dfrac{\text{sales}}{\text{fixed assets}}$	$\dfrac{2{,}000}{550} = 3.64$	$\dfrac{2{,}000}{650} = 3.08$
$\dfrac{\text{sales}}{\text{working capital}}$	$\dfrac{2{,}000}{500} = 4.00$	$\dfrac{2{,}000}{250} = 8.00$

Because Pike has a lower amount invested in fixed assets, that company has the better sales to fixed asset ratio. A further breakdown into types of fixed assets might be more revealing.

However, excessive working capital investment by Pike gives Newton the better overall asset turnover ratio.

1 A quarter of the value of buildings and machinery shown in a balance sheet relates to progress payments on a new factory that has not yet started to produce. What effect will this have on the sales to capital employed ratio?

2 Why is it useful to break down the ratio of sales to capital employed into asset categories?

(Answers in Appendix E)

2.5 Can the business pay its way?

If you are unable to meet your current commitments either out of cash resources or by borrowing, you are *technically* insolvent. You could possibly pay your debts by selling some possessions or property, but even this drastic action may not be enough. Your total liabilities would then exceed your total assets, and you would be *legally* insolvent.

This need for cash (or liquidity) applies no less to a business, and its 'liquidity' ratios can give some indication of its capacity to pay current debts. The ratios are concerned with current assets and current liabilities, the term 'current' implying that the value will be received or paid within one year.

Current ratio

This is calculated by dividing total current assets by total current liabilities. It has been referred to as the '2 to 1' ratio because banks tend to look favourably, as regards credit, upon firms who maintain the ratio at that level.

Pike and Newton show the following current ratios:

	Pike	*Newton*
$\dfrac{\text{current assets}}{\text{current liabilities}}$	$\dfrac{1,000}{500} = 2{:}1$	$\dfrac{650}{400} = 1.63{:}1$

Do you think that, as Pike has the higher ratio, it is more liquid than its competitor?

It would be if both stock and debtors could be converted into cash *within the same time*. It is likely, however, that Pike is holding too much stock, and that a proportion of her debtors are delaying payment of their debts. For these reasons the current ratio may not be a very sound indicator of liquidity.

'Quick' or 'acid test' ratio

A much better measure of solvency, this ratio relates current assets (*less* stock) to current liabilities. Stock is left out of the reckoning because it is not quickly turned into cash; although this is not so in retailing businesses.

In general one would look for a 1:1 ratio to show that cash or near-cash matches debts payable.

EXERCISE 2.8

Calculate Pike's and Newton's acid test ratios.

	Pike	*Newton*
$\dfrac{\text{current assets (\textit{less} stock)}}{\text{current liabilities}}$	$\dfrac{400}{500} = 0.8{:}1$	$\dfrac{300}{400} = 0.75{:}1$

Rather surprisingly, both companies seem to be at risk in this respect. Things may not be as black as they look, however, for tax payable may not be due for some months, by which time cash will have accumulated from operations to meet the bill. If tax is payable immediately then both companies have liquidity problems, and may have to resort to further temporary borrowing.

Stock turnover

Stock has a considerable influence upon the effective use of resources and liquidity ratios, which we have already considered; but it can be examined even more closely.

Cost of sales in a period, divided by the cost of stock normally held, reveals the *velocity* or *turnover* of stock moving through the business. It is normally expressed as an index, e.g. '10 times'. An alternative calculation of (cost of stock ÷ cost of sales) × 365 shows how many days' sales the stock held represents. The lower the stock relative to sales, the less capital is tied up, as long as there is sufficient stock to maintain deliveries to customers. A low index or high number of days' stock held might be caused by the inclusion of obsolete or slow-moving items, or simply over-production or bad buying.

Too high an investment in stock will therefore not only result in the deterioration of profit to capital employed, but may also be a prime cause of liquidity problems.

1 Calculate the stock ratios of Pike and Newton in terms of both turnover and time.

	Pike	*Newton*

$$\textit{Turnover:} \quad \frac{1,400}{600} = 2.3 \text{ times} \qquad \frac{1,500}{350} = 4.29 \text{ times}$$

$$\textit{Time:} \quad \frac{600}{1,400} \times 365 = 156 \text{ days} \qquad \frac{350}{1,500} \times 365 = 85 \text{ days}$$

Newton is patently managing its stock more efficiently than Pike.

Stock can be further analysed, particularly in manufacturing firms, into raw materials, work in progress, and finished goods. By relating each of these categories to cost of sales, one could discover whether raw materials were being overstocked, whether there are bottlenecks in production or whether there is a decreased demand for the finished product.

Average debt collection period

As with stock, an excessive investment in debtors will lower the return on capital employed, and may also contribute towards the liquidity problems of a business.

The length of time currently being taken by customers to pay their debts can be calculated as:

(debtors ÷ credit sales for the period) × 365

Note that the denominator is credit sales, as debtors cannot be associated with cash sales.

Calculate the average collection period for the Pike and Newton companies, and suggest reasons for any difference between them.

Pike: (400 ÷ 2,000) × 365 = 73 days
Newton: (250 ÷ 2,000) × 365 = 46 days

Here again, Newton appears to be managing its assets better than Pike. If, say, 55 days is the normal period allowed to customers to pay their debts, then Pike has some explaining to do. Her credit control or debt collection procedures could be at fault.

Conversely, although Newton appears to be efficient, his over-zealous collection of debts *within* the normal credit period may be causing him some loss of customers.

Average creditors' payment period

Businesses are normally expected to allow their customers time to pay their debts. Conversely they expect the same treatment from their suppliers of raw materials and services. The average credit period allowed by suppliers is calculated as:

$$\text{(creditors} \div \text{purchases for the period)} \times 365$$

In our illustrative example a separate purchases figure is not given, but as the cost of sales includes materials and services, it can be used to make a comparison between our two companies.

EXERCISE 2.11

What are Pike's and Newton's average creditors' payment periods?

> ***Pike:*** $(250 \div 1,400) \times 365 = 65$ days
> ***Newton:*** $(150 \div 1,500) \times 365 = 37$ days

Pike again shows up badly, and presuming that the normal credit period is 37 days, it rather looks as though it is delaying payment to suppliers to help overcome its cash problem.

(See also Chapter 19, 'Cash Operating Cycle'.)

QUESTIONS 2.3

1 Why is the current ratio sometimes referred to as the '2 to 1' ratio?

2 'The acid test ratio is a better measure of liquidity than the current ratio.' Do you think this is always the case?

3 The following figures relate to an electrical appliance wholesaler. The stock at the beginning and at the end of the year were the same.

	£		£
Sales	1,500	*Current assets:*	
Cost of sales	1,000	Stock	125
Gross profit	500	Debtors	250
		Cash	225
		Current liabilities:	
		Trade creditors	200

Calculate the current and acid test ratios, stock turnover, average debt collection period and average creditors' payment period. Comment briefly on the firm's liquidity position. What have stock and debtors to do with liquidity?

(Answers in Appendix E)

2.6 Has the business overborrowed?

In section 2.5 we used ratios to measure a firm's ability to meet *short-term* obligations. It is equally important to know that a business is not over-burdened with *long-term* debt. Such borrowing does eventually become a short-term repayment or replacement problem, and meantime there is the short-term commitment to pay annual interest on the loan.

The advantage of long-term borrowing is that business owners are able to expand without having to contribute additional funds themselves. They resort to borrowing only if they expect that the profit generated from its use will add to their wealth after the loan interest has been paid.

An analysis of the risks of borrowing are discussed in Chapter 14.

Long-term debt to net assets

The reliance of a firm on long-term borrowed capital can be measured by relating long-term debt to total assets less current liabilities. The following are the borrowing (or gearing) ratios of Pike and Newton:

	Pike	*Newton*
long-term debt/net assets	50:1,050 or 1:21	300:900 or 1:3

This shows that £1 in every £3 of Newton's net assets is financed by long-term borrowing. Pike's borrowing is negligible. Newton is heavily dependent upon borrowing, and if the ten-year loan was repayable at an early date, he could be in financial trouble.

Total debt to total assets

A more comprehensive ratio that shows a firm's dependence upon borrowed money includes *all* current liabilities as debts. This measurement is particularly significant to suppliers who are highly sensitive to risk when granting credit. For our two companies, the relevant ratios are:

	Pike	*Newton*
long-term debt/net assets	550:1,550 or 1:2.82	300:1,300 or 1:1.86

When these figures are compared with the long-term debt ratios, suppliers will see that, although Newton has a higher proportion of long-term debt, Pike is relying upon debt finance far more than was previously revealed. This is confirmed by comparing the two companies' average creditors' payment periods.

Interest cover

The chance of not being able to repay a long-term loan is a relatively *long-term* risk. The *short-term* risk relates to interest payments. To measure the interest paying capacity of a business we calculate how many times interest payable is covered by pre-tax, pre-interest profit.

EXERCISE 2.12

1 Calculate how many times Pike's and Newton's loan interest payable is covered by profit.

	Pike	*Newton*
$\dfrac{\text{pre-tax, pre-interest profit}}{\text{interest paid}}$	$\dfrac{350}{6} = 58$ times	$\dfrac{295}{45} = 6.5$ times

Pike appears to have plenty of reserve borrowing capacity. Interest cover is generally expected to be at least five times, and Newton has little margin over this. Generally the more stable and growing profits are, the lower this ratio could be.

QUESTIONS 2.4

1 What are the twin risks of overborrowing?

2 Which of the following measures a firm's reliance upon long-term borrowing, and which interest cover?
  a Interest paid divided into profit before tax and interest;
  b Total assets divided by total debt;
  c Fixed assets divided by total liabilities;
  d Long-term debt related to net asset value;
  e Interest paid divided into after-tax profit.

(Answers in Appendix E)

2.7 What dividend should we pay to shareholders?

If you examine the profit and loss accounts of Pike and Newton, you will note that dividends paid are modest in each case, and are substantially covered by available profit.

EXERCISE 2.13

Calculate the number of times that dividends are covered by the 'Shareholders' profit' of Pike and Newton.

$$\textit{Pike}:\ 172 \div 10 = 17.2\quad \textit{Newton}:\ 125 \div 5 = 25$$

In each case, it is clear that a policy of retention and re-investment of profit is being followed. However, as shown in section 2.6, while Pike could expand to advantage by borrowing, Newton does not have the same borrowing flexibility.

Dividend policy and its effect on share valuation is discussed further in Chapter 16.

2.8 Limitations of ratio analysis

Ratios can be useful indicators of adverse or encouraging business trends, but they are only *starting-points* in the quest for information. They do not tell *what* is going right or wrong; they merely invite further questions.

In particular, the following points must be noted when analysing financial statements by using ratios:

- One year's figures are insufficient; *trends* are gleaned from a comparison of at least five years.
- When comparing with other firms, ensure that the *bases* upon which the ratios have been calculated are the same. For instance, asset valuation bases might differ.
- Valid comparisons can only be made with firms of the *same size* and *activity*.
- The bases used to calculate ratios should be *consistent*.
- The ratios discussed in this chapter are *not exhaustive*. Further useful ratios will be met in later chapters.
- Note that ratios do not stand in isolation – they are *interrelated*. For example, poor profitability will affect liquidity.
- Ratios relate to a particular *point in time*. Seasonal factors can distort them, and these should be known.
- Figures can be 'window-dressed'; that is, made to look *better than they really* are. For example, loans can be repaid temporarily, and then renegotiated after the production of the financial statements.

TO SUM UP

- The investment and financing decisions of a business will be reflected in its periodic operating statements revealing actual against budgeted results. In this chapter you have seen that financial ratios calculated by reference to these statements, and subject to further investigative analysis, can yield significant information regarding operating performance and financial status. We also saw how such ratios can be applied to compare the performances of two similar businesses.

- However, ratios are only as good as the figures upon which they are calculated. To be credible, bases of comparison must be consistent and unbiased.

Listed below are various financial ratios of JP Tools, an average-sized company in its industry, calculated from last year's accounts. The industry average is also shown for comparison.

	JP Tools	Industry average
Profit to shareholders' capital	17%	15%
Profit to management's capital	29%	28%
Profit to sales	16%	14%
Sales to capital employed	1.8×	2.0×
Sales to fixed assets	4.0×	4.0×
Sales to working capital	5.0×	6.0×
Current ratio	1.8:1	2.0:1
Acid test ratio	0.9:1	1.2:1
Stock turnover	5.0×	6.0×
Average debt collection period	48 days	42 days
Average creditors' payment period	55 days	49 days
Long-term debt to net assets	1.0:3	1.0:4
Total debt to total assets	1.0:2	1.0:2.5
Interest cover	4.0×	6.0×

Note: × = times

Specify the ratio(s) most applicable to each of the situations outlined below, and in each case comment upon the way the comparison between JP Tools and the industry average effects the issue at stake. Assume that each of the circumstances is independent of the others.

1 JP Tools has requested its bank to lend it £50,000 for a two-year period.

2 A new supplier to JP Tools is considering what terms to apply to that company.

3 An investor requires to know whether JP Tools is a worthwhile investment.

4 Because of expansion, JP Tools is seeking substantial additional long-term capital.

(Answers in Appendix E)

FURTHER READING

Arnold, G. (2002) *Corporate Financial Management*, Financial Times Pitman, chapter 18.
Pine, R. and B. Neale (2003) *Corporate Finance and Investment*, Prentice Hall, chapter 2.
McLaney, E.J. (2000) *Business Finance: Theory and Practice*, Prentice Hall, chapter 3.
Samuels, R., F. Wilkes and R. Brayshaw (1999) *Management of Company Finance*, Chapman & Hall, chapter 3.

PART

II Investment Decisions

Investment appraisal – non-discounting

INTRODUCTION

- The whole of Part II is concerned with capital investment decisions. In this chapter we examine the accounting rate of return and payback approaches to investment appraisal, which both rely on the information provided by the traditional profit and loss account, and which are still much used in practice.

- Both of these methods are theoretically flawed, however, because they fail to take account of the timing of cash flows.

- We will examine how compound interest is applied, not only to deal with this problem, but to other aspects of finance.

LEARNING OBJECTIVES

When you have completed this chapter you should be able to:

1 Explain the nature and importance of investment decisions.

2 Describe the accounting rate of return and payback methods of appraising investments.

3 Appraise investment project data by applying the accounting rate of return and payback approaches.

4 Explain the merits and drawbacks of these two methods of approach.

5 Explain and illustrate how compound interest deals with the cash flow timing problem in investment decisions.

6 Explain and illustrate how compound interest applies to other aspects of finance.

3.1 The importance of effective investment decisions

To satisfy the ever-expanding social and economic aspirations of its people, a nation must plan to increase its wealth. This can be achieved only if a substantial part of the national income is channelled into investment, rather than immediate consumption.

Swiftly changing technology in a highly competitive international trading environment also calls for a growing proportion of resources to be diverted into research and development of new, high-technology products.

Governments can influence such investment by providing financial assistance and by creating demand from the public sector; but industry must also play its part by seeking opportunities for investment, ensuring that scarce capital is directed into the most productive uses.

Within each firm, investment decisions are part of an overall strategic plan aimed at achieving the business objective. Care is essential in the appraisal of projects for two main reasons:

- Investment involves a *complete commitment of scarce resources* for a long period, a commitment that may be impossible or extremely difficult to reverse.
- An ever-increasing trend towards the creation of larger business units by amalgamation and globalisation means that serious economic and social consequences can flow from bad investment decisions.

3.2 The nature of investment decisions

Next year's harvest is possible only if some of this year's crop is withheld from consumption to provide the seed for next year's crop.

The finance so essential to all businesses, to invest in buildings, plant, machinery and other assets, is available because they have either withheld profit from distribution as dividends to shareholders, or because they have access to someone else's savings.

Savings are the lifeblood of investment.

EXERCISE 3.1

Mrs Burrows was a prudent lady who had always put by some of her income for a 'rainy day'. She kept her savings in an old stocking under the floorboards of her house, because she did not trust other people to look after her money. What would be your advice to her?

Apart from reminding her to check her stockings for holes, and warning her that there is a very real possibility that her money might be stolen, you would probably tell her that she could do much better by putting it into some kind of savings account. It would be safeguarded and she would still have easy access to it. In addition, she would be paid interest to reward her for deferring consumption of her savings, to compensate her for loss of value due to inflation to some extent, and for whatever risk of loss might be associated with the savings bank.

If Mrs Burrows followed this advice she would be *investing* her money. She would be 'locking up' her savings in anticipation of receiving future cash in the form of interest and the ultimate return of her original investment.

Mrs Burrows' example illustrates the essence of all investment, whether by individuals or by businesses. Let us suppose that she was expecting a 10% return on an investment of £1,000. If she was paid a *certain* £100 at the end of each year for five years, at the end of which time her £1,000 was returned, she would patently have earned a return of 10% per year – ignoring inflation and taxation.

Business investments also normally require an *initial* outlay of cash on such assets as buildings, machinery and raw materials; but thereafter the cash flows generated in each year by the project are part interest and part return of initial capital invested. The acceptability or otherwise of each project is not as easy to assess as Mrs Burrows' investment. Cash flows will probably be irregular and difficult to forecast because different projects are subject to varying degrees of risk.

A further problem is to determine the *required rate of return* on business investments. Mrs Burrows was happy to receive 10% because this was equal to the best alternative opportunity to invest her money at similar risk. Likewise, shareholders in, or lenders to, companies will expect returns on the money that they have invested commensurate with the risks involved. Shareholders will look for a higher return than lenders because, whilst the latter enjoy the safety of a fixed and contractually payable sum, shareholders can receive dividends only if there is any profit remaining after all prior claimants have been paid.

The expected yield rate on investments within a company must therefore satisfy the *cost of capital* requirements of the shareholders and lenders who provide the funds for that investment. We will be examining the question of cost of capital more closely in Chapter 15.

3.3 Methods of appraisal

Accounting rate of return

In the first year in her computer business, Mary Pike relied upon a young, unqualified accountant to keep accounts and provide information for decision-making. However, growth in future years was anticipated to be so great that she engaged an experienced, qualified accountant as her financial manager.

One of the first areas examined by the new accountant, Jim Bowles, was investment appraisal. He discovered that investment decisions were made generally by forecasting the average annual profit after depreciation, over the life of each project, and then expressing that average figure as a percentage of the total capital invested in the project.

Although this method appears to be consistent with the return on management's capital employed ratio (see Chapter 2) Jim was determined to show that this 'accounting rate of return' approach could be totally misleading; he produced the following figures by way of illustration:

Project		A £	B £
Capital invested, beginning of year 1		11,000	11,000
Profit before depreciation:	Year		
	1	1,000	6,000
	2	2,000	5,000
	3	3,000	3,000
	4	5,000	2,000
	5	6,000	1,000

'To keep the calculations simple, I will ignore taxation for the time being,' Jim explained to Mary.

He then produced the following calculations to show the accounting rate of return for each of the projects A and B:

Project	A £	B £
Total profit over 5 years	17,000	17,000
less depreciation (total over 5 years)	11,000	11,000
	6,000	6,000
Average profit per year	1,200	1,200
Accounting rate of return:		
(1,200 ÷ 11,000) × 100	10.9%	10.9%

'As both projects yield a rate considerably below our minimum required rate of return of 15%, they would be rejected if we used this method of appraisal,' Jim said. 'But are they as equal as they appear?'

'Probably not,' replied Mary, '*B*'s forecast profits are the exact reverse of *A*'s, which rather implies that *cash* will be received earlier in the life of that project. This would make *B* more attractive, as the early cash flows can be re-invested sooner – to generate more cash.'

'Right,' said Jim, 'and you are correct to imply that *profit*, which is measured by applying accounting principles, should not be confused with cash flow.

'The revenue reported in the profit and loss account of an accounting period, generated from the sale of goods or services, may not all be received in that period. Conversely, costs deducted from that revenue may not be paid in that period. The capital cost of machinery, for example, is usually paid for at the *commencement* of a project, but is charged against profit, on some proportionate basis, over the life of that project.

'The accounting rate of return approach is therefore unreliable, because it ignores the *timing* of cash flows.'

---

1 Calculate the accounting rate of return for an investment of £5,000 which yields profit before depreciation as follows: year 1, £1,000; year 2, £2,000; year 3, £5,000.

2 Would your rate of return be different, if the timing of profit was reversed?

3 What is the major drawback of using the accounting rate of return as an investment appraisal criterion?

(Answers in Appendix E)

Payback

'Clearly, the accounting rate of return is unsatisfactory for more than one year's assessment,' continued Mary. 'Our approach must take early cash flows into account if only because our present rate of expansion is demanding more and more cash.'

Jim agreed. 'What you are suggesting is that we should look for early payback of capital invested in projects, and this is a criterion that many companies use – either on its own, or in conjunction with some other method.'

EXERCISE 3.2

Assuming that the figures used in the *A* and *B* illustration are *cash flows* not profit – calculate how long it would be before each of the projects recovers its capital invested.

A: 4 years (cash flow for the first four years = £11,000)
B: 2 years (cash flow for the first two years = £11,000)
'As *B* has the shorter payback period it would be preferred to *A*, but it would only be acceptable itself, if it met some previously agreed payback standard of, say, two years.

'The method is simple,' continued Jim, 'but its biggest weakness is that it ignores cash flows after capital is recovered. Let me illustrate this point by introducing another project, *C*, which has the same capital investment of £11,000, and the following cash flows:

Year 1	2	3	4	5
£5,000	£6,000	£2,000	£1,000	nil

'Note that *C* has the same payback period as *B*, and would therefore be just as acceptable on that basis, but that its following cash flows are not as valuable of those of *B*. In addition, even the cash flows within the payback period are reversed – *B* being superior in this respect.'

Jim then summarised the defects of payback as follows:

- Cash flows after the recovery of capital outlay are ignored.
- The incidence of cash flows within the payback period are not taken into account.
- Large capital investments are equated with small ones, if they have the same payback period.

'Payback is still used in practice however, because:

- It is easy to understand and apply;
- When later cash flows are difficult to forecast, it is an appealing way of dealing with the uncertainty;
- It can add some useful information when used in conjunction with more sophisticated methods.

3.4 £1 is worth more now than in a year's time

'It is quite obvious to me now, Jim, that the *timing of cash flows* is at the very heart of investment decisions,' observed Mary.

'If we ignore the question of uncertainty in connection with cash flows for the time being, then you are quite right,' the accountant responded. 'Accounting rate of return ignores timing in cash flows completely, whilst payback only recognises the importance of timing up to the point when capital invested is recovered.

'We somehow have to incorporate the *time value* of money into our investment appraisal procedure.

'If you were offered the alternative of being paid £1 now or £1 in one year's time, there is no doubt that you would opt for £1 now, because most of us prefer *present to postponed* consumption. However, if you were able to invest that £1 at a rate of interest that compensates you adequately for the delayed consumption, then you would be equally indifferent between receiving £1 now and that sum plus interest in the future. At 10% interest you would be happy to receive £1 now, £1.10 in one year, or £1.21 in two years.

'This can be illustrated:

	£
Invested now	1.00
10% interest end year 1	0.10
Sum at end of year 1	1.10
10% interest end year 2	0.11
Compound sum at end of year 2	1.21

'And this can be written as an equation:

$$A = P \times (1 \times i) \times (1 + i)$$

or

$$A = P(1 + i)^n$$

where

> A = the sum received at a future date
> P = the amount invested now
> i = the rate of interest expected
> n = the number of years hence the sum is receivable

'You will probably recognise this as the *compound interest* equation, and also recall that it can be converted into a formula to ascertain the *present value* (P) of a known or forecast amount receivable in n years' time, expressed as:

$$P = A \div (1 + i)^n$$

'Applying the compound interest formula to the figures used above we have:

$$A = 1(1 + 0.10(1 + 0.10))$$

$$A = 1(1 + 0.10)^2$$

$$A = 1.21$$

'Or, applying the present value equation:

$$1 = 1.21 \div (1.10)^2$$

'Using the last equation, an equivalent *present value* can be calculated for any sum receivable in the future, assuming an appropriate rate of compound interest.'

Jim paused, then asked Mary to calculate, to three places of decimals, the present values of individual £1s receivable at the end of one, two and three years, at 10% compound interest.

EXERCISE 3.3

Calculate Mary's answers.

One year	*Two years*	*Three years*

$$P + \frac{1}{(1.10)} = 0.909 \qquad P = \frac{1}{(1.10)^2} = 0.826 \qquad P = \frac{1}{(1.10)^3} = 0.751$$

'Very good,' complimented Jim. 'Now see if you can prove that £0.751 received now is the equivalent of £1 in three years' time, at 10% compound interest, by successively adding interest at the end of each year.'

EXERCISE 3.4

Complete this assignment for Mary.

	£
Invested now	0.751
10% interest end year 1	0.0751
Sum at end of year 1	0.8261
10% interest end year 2	0.08261
Sum at end year 2	0.90871
10% interest end year 3	0.090871
Sum at end year 3	0.999581*

*Not quite £1 because £0.751 is approximate.

3.5 The importance of compound interest

Jim then explained that a good knowledge of the application of compound interest is essential to an understanding of financial theory and practice.

'However, we do not have to explore the mathematics involved beyond what we have already discussed in the previous two pages, because tables exist that can help us.'

He then produced Appendixes A and B, showing:

- The compound value at the end of successive years, of £1 invested now, at various interest rates (Appendix A, p. 319);
- The present values of £1 received or paid, at the end of successive years, at increasing rates of interest (Appendix B, p. 322).

'In each of the tables you will note that interest rates are set out in columns, and the number of years in rows. Appendix A shows the *compound value interest factor (CVIF)* of £1, at the intersection of the appropriate interest rate column and the time period row. Likewise, Appendix B tabulates the *present value interest factor (PVIF)* of £1 at the relevant intersection of interest rate and time,' he continued.

Calculate the compound value of £200 after four years, at 12% compound interest.

From Appendix A, read the *CVIF* for four years at 12% = £1.574
Therefore *compounding* £200 × 1.574 = £314.80 at the end of four years.

By reference to Appendix B, calculate the present value of £314.80 receivable at the end
of year 4 at 12% compound interest.

From Appendix B the *PVIF* at year 4 at 12% is £0.636
Therefore *discounting* £314.80 × 0.636 = £200, which illustrates the connection
between compounding and discounting.

'You can see that Appendix B in particular, can help us in the cash flow timing
problem, by enabling us to convert all future cash flows to *present value*, and thus
providing a common basis for evaluating proposed investments.'

Jim then asked Mary to consider a succession of annual cash flows.

Using Appendix B, tabulate the total present value of £200 received at the end of each
of the next five years, at 8% interest.

Mary produced the following tabulation:

Year	Cash flow	PV factor	Present value
1	200	0.926	185.20
2	200	0.857	171.40
3	200	0.794	158.80
4	200	0.735	147.00
5	200	0.681	136.20
Total present value			£798.60

and pointed out that this calculation could have been simplified by multiplying the
annual sum of £200 by the total of the five years' PV factors, i.e. £200 × 3.993 =
£798.60.

'Quite right,' encouraged Jim, 'and you have also probably guessed that we have
another convenient Appendix, C (p. 325) which shows us the present value of a £1
annuity for any number of years at progressive interest rates.'

'An *annuity* is a fixed annual sum, paid for a specified number of years, assuming a particular interest rate. Its present value (*PVa*) is computed by multiplying the annuity (a) by the relevant PV interest factor (*PVIFa*), which in this case is at the intersection of an 8% interest rate and five years, i.e. 3.993, and confirming the figures shown above:

$$PVa = a \times PVIFa = £200 \times 3.993.$$

'While this last equation is applicable to investment decisions involving *fixed* annual cash flows, it can also be usefully applied to other financial problems, e.g. the payment of a pension, or the repayment of a loan. In each of these cases, a present value (*PVa*) is known – the fund out of which the pension is to be paid, or the loan which has to be repaid by instalments. By simply transposing the present value equation we have a = *PVa* ÷ *PVIFa*. Given that the number of years and the interest rate are known, the PVIFa can be read from Appendix C, and substituted in the last equation to give the value of *a*.'

EXERCISE 3.8

Calculate the annual pension payable out of an accumulated fund of £100,000, for fifteen years at an interest rate of 5%.

$$\text{Pension payable} \quad \frac{\text{Pension fund}}{PVIFa} = \frac{100,000}{10.380} = £9,634$$

Jim then gave a further example of how the present value of an annuity equation can be manipulated:

'When an annuity is known, together with its present value, it follows that its *PVIFa* = *PVa* ÷ a. Knowing this, we can ascertain either the interest rate applied or the time factor, whichever is the unknown. For example, an annuity of £1,554 has a present value of £12,000 at an interest rate of 5%. Its *PVIFa* is therefore £12,000 ÷ 1554 = 7.722. To find the number of years for which the annuity is to be paid, look down the 5% interest column in Appendix C for the nearest factor to 7.722. This is on the 10-year row.'

EXERCISE 3.9

Your bank is willing to lend you £10,000, subject to you repaying it by instalments of £2,504 at the end of each of the next five years.
What interest rate would the bank be charging you?

$$PVIFa = \frac{PVa}{A} = \frac{\text{Loan}}{\text{Annual instalment}} = \frac{10{,}000}{2{,}504} = £3.993$$

Then reading along the *5-year row* (Appendix C) for 3.993 = an interest rate of 8%.

To round off their discussion of the importance of compound interest in financial decision-making, Jim explained that in some circumstances we may need to ascertain the terminal value of an invested annuity at compound interest, at the end of a set period of time. For example, to provide a fund to repay a loan, or to make a special purchase at that time. He then produced another Appendix, D (p. 328), which tabulated the compound value interest factors (*CVIFa*) of an annuity of £1, at the end of each of a number of years, at progressive interest rates. The terminal value of such an investment can be represented by the equation: $St = a \times CVIFa$ where St is the terminal value at the end of a specified period of time, a is the annuity and *CVIFa* the relevant compound interest factor.

EXERCISE 3.10

Calculate how much £300, invested in a savings account at the end of each of ten years at 6% interest, would amount to.

Applying the equation $St = a \times CVIFa$, we have $St = £300 \times 13.181 = £3{,}954.30$

TO SUM UP

■ In this chapter we have seen how accounting rate of return and payback can mislead in the evaluation of investment projects, because they ignore the timing of receipts and payments.

■ However, when these cash flows are converted to present values, they provide a more credible common basis for making investment decisions. This will be developed further in Chapter 4.

■ The importance of compound interest in recognising the time value of money in other areas of financial decision-making was also explained and illustrated.

QUESTION 3.2

1 Grafton Sports Ltd are considering the development of one of two alternative projects, each of which would require an initial investment of £9,000.

The estimated cash flow from each project is as follows:

▶

▶

Year	Project A £	Project B £
1	5,000	1,000
2	4,000	1,000
3	2,000	1,500
4	1,000	2,500
5	–	4,000
6	–	6,000

Required:
a   Calculate the ARR for each project.
b   Calculate the payback period for each project.
c   Which project would the company opt for using (i) ARR, or (ii) Payback, as the basis for its decision?
d   State the arguments for and against the use of each of these decision criteria.

2 Your bank have offered you an immediate loan of £50,000 at 8% interest, subject to your repaying it by equal annual instalments at the end of each of the next six years.
Required:
What would be the amount of each annual instalment?

3 One of your friends owes you £5,000, and has agreed to repay you by equal instalments of £2,010, at the end of each of the next three years.
Required:
What rate of interest would he be paying you?

4 Your parents have agreed to finance a celebratory trip abroad when you graduate in three years' time. The trip is estimated to cost £3,000 at that time, and will be built up either by them paying you (a) three end of year deposits into a savings account paying 5% interest, or (b) one single deposit now into the same savings account, which would be left to accumulate to the required amount at the same interest rate.
Required:
Calculate what the annual deposit should be under alternative (a), and the single deposit under alternative (b).

(Answers in Appendix E)

FURTHER READING

Arnold, G. (2002) *Corporate Financial Management*, Financial Times Pitman, chapter 4.

Lumby, S. and C. Jones (1999) *Investment Appraisal and Financial Decisions*, Chapman & Hall, chapters 3 and 4.

McLaney, E.J. (2000) *Business Finance: Theory and Practice*, Prentice Hall, chapter 4.

Pike, R. and B. Neale (2003) *Corporate Finance and Investment*, Prentice Hall, chapters 5 and 6.

Samuels, R., F. Wilkes and R. Brayshaw, (1999) *Management of Company Finance*, Chapman & Hall, chapters 4 and 6.

4 Investment appraisal – discounting

INTRODUCTION

- In this chapter we discuss how cash flow discounting is fundamental to the net present value and yield rate methods of investment appraisal.

- We compare the two approaches, and show how, in some circumstances, yield rate could mislead the decision-maker.

LEARNING OBJECTIVES

When you have completed this chapter you should be able to:

1 Describe and illustrate the net present value and yield rate methods of investment appraisal.

2 Define opportunity cost in relation to the investment discounting rate.

3 Explain why net present value and yield rate might lead to opposing investment decisions.

4 Show how the concept of present value can be applied to the asset replacement decision.

4.1 Discounted cash flow – net present value

Jim Bowles continued his discussion with Mary.

'You will recall that the basic flow in accounting rate of return and payback was that they did not take account of the timing and therefore the true value of cash flows.

'We discussed how cash flows can be discounted to a common point in time, i.e. to present value. It follows that the forecast cash flows of a proposed investment can be discounted to a *single* net present value (NPV) upon which we can make our investment decision. An NPV of zero or greater would be acceptable, whilst a negative NPV would indicate rejection.

'For example, at an interest rate of 10%, £1,000 received at the end of three years, would repay an investment of £751 now, as well as paying compound interest on the investment for those three years. It would have a zero NPV, and just be acceptable (1,000 × 0.751) – 751 = £0 NPV.'

'On the other hand, if the same investment returned only £900 at the end of Year 3, it would have a negative NPV of (900 × 0.751) – 751 = –£75 NPV and not be acceptable.'

Mary confirmed that she understood the importance of the *amount* and *timing* of cash flows.

'But given that present value factors change at different interest rates, it is obviously important for us to apply an appropriate discount rate.'

Jim agreed. 'If we had used a 12% instead of a 10% rate in the examples that we have just considered, the present value factor would have been 0.712, and both would have returned *negative* NPVs, and have been rejected.

'We should use a rate that is not less than we could obtain from an alternative investment opportunity of similar risk, i.e. the *opportunity cost*. In addition, we should accept only projects with *positive* NPVs, in order to maximise the value of your business.'

In the above example, it is more likely that the £751 investment would generate an irregular pattern of cash flows over the three years, and that the present value of those cash flows would be more or less than £751. The initial capital invested would be over- or under-recovered. The following illustrates this point:

	Cash flow £	Present value factor @ 10% £	Present value £
Beginning year 1	–751	1.000	–751
End year 1	+400	0.909	+364
End year 2	+350	0.826	+289
End year 3	+300	0.751	+225
Net present value (NPV)			£+127

'Because the forecast cash flows from this investment yield a *surplus* net present value (NPV), it would be accepted. Conversely, if the net present value shows a *deficit*, the project would not go ahead.'

Another way of showing this is to treat the initial sum invested as a loan which is gradually recovered over the life of the project, after accounting for interest *on the outstanding balance* of the loan each year – rather like a mortgage loan on a house. The following figures illustrate this treatment:

	Cash flow A £	Interest @ 10% on outstanding balance B £	Repayment of capital A–B £	Investment balance outstanding £
Beginning year 1				–751
End year 1	+400	–75	+325	–426
End year 2	+350	–43	+307	–119
End year 3	+300	–12	+288	+169

'The above table reveals a surplus at the end of three years of £169, which has a present value of £127 at 10% (£169 × 0.751), the same as the NPV in the previous table.'

'Can I check that I have understood you correctly?' interrupted Mary. 'Let me interpret the last two sets of figures.

'If the cash flow generated by an investment during its life recovers the original capital, plus interest at the required rate of return on the outstanding capital at the commencement of each year, then the project is acceptable.'

'That's right,' agreed the accountant. 'In a nutshell – an investment which yields an NPV of zero or greater is acceptable, whereas one that results in a negative NPV should be rejected.'

QUESTION 4.1

For convenience, the figures shown in the accounting rate of return illustration in Chapter 3 are repeated below.

Using a required rate of return of 15%, and assuming that the figures are cash flows not profit, determine whether projects A and B are acceptable or not.

Project		A £	B £
Capital invested, beginning of Year 1:		11,000	11,000
Cash flows:	Year 1	1,000	6,000
	2	2,000	5,000
	3	3,000	3,000
	4	5,000	2,000
	5	6,000	1,000

(Answers in Appendix E)

4.2 Discounted cash flow – yield rate (or internal rate of return)

Mary resumed the discussion: 'You have convinced me that our accounting rate of return approach could lead to wrong decisions, Jim, but I would feel lost not knowing what the rate of return on a project is. A positive NPV is fine but it cannot compare directly with financial market rates of return.'

'That's fair,' Jim said, 'but a yield rate can, in fact, be calculated. You will appreciate that a project with a *positive* NPV must be yielding a rate that is higher than the minimum rate of return, whereas a *negative* NPV means that the yield is less than the required rate. At zero NPV all the capital invested in a project has been recovered, and interest has been paid on the outstanding capital at the beginning of each year of the project's life.

'In order to "home in" on that yield it is necessary first to try a discounting rate and then, according to whether the NPV is above or below zero, choose a higher or lower rate, which we hope will result in the NPV being the "other side" of zero. It really is a question of trial and error.

'The following example illustrates the approach:

	Cash flow £	First trial Factor @ 12%	PV £	Second trial factor @ 9%	PV £
Year 0	–100	1.000	–100	1.000	–100
1	+60	0.893	+53.58	0.917	+55.02
2	+55	0.797	+43.84	0.842	+46.31
Net present values			–2.58		+1.33

'The yield rate of these cash flows is somewhere between 9% and 12%, and can be found by linear interpolation. This simply means that we add an arithmetic proportion of the difference between the two trial rates to the lower rate, according to how much the NPV of the latter is from zero, as shown below:

$$9\% + \left(\frac{1.33}{1.33 + 2.58} \times 3\% \right) = 10\% \text{ (approx.)}$$

'In this example, the investment would be approved as long as the required rate of return is less than or equal to 10%. The discounted cash flow (DCF) yield rate method compares that rate with the required rate. If the yield rate is higher than the required rate, the project is acceptable; if it is less, the project should be rejected.'

1 Draw a graph of the net present values (NPVs) of the above project at progressively increasing rates of interest, commencing with 1%. Plot NPVs on the vertical axis and rates of interest on the horizontal axis.

2 Does your graph confirm the yield rate calculated above?

1

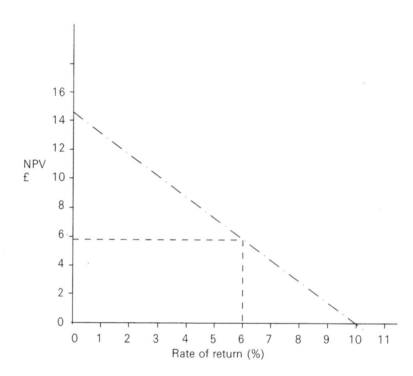

Figure 4.1
Graph of NPVs at increasing rates of return

2 The NPV curve which, strictly speaking, should be curvilinear, cuts the horizontal (i.e., zero NPV) at 10%, thus confirming our previous calculation of yield rate.

1 Calculate the yield rates of projects *A* and *B* used in the Question on p. 48.

2 Explain whether you think the yield rate method will result in the same accept or reject decision as NPV.

Notes: (a) Use year 0 for the beginning of year 1 in all future assignments in this book. (b) Put a minus sign immediately before *negative* cash flow; other cash flows will be treated as positive.

(Answers in Appendix E)

The yield rate can normally be determined only by trial and error, but a shortcut approach can be used when cash flows are assumed to be the same (i.e., an annuity). The present value of an annuity of £1 for increasing annual periods at various rates of interest can be found in Appendix C, the annuity factors simply being the cumulative totals of the factors to be found in each column in Appendix B. The present value of an annuity is the annual sum receivable multiplied by the appropriate annuity factor.

You will recall that the yield rate equates the cash flows of a project to zero. In the case of an annuity, if we divide the capital outlay of the project by the annual sum, we arrive at the annuity factor. Then referring to Appendix C, if we look along the row relating to the life of the project to find the annuity factor just calculated, the yield rate will be the column in which that factor can be found.

For example, if capital outlay is £3,791 and cash inflows £1,000 for each of five years, the annuity factor is £3,791 ÷ £1,000 = 3.791. Looking along the five-year row, the factor nearest to 3.791 is the 10% discount column. This is the yield rate.

4.3 NPV or yield rate – which should we use?

When we apply the *yield rate* method to discover whether an investment is worthwhile, we ascertain the rate of return that discounts the cash flows of a project to zero. If that rate is higher than the *required* rate of return the project is acceptable.

Using net present value (NPV), any project with a *positive* NPV after applying the *required* rate of return to the cash flows is deemed acceptable. It follows that, if NPV is positive, the yield rate must be more than the required rate of return to discount the cash flows to zero.

Figure 4.1 (p. 50) shows the relationship between NPV and yield rate. It shows that if the minimum rate if 6%, NPV is positive at £5.60. The curve on the graph is seen to cut the horizontal axis (zero NPV) at 10%, which is higher than the minimum required rate. Whichever method is used, an 'accept' decision is indicated.

Most investment decisions feature independent projects whose viability will be judged according to whether they can meet the required rate of return criteria. In these circumstances both NPV and yield rate point to the same decision.

However, when we have to decide between two or more mutually exclusive investments (see below), yield rate may rank the alternatives differently from NPV. This may be caused by the different timing of the alternative cash flows, but as yield rate is simply the rate at which cash flows are discounted to zero NPV and not the required *opportunity* rate, it does not indicate how much additional wealth has been created by each of the alternatives. Only NPV can do this!

4.4 Mutually exclusive investments – with equal capital outlays

One way for a business to expand is to purchase the assets of a similar business. A decision to do this would, of course, be preceded by a rigorous investment appraisal procedure, and it is possible that the choice might lie between two alternative companies. The two alternatives would be *mutually exclusive*, in that the choice of one will exclude the other.

Similarly, whether to buy one machine or another, or build one type of factory or another, are also examples of mutually exclusive proposals.

EXERCISE 4.2

A company is faced with the choice of one of two investment opportunities, A or B. The capital cost of each is £200 and their estimated cash inflows are:

	A	B
Year 1	40	200
2	240	60

Assuming a cost of capital of 7% calculate **a** the NPV, and **b** the yield rate, of each project. Which project would you choose?

a NPV:

		A		B	
Year	DCF factors @ 7% £	cash flow £	Present value £	Cash flow £	Present value £
0	1.000	−200	−200	−200	−200
1	0.935	40	37	200	187
2	0.873	240	210	60	52
Net present values			47		39

b Yield rate – A:

		Trial @ 15%		Trial @ 22%	
Year	Net cash flow	Factor	PV	Factor	PV
0	−200	1.000	−200	1.000	−200
1	40	0.870	35	0.820	33
2	240	0.756	181	0.672	161
			16		−6

By interpolation 15% + [(16 ÷ 22) × 7%] = 20.1%

Yield rate – *B*:

Year	Net cash flow	Trial @ 20%		Trial @ 28%	
		Factor	PV	Factor	PV
0	−200	1.000	−200	1.000	−200
1	200	0.833	167	0.781	156
2	60	0.694	42	0.610	37
			9		−7

By interpolation 20% + [(9 ÷ 16) × 8%] = 24.5%

Comparison between the two methods

Using NPV, the choice would be *A*. Using yield rate, the choice would be *B*.

How can we resolve this conflict in ranking? First, a diagram will help to show how the problem arises. In Figure 4.2 the NPVs of each of the proposals have been plotted at progressive rates of return.

Note how the slope of *A*'s curve is steeper than that of *B*. This more accelerated fall in value is because the *later* heavy curve cash flow of *A* is discounted more than the earlier cash flow of *B*. However, up to about 13% *A* remains superior to *B*, and if the required rate of return were below 13%, *A* would be chosen. For all rates beyond 13%, *B* comes out on top whether NPV or yield rate is used.

As the specified rate of return is 7%, and this is below 13%, *A* is the 'best buy', *because it adds more value to the business* after meeting the cost of capital.

Thus, the choice between mutually exclusive projects can best be made by using the NPV method because it will always result in choosing the alternative that adds the greater value to a business.

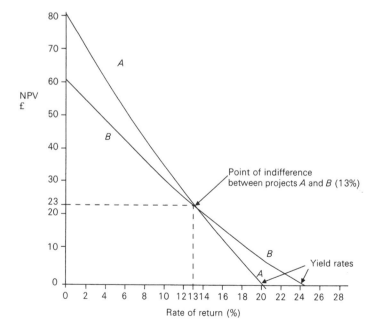

Figure 4.2 Mutually exclusive projects

4.5 Mutually exclusive investments – with different capital outlays

The following figures compare the NPVs and yield rates for investment proposals X and Y. The two projects are mutually exclusive:

Project	Asset cost £	Cash flow per annum £	Life	NPV @ 8% £	Yield rate %
X	5,000	1,200	10 yrs	3,052	20
Y	10,000	2,200	10 yrs	4,762	17

Again, we have reversals of ranking between the two DCF approaches. X has the higher yield rate, Y the greater NPV.

In this case a normal reaction might be to suggest that, although Y has the higher NPV, the additional value results from committing a further £5,000 capital to that project. If this addition could be invested in a project similar to X, total NPV could then be greater than if the whole £10,000 were sunk into Y.

This argument might be acceptable, but only if finance is restricted for some reason. Without such a constraint Y must be chosen because:

- all the capital invested in that project is recovered;
- interest has been provided at the required rate of return;
- there is a net addition of £4,762 to the wealth of the company.

If there *is* another worthwhile investment requiring £5,000, then as long as that project satisfied the cost of capital of 8%, and the finance is available, it should proceed independently of Y.

The weakness of the yield rate approach, as regards mutually exclusive investments, is that it is only a *relative* measure of profitability. Whether the investment if £100 or £1 million the yield rate could be the same. Net present value, on the other hand, is an *absolute* measure of profitability.

EXERCISE 4.3

From the above example it can be inferred that the £5,000 additional capital invested in Y has generated a cash flow of £2,200 – £1,200 = £1,000 per annum for ten years.

a Calculate the NPV and yield rate of this *incremental* investment of £5,000.
b What does the result of your calculations imply?

a NPV:

$$(£1,000 \times 6.710^*) - £5,000 = £6,710 - £1,710$$

*Annuity factor at 8%. (See Appendix C)
   Yield rate:

@ 12% (£1,000 × 5.650) – £5,000 = £650
@ 18% (£1,000 × 4.494) – £5,000 = –£506
By interpolation 12% + [650 ÷ (650 + 506) × 6%] = 15% (approx.)

b The increment £5,000 has yielded an NPV of £1,710 (this can be checked by reference to the original table) and a yield rate of 15%. The latter is better than the cut-off rate of 8%, and confirms that Y is superior to X, for it does everything that X can do, and also adds further value of £1,710 to the firm.

Given a choice between mutually exclusive investments, the NPV approach is safer to use than yield rate, but if knowledge of the latter is needed by management, it can be calculated on the incremental method demonstrated in the last exercise.

QUESTION 4.3

The Phew Cosmetic Co. has to decide which of two tube-filling machines it should purchase. The computed DCF data relevant to each is as follows:

| Machine | Capital cost £ | Net cash inflows | | | Yield rate % |
		Year 1 £	2 £	3 £	
A	150,000	100,000	60,000	43,500	20
B	204,000	120,000	100,000	50,000	18

The managing director suggests that because machine A has the higher yield rate at lower capital cost, it should be preferred to B.

a Calculate the NPV of each proposal, assuming a cost of capital of 10%.
b Which of the machines would you choose based upon NPV?
c Which of the two DCF methods would you advise the managing director to use, and why?
d Is it possible to use yield rate to determine the better machine?
e If the cost of capital was 15%, would your advice be different?

(Answers in Appendix E)

4.6 Projects having more than one yield rate

Most investments follow the pattern of an initial capital outlay followed by a series of cash inflows.

Very rarely, however, a project may have further *negative* cash flows during its life. For example, an open-cast mining operation requiring an expensive reinstatement of the land after the coal has been extracted could result in a negative cash flow in one year. In such cases it is possible for the project to have as many yield rates as there are changes in arithmetic signs during the cash flow series.

If yield rate is preferred by management, how is this problem to be overcome?

EXERCISE 4.4

Using rates of return of 10% and 25% calculate the net present values of the following cash flows:

	Year		
	0 £	1 £	2 £
	–1,000	2,350	–1,375

	Year			
	0 £	1 £	2 £	NPV £
PV @ 10%	–1,000	2,136	–1,136	0
PV @ 25%	–1,000	1,880	–880	0

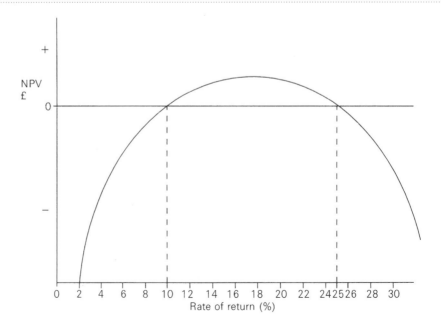

Figure 4.3
Multiple yield rates

As you can see, two yield rates are possible here! Figure 4.3, which charts the NPVs of the cash flows at increasing rates of return, illustrates how this comes about.

Clearly there is no unique yield rate – there are two! However, NPV to the rescue! At required rates of return of between 10% and 25%, NPV is positive and therefore acceptable, outside these the project does not meet the required rate.

4.7 Projects with unequal lives

Whatever the estimated lives of *independent* investment proposals , each one should be appraised upon its own merits, and accepted or rejected according to whether:

- it comes within the *overall strategic plan* of the company;
- it meets the *minimum rate of return*.

A problem of ranking projects according to profitability arises, however, when finance is restricted and capital has to be shared between competing projects. How this problem might be resolved is discussed later in this chapter.

But what of mutually exclusive projects with different lives? The achievement of the common objective by one of the alternatives before the other may present some advantage when the supply of finance is restricted, if the earlier released capital can yield some immediate benefit on another project.

If finance is freely available for all other projects, this benefit is illusory. The choice can then be made by opting for the one that adds more value to the firm – except when the customer specifies a date of completion for the project which can only be attained by the one with the shorter life.

QUESTION 4.4

Corax Construction plc have received an enquiry for most urgent repair work to a reservoir. They estimate that the job can be completed in either two or three years at a contract price of £200,000, payable upon completion of the work.

Initial cost of machinery and plant would be £50,000 or £29,000 according to whether the work was completed in two or three years respectively; with other costs as follows:

Completion time	Year		
	1 £	2 £	3 £
2 years	55,000	55,000	
3 years	40,000	40,000	40,000

The plant and machinery would have no residual value at the of the contract.

Using a rate of return of 10%, but ignoring taxation, calculate which alternative is more attractive.

(Answer in Appendix E)

4.8 How often should assets be replaced?

The replacement of plant, machinery and other equipment comprises the largest group of investment decisions made by industry. The question of when, and how frequently, such assets are replaced is just as important as deciding what asset to use as replacement. As replacement is a question of timing, this is a special case of choosing between assets with different lives. A common example will illustrate the problem.

Next to buying a house, the largest capital expenditure for most people is the purchase of a car. Unlike houses, cars have short lives and have to be replaced frequently.

EXERCISE 4.5

Given that you normally replace your car with a similar one, what are the major financial factors to take into account in deciding to replace your vehicle?

Your biggest problem is probably one of finance; but assuming that is readily available, you would intuitively feel that the optimum time to replace is when costs are at their lowest. The major financial factors to consider are:

- *initial cost* – as an annual cost this reduces the longer the vehicle is kept;
- *maintenance* – increases as the car ages and parts become worn;
- *trade-in value* – reduces with the age of the car (unless you keep it until it becomes an antique!).

Assume that you can buy a car for £5,000 and that its operating costs and trade-in values for four years, at present prices, are as follows:

Year	Operating costs £	Trade-in values £
1	100	4,000
2	200	3,500
3	350	3,000
4	500	2,400

One method of solving the minimum cost problem is to schedule the costs and trade-in values of replacing the car annually, every two years, every three years and every four years. In our example, costs would have to be scheduled for twelve years (the lowest common multiple of 1, 2, 3 and 4) and comparison made between the *present values of the total costs* of 12 one-year, 6 two-year, 4 three-year and 3 four-year replacement cycles.

Adjustments would have to be made for inflation, and the cost of capital and taxation forecast for the twelve-year period – a rather unwieldy and daunting task.

A simpler alternative approach is not to adjust present costs and values for inflation, and to match this by discounting the cash flows for the four alternative life cycles, at a rate which also excludes inflation.

Assuming a 10% cost of capital (excluding inflation) for the next four years, and ignoring taxation for the sake of simplicity, the present values of costs associated with the different lives are shown below:

Year	Cash flows	DCF factors @ 10%	1 £	2 £	3 £	4 £
			Present values of different lives – years			
0	−5,000	1.000	−5,000	−5,000	−5,000	−5,000
1	−100	0.909	−91	−91	−91	−91
2	−200	0.826		−165	−165	−165
3	−350	0.751			−263	−263
4	−500	0.683				−342
Trade-in values:						
1	4,000	0.909	3,636			
2	3,500	0.826		2,891		
3	3,000	0.751			2,253	
4	2,400	0.683				1,639
Present value of net costs			−1,455	−2,365	−3,266	−4,222

Mistakenly, it might be thought that if we divide the present value of each optional life by the appropriate number of years we arrive at the average annual cost. This assumes, however, that the *present value* of equal amounts paid in each of, say, two years, is their sum.

At 10% the present value of £1 paid in each of two successive years is £1.736. Conversely, the *equivalent annual payment* for those two years is not £1.736 ÷ 2, but £1.736 ÷ 1.736. The latter is the *annuity factor* at 10%. Annuity factors at other rates of interest can be found in Appendix C.

To find the *equivalent annual cost* for each alternative life, divide each present value by the annuity factor appropriate to the number of years as follows:

	1 £	2 £	3 £	4 £
	Life years			
Present value costs	−1,455	−2,365	−3,266	−4,222
Annuity factor @ 10%	0.909	1.736	2.487	3.170
Equivalent annual cost	−1,601	−1,362	−1,313	−1,332

Cost is lowest at the end of three years; therefore replacement should take place every three years to keep costs to a minimum.

When to replace with different assets

If we are considering *when* to replace an asset with an *identical* asset, the equivalent annual cost approach discussed in the last section can be used. Replacement assets, however, are very often different from existing assets, both as regards costs and productivity. When these differences are substantial, the replacement decision must be based upon a comparison of replacement cost with the present value of *cost savings* plus the *contribution* from additional sales.

In other cases the decision can be made, first, by ascertaining the *minimum equivalent annual cost* of continuing to operate the existing asset for one, two, three or more years; then comparing this with the *lowest* equivalent annual cost of the replacement machine.

For example, the figures below relate to an existing machine:

Years	0 £	1 £	2 £	3 £
Sale value of machine	3,000	2,000	1,200	500
Operating costs		1,000	1,600	1,900

EXERCISE 4.6

Assuming a cost of capital of 10% and ignoring taxation, calculate the equivalent annual costs of running the machine for a further one, two and three years.

Hint: treat the present sale value of the machine, £3,000, as an initial cost of continuing for *each* of the alternative periods. Otherwise, schedule the figures in exactly the same way as illustrated in the last section.

Year	Cash flows £	DCF factors @ 10%	Present values of continuing for			(Years)
			1 £	2 £	3 £	
0	−3,000	1.000	−3,000	−3,000	−3,000	
1	−1,000	0.909	−909	−909	−909	
2	−1,600	0.826		−1,322	−1,322	
3	−1,900	0.751			−1,427	
Trade-in values:						
1	2,000	0.909	1,818			
2	1,200	0.826		991		
3	500	0.751			376	
Present value of net costs			−2,091	−4,240	−6,282	
Annuity factor @ 10%			0.909	1.736	2.487	
Equivalent annual cost			−2,300	−2,442	−2,526	

Having obtained this information, we compare it with the equivalent annual costs of the replacement machine.

For example, if the minimum annual cost of the new machine is £2,000 for a five-year life, the existing machine should be replaced immediately, as its lowest annual running cost is £2,300 at the end of the first year.

TO SUM UP

■ Net present value (NPV) and yield rate are time-related approaches for assessing proposed investments, and both signal the same decisions in dealing with *single* investments.

■ However, in the case of mutually exclusive proposals, the two rules could suggest opposing decisions. In these circumstances, NPV is normally preferred because it indicates how much additional wealth will be generated by the investment. This accords with the business objective of wealth maximisation.

QUESTIONS 4.5

1 Assume that the new machine referred to in Exercise 4.6 has a five-year life, and that its minimum equivalent annual cost is £2,460 in year 4. When would you replace the existing machine?

2 Appraisal data relevant to two mutually exclusive projects is given below:

Project	Annual cash flow £	Capital cost £	Life years	NPV @ 8% £	Yield rate %
A	100	502	10	169	15
B	144	780	10	189	13

  a Which project would you choose, and why?
  b If a manager insisted that yield rate be used for appraisal purposes, how would you demonstrate its use?

3 A series of investment cash flows could yield more than one rate of return. When might this be so? How can such an investment be appraised?

4 The optimum replacement cycle for assets that are in continuous use by an organisation, and are replaced by similar assets, such as cars, can be calculated by:
  a dividing the net present value of costs of each possible life by the appropriate number of years;
  b choosing the life with lowest arithmetic average operating costs;

▶

c dividing the net present value of costs of each possible life by the appropriate annuity factor;

d dividing the total net costs of each possible life by the appropriate number of years.

Which of **a**, **b**, **c** or **d** is correct?

(Answers in Appendix E)

FURTHER READING

Arnold, G. (2002) *Corporate Financial Management*, Financial Times Pitman, chapters 2 and 3.

Lumby, S. and C. Jones (1999) *Investment Appraisal and Financial Decisions*, Chapman & Hall, chapters 4, 5 and 6.

McLaney, E. (2000) *Business Finance: Theory and Practice*, Prentice Hall, chapters 4 and 5.

Pike, R. and B. Neale (2003) *Corporate Finance and Investment*, Prentice Hall, chapters 3, 5 and 6.

Samuels, R., F. Wilkes and R. Brayshaw (1999) *Management of Company Finance*, Chapman & Hall, chapters 4 and 5.

Investment appraisal – cash flow

INTRODUCTION

- In this chapter we examine the concept of 'cash flow' a little more closely.
- We then look at how the recovery of working capital, and the imposition of taxation are incorporated into investment cash flows.
- Finally, we discuss how inflation affects cash flows over time, and consider the adjustments that can be made to deal with its impact on investment decisions.

LEARNING OBJECTIVES

When you have completed this chapter you should be able to:

1 Describe and apply the main rules for determining the cash flows relevant to a proposed investment.

2 Explain the cash flow effects of an investment in working capital.

3 Describe and illustrate the effects of taxation on investment cash flows.

4 Define and calculate from given data, the 'money' and 'real' rates of inflation.

5 Explain and incorporate the effects of inflation on investment cash flows.

5.1 What do we mean by 'cash flow'

Forecasts of market size, market share, selling prices, cost of capital and operating costs involve skilled and painstaking work before final figures emerge. The arithmetic of DCF is simple but if the underlying figures and assumptions are suspect, the relative sophistication of discounting will be wasted.

When compiling proposed investment cash flows, three principles apply:

- Include *incremental* cash flows only; that is, those that will occur because the project goes ahead. Accordingly, costs such as rent and rates, which are already incurred or committed, will not be included in individual projects. This would not be so, of course, if a new building were to be rented specifically for a new project.

▪ Include any *cash flow changes* caused by the investment decision. For example, a warehouse that might be used for a proposed project could alternatively be let. The rent foregone is an opportunity cost treated as a cash flow resulting from the investment decision. All cost savings and increases in sales receipts will be included.

▪ Do not confuse *profit with cash*. In particular, depreciation is normally deducted as a cost in profit measurement each year. In investment terms, depreciation should not be treated as an *annual* cash flow, because it relates to assets normally purchased and paid for at the commencement of a project.

The relationship between cash flow and profit measurement requires a closer examination. The statement below shows the orthodox calculation of profit attributable to a proposed investment, followed by some notes regarding its compilation:

	Year			
	1 £	2 £	3 £	4 £
Sales	10,000	8,000	8,000	6,000
Variable costs	5,000	4,000	4,000	3,000
Fixed costs	2,500	2,500	2,500	2,500
Net profit	2,500	2,500	1,500	500

Notes:

1 Included in fixed costs each year are amounts for:
   a *depreciation* of £1,500 for a new machine to be bought especially for the project at a total of £6,000;
   b hire of machine specifically for the project – £500;
   c an allocation of the establishment and administration costs which are already incurred – £500.

2 Variable costs includes £600 wages payable to skilled workers who would be idle but still employed by the company if this project did not proceed.

3 Sales of £2,000 in year 1 will not be paid for by a customer until the end of year 2.

4 If the project did not go ahead, the space it would otherwise occupy could be let for an annual rental of £300.

5 If the new machine was bought, an old machine would be sold for £400.

6 The new machine would have a scrap value of £500 at the end of year 4.

Make a brief note of how each of the items listed above should be treated in your compilation of *investment* cash flows, bearing in mind the principles mentioned earlier in the section.

1 a *Depreciation* – exclude from annual cash outflows. Cost of the machine to be shown as purchased at the beginning of year 1.
   b *Machine hire* – include as an incremental cash outflow.
   c *Allocated administrative costs* – exclude as a cost; will be expended anyway.
2 *Skilled workers' wages* – exclude; will be paid to workers regardless of this project.
3 *Sales* – transfer £2,000 to year 2 cash inflow.
4 *Rent receivable* – *opportunity cost*; include as an outflow.
5 *Sale of old machine* – bring in as a cash inflow at the commencement of the project.
6 *Salvage value of new machine* – bring in as an inflow of cash at the end of the project's life.

Assuming a rate of return of 15%, and using the adjusted relevant cash flows in the above example, show by calculating the net present value, whether the new machine should be purchased.

		Year				
	0	*1*	*2*	*3*	*4*	*NPV*
Capital cost	⎰−6,000 ⎱ −400					
Sales		8,000	10,000	8,000	6,000	
Variable costs		−4,400	−3,400	−3,400	−2,400	
Machine hire		−500	−500	−500	−500	
Rent (opportunity cost)		−300	−300	−300	−300	
Machine salvage					500	
Net cash flow	−5,600	2,800	5,800	3,800	3,300	
DCF factor @ 15%	1,000	0.870	0.756	0.658	0.572	
Present values	−5,600	2,436	4,385	2,500	1,888	5,609

Notes:
1 Capital or revenue cash outflows at the start of the project are shown as 'year 0', since they are assumed to have occurred on 1 January in the first year.
2 Although it does not apply to this project, capital outflows occurring other than at the beginning should be included in the year in which they happen.

3 Revenue cash flows, in or out, are assumed to take place at the year end, to coincide with the discount rate factors which also relate to the year end. This is normally an acceptable approximation but, if shorter-period discounting is more appropriate to certain types of investment decisions, tables of such rates can be obtained.

QUESTION 5.1

State, with reasons, whether each of the following items should be included in the forecast cash flows of an investment proposal:

a Depreciation of the machine to be specially purchased for the project;

b Cost savings resulting from the implementation of the project;

c The salary of a supervisor who is currently employed by the firm, and who will continue to be so;

d An increase in the sales of other products, consequent upon going ahead with the new project;

e The book value of an existing machine which will be replaced by the new machine.

(Answers in Appendix E)

5.2 Working capital

The resources used by an investment, particularly in manufacturing businesses, include not only buildings, plant and machinery but also increases in working capital; extra stocks of raw materials and work in progress to support the manufacturing operations; additional stocks of finished goods and debtors to support the selling function. Cash will be expended in the early years of a project to build up these resources but, because it is working capital and not machinery that will be worn out by the end of the project life, most of it will be recovered – probably in the project's last year, save for losses normally associated with working capital, such as bad debts and stock spoilage or waste.

QUESTION 5.2

Paul Schofield wants to lease a shop for three years to sell cassette tapes and CDs. The shop rental is very low at £500 per annum payable in arrears, but he estimates he will have to purchase initial stock costing £10,000. Thereafter, he will replenish stock sold on a weekly basis.

He estimates the net cash flow from product sales – that is, cash sales less the direct cost of the goods sold – will be:

▶

▶

	£
Year 1	7,000
Year 2	8,000
Year 3	9,000

Assuming that he will recover 90% of his stock value by the end of year 3, and that other annual operating costs will be £3,000, should Paul open his shop? His required rate of return is 18%.

(Answer in Appendix E)

5.3 The effect of taxation on cash flows

Inexorably, the Inland Revenue will take their slice from investment cash flows. It is true that, as individuals, we are entitled to certain personal allowances against income, but beyond that taxation will reduce our net cash flows, at the standard rate of income tax at first, then at progressively higher rates.

Limited companies pay corporation tax on their assessable profits at a standard rate, currently 30% (2003/4), with some relief for companies not reaching a certain level of profit.

Some relief, however, is afforded to businesses which, though not allowed to deduct depreciation from profit, are allowed to deduct capital allowances against profit for new plant and machinery, industrial buildings, equipment and motor cars at the following rates (2003/4).

	Capital allowances on cost
Plant, machinery and equipment	25% per annum on reducing cost
Motor cars	25% per annum on reducing cost
Industrial buildings	4% per annum on cost over 25 years

Note: For 2003/4 small and medium-sized businesses have a first year allowance of 40% of the cost of new plant and machinery, followed by 25% per annum on the reducing balance of cost.

It will be appreciated that tax rates and allowances are changed from time to time. In line with other project cash flows, it is important that effect is given to taxation when it is actually paid. A one-year time-lag is normally associated with taxation payable on project cash flows. Conversely, capital allowances on project assets will *reduce* the taxation payable, and should be recorded as cash inflows, again time-lagged by one year after the relevant assets are paid for. This implies that any capital asset purchased *during* year 1 will affect tax paid in year 2.

Further, when assets which have previously attracted capital allowances are eventually sold for scrap or are traded in, tax is payable on the amount received.

As an example of the effect of taxation upon investments, the cash flows shown in the Exercise 5.2 (p. 65) are repeated below, with an assumed corporation tax rate of 50% applied to capital allowances, and net revenue cash flows:

			Year				
	0	1	2	3	4	5	NPV
Capital cost	−5,600				500	−250	
Capital allowances			2,800				
Taxable net cash flows		2,800	5,800	3,800	2,800		
Corporation tax			−1,400	−2,900	−1,900	−1,400	
Net cash flow	−5,600	2,800	7,200	900	1,400	−1,650	
DCF factor @ 15%	1,000	0.870	0.756	0.658	0.572	0.497	
Present values	−5,600	2,436	5,443	592	801	−820	2,852

Even after adjustment for taxation this proposal still looks good, thanks largely to the early cash inflow from the capital allowance. A point to note from this example is the additional year 5 brought in to accommodate the negative cash flows arising from the tax payment time-lag, the assumption being that the company is in an overall tax-paying position in that year, and indeed in every year of the project's life.

If the company had not been paying tax on its overall activities at the start of the project, and perhaps for a year or two more, so that the otherwise taxable cash flows of this project were absorbed by losses elsewhere, corporation tax would not be shown as paid for those years. Likewise the capital allowances would be carried forward until a year in which profits exist for them to be set off against.

QUESTIONS 5.3

1 Explain whether the taxation effects of the following either increase or decrease the net present value of an investment:
   i   capital allowances;
   ii cost savings;
   iii incremental costs.

2 'When compiling investment cash flows, adjustments for taxation allowances or deductions are made in the same year as the cash flows to which they relate.' Is this statement correct? Explain.

3 At the end of its useful life it is expected that an electric kiln can be sold for £5,000. Its cost now is £50,000. In the investment appraisal cash flows, would it be correct to show £45,000 as the net cost of the kiln in year 0?

4 If the company contemplating installing the kiln is expected to be in its current non-tax-paying position for the next four years, what affect would this have on your answer to question 3?

(Answers in Appendix E)

5.4 Investment appraisal and inflation

If businesses are to prosper they must manage inflation successfully. They must ensure that costs are controlled and that any unavoidable increases in costs of materials, labour and overheads are anticipated and reflected in selling price policy.

If the rate of inflation is expected to be zero for the foreseeable future, investors will expect rates of return on their investments solely related to the *risks* to which their money is exposed – risks both of operations and time. An investor may happily accept such a *real* rate of return of, say, 5% knowing that his £100 investment will grow to £105 in one year.

However, if the general level of prices is expected to increase by 10% in the coming year, the investor would look for a return of approximately 15% to maintain his purchasing power in real terms. The 15% he would receive is known as the 'money' or 'nominal' rate of interest. If the inflation forecast proved to be correct, the 'real' rate of return would be his risk-related 5%. If, on the other hand, the inflation rate was 12%, the investor's real rate of return would be only 15% – 12% = 3%.

A more accurate *real* rate can be calculated by using the following formula:

$$r = ((1 + m) \div (1 + p)) - 1$$

where

r = the real rate of return
m = the money rate of return
p = the rate of inflation

Substituting the figures in the last line of the previous paragraph, we have:

$$r = [(1 + 0.15) \div (1 + 0.12)] - 1 = 2.7\%$$

To find the money rate of interest when the real rate and the inflation rate are given, the above formula can be translated to:

$$1 + m = (1 + r)(1 + p)$$

Thus if the real rate is 6% and inflation expected to be 8%, investors would look for a money rate of return of:

$$1 + m = (1 + 0.06)(1 + 0.08)$$

and

$$1 + m = 1.14$$
$$m = 0.14 \text{ or } 14\%$$

If business projects cannot satisfy investors' expected *money* rates of return, finance will not be forthcoming. It follows that investment cash flows must be stated in *money* terms, at the actual £s expected to flow during each period of a project's life, *because the required rate of return incorporates expectations of inflation over the same period*. We will then be matching inflation-adjusted cash flows with an inflation-priced rate of return.

EXERCISE 5.3

Ultra Engineering plc wants to purchase a machine costing £80,000 to produce a component for the motor car industry. At *present prices and costs* annual cash inflows from this five-year venture are expected to be £20,000, and at the end of five years the machine could be sold for £5,000 at present prices. The company's target rate of return over this five-year period is 12%. Using only the information given, show by calculating its NPV whether the project should be accepted. Ignore taxation.

Year	Machine £	Annual cash flow £	PV factors @ 12% £	Present value £
0	−80,000		1.000	−80,000
1–5		20,000	3.605*	72,100
5	5,000		0.567	2,835
Net present value				−5,065

*Annuity factor for five years, see Appendix C.

On the basis of the information given, the investment should not proceed because it yields a negative NPV.

However, we may not have been consistent in our appraisal if inflation is expected to continue at a compound rate of 5% per annum during the next five years. The target rate of 12% presumably takes inflation into account, and therefore the project cash flows ought also to be adjusted for inflation.

EXERCISE 5.4

Reappraise the Ultra proposal taking into account a 5% compound rate of inflation on all cash flows.

Year	Machine £	Annual cash flows £	Net cash flow £	PV factors @ 12% £	Present value £
0	−80,000		−80,000	1,000	−80,000
1		20,000 × 1.05 = 21,000	21,000	0.893	18,753
2		21,000 × 1.05 = 22,050	22,050	0.797	17,574
3		22,050 × 1.05 = 23,153	23,153	0.712	16,485
4		23,153 × 1.05 = 24,310	24,310	0.636	15,461
5	6,381*	23,310 × 1.05 = 25,526	31,907	0.567	18.091
Net present value					6,364

*$5,000 (1.05)^5 = £6,381$

Inflation does not affect all cash flows at the same rate. For example, capital allowances are delayed in their effect upon tax cash flows, but as they are related to a *fixed* number of £s, no adjustment for inflation is made when the allowances are eventually deducted from tax paid.

Selling prices that are fixed by long-term contract, real wages and costs of energy-related resources are all examples of cash flows that may deviate from the general movement in the level of prices during the life of a project.

The section on working capital indicated that additional stocks of materials might be occasioned by the acceptance of a new project. Such stocks will have to be replaced continually at inflated prices, but this can be taken care of in the forecast cash flow related to purchases. In the final year of a project, the rundown of these stocks will be shown as an inflation-adjusted cash inflow, and not at the prices paid at the commencement of the project.

TO SUM UP

■ In this chapter we have seen that the cash flows relevant to an investment project are only those that are triggered by the decision to proceed with that project. For example, they do not include costs of resources, such as rented warehouse property, that the investing organisation is already committed to incur.

■ We also saw how the recovery of working capital, the amount and timing of project taxation and inflation can affect project cash flows significantly.

QUESTIONS 5.4

1 a Using the appropriate formula, calculate to three places of decimals the real rate of return on a security if the money rate is 19% and the rate of inflation 12%.

   b Using the same formula, calculate the money rate required to satisfy a real rate of 4% with a rate of inflation of 10%.

▶

▶

2 'If a company's required rate of return is applied to investment cash flows compiled at today's prices, the resulting NPV will indicate whether or not to accept the proposal.' Is this statement correct? Explain.

3 Pike Electronics were attempting to break into the video game market. Mary Pike designed a low-cost box and display, with associated electronics, and ten original video games can be purchased from a software house, at a cost of £50,000.

Machinery to manufacture the video boxes will cost £100,000 now, but at the end of five years will only fetch £5,000 at today's prices, on the second-hand market. Additional working capital of £20,000 will be required immediately, all recoverable at the end of year 5.

Factory space to manufacture the games can be created by giving up space devoted to manufacture of a component that would currently cost £1,000 a year more to purchase from an outside supplier. Machinery used in the making of this component would be sold for £10,000 immediately.

At present, rates, heating and lighting costs on this part of the factory are £500 per annum.

Sales are forecast at 2,000 video games a year for five years, and each game would be sold for £80 in the first year. It is expected, however, that this price can be raised by £5 in each of the following four years, to recoup rising costs, despite increasing competition.

The variable manufacturing and selling cost of each video game, at present prices of materials, labour and overheads, is £50. Additional supervisory costs of £2,000 per annum (at current cost) would be needed for the new project.

5% inflation is expected in each of the five years.

Pike will continue to be in a tax-paying position for the next six years, and she currently pays corporation tax of 50% on her assessable profits.

Machinery attracts 100% capital allowances, whilst the software purchases can be written off against profits for taxation purposes, in equal instalments over five years.

Pike requires a rate of return of 15%.

Required:

Prepare net present value calculations to help Mary Pike decide whether she should proceed with this project.

(Answers in Appendix E)

FURTHER READING

Arnold, G. (2002) *Corporate Financial Management*, Financial Times Pitman, chapters 3 and 5.

Lumby, S. and C. Jones (1999) *Investment Appraisal and Financial Decisions*, Chapman & Hall, chapter 7.

McLaney, E.J. (2000) *Business Finance: Theory and Practice*, Prentice Hall, chapter 5.

Pike, R. and B. Neale (2003) *Corporate Finance and Investment*, Prentice Hall, chapter 6.

Samuels, R., F. Wilkes and R. Brayshaw (1999) Management of Company Finance, Chapman & Hall, chapter 5.

6 Dealing with risk in investment decisions

INTRODUCTION

■ Climbers on Everest are said to take 'calculated risks'. They reduce the chance of failure by rigorous training. They use the best equipment, plan their expeditions to a fine degree, attempt only viable, if dangerous, routes on the mountain and climb only in acceptable weather conditions. When they have reduced risk to an acceptable level, they proceed with their venture.

■ Most of us prefer the lower slopes; the satisfaction is not so great, but neither is the risk.

■ Although the relationship between reward and risk was introduced in Chapters 1 and 2, when we considered investment appraisal in Chapter 4 we unrealistically assumed that future cash flows are known with certainty. Now this may be so with a fixed-interest government security, but it certainly will not be the case with a speculative goldmining operation. Investors should therefore consider not only the net present value (NPV) of a project, but also the risk that its NPV could vary according to the economic political and other conditions prevailing at the time of the operations. People who subject their capital to high risk will expect high rewards.

■ However not everyone is prepared to take the same chances. Our *risk preferences* vary, and as investors we must judge that the likelihood of loss, set against the likelihood of gain, is an *acceptable* risk.

■ In this chapter, we discuss how the rational investor, like the mountaineer, might take account of the uncertainties accompanying his decisions by:

1 measuring and analysing the risk involved;

2 reducing avoidable risk;

3 matching unavoidable risk to his or her own risk preferences.

When you have completed this chapter you should be able to:

1 Explain the nature of risk.

2 Discuss and illustrate the application of statistical analysis in the measurement of risk.

3 Describe and apply sensitivity analysis to proposed investment cash flows.

4 Discuss payback as a risk-screening device.

5 Explain the application of risk-adjusted discount rates to investment cash flows.

6 Discuss how risk can be reduced by appropriate administrative action or diversification.

7 Explain how an investor in Stock Market securities may use the *capital asset pricing model* (CAPM) to adjust the risk of his or her investment portfolio.

6.1 Utility – the essence of risk

£1 to a starving man yields him more satisfaction than it would to a rich person. Conversely the starving man has a lot more to lose if the £1 is not available to him.

EXERCISE 6.1

Suppose you are offered two alternative opportunities to invest £5,000 for one year. Which of *A* or *B* below would you choose, assuming that you recover your £5,000 in each case?

Alternative *A* would yield a *certain* net return of £3,000. Alternative *B* has a 0.5 probability of a net return of £2,000, and a 0.5 probability of a net return of £4,000.

Most people, being risk-averse, would choose alternative *A*, and if asked why, they would probably reply that they preferred the *certain* to the uncertain return. They would be implying that the half-chance of gaining £1,000 (i.e. £4,000–£3,000) would not be sufficient to compensate them for the half-chance of losing £1,000 (i.e. £3,000–£2,000). They would lose more satisfaction than they would gain.

This attitude can be understood more clearly by considering how much extra enjoyment you obtain from spending additional increments of £1,000. The first £1,000 spent upon the basic needs of food, shelter, clothing and warmth would give you tremendous satisfaction; but when these fundamental requirements have been met, each successive £1,000 yields less and less satisfaction.

In economic theory, satisfaction value is referred to as *utility*, and the concept can be illustrated by ascribing *assumed* utility values to increasing sums of money as follows:

Monetary value £	Utility value	Marginal utility per incremental £1,000
0	0	
1,000	10	10
2,000	19	9
3,000	27	8
4,000	33	6
5,000	38	5

Note:

a Each incremental £1,000 yields progressively less utility.

b Alternative *A* in our original investment opportunity has a utility value of 27.

c The weighted average utility of alternative *B* is $(0.5 \times 19) + (0.5 \times 33) = 26$, showing that its lower utility is less attractive than the certain £3,000 of alternative *A*. Putting it differently, the possible gain of 6 units of utility (i.e. 33–27) is more than offset by a possible loss of 8 units (i.e. 27–19).

The utility and monetary values scheduled above are plotted in Figure 6.1, revealing that utility increases at a diminishing rate as wealth increases, but decreases at an increasing rate as wealth is lost. It portrays the utility function of a risk-averse investor, but does not apply to all investors. Risk preferences vary between individuals, and so do their utility functions.

EXERCISE 6.2

What would be the utility value of another investment, *C* which promises a 0.5 probability of £1,000 and a 0.5 chance of £5,000?

$$\text{Utility value} = (0.5 \times 10) + (0.5 \times 38) = 24$$

Notice how, as the expected money values of *A*, *B* and *C* grow wider apart, utility diminishes. From this, we can infer that the risk of an investment is related to the dispersion of its possible outcomes.

Utility theory attempts to measure this risk, but however conceptually sound the connection between utility and risk, it does not offer a very practical way of measuring, analysing and dealing with risk.

6.2 Probability and risk

Investment decisions are concerned with *future* cash flows, and whilst these are relatively easy to forecast in the case of fixed-interest bonds, more difficulty is

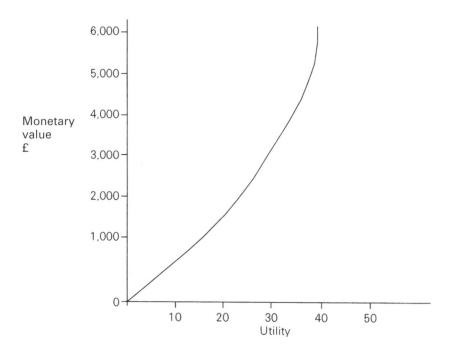

Figure 6.1
Utility function of
a risk-averter

encountered when estimating those of commercial projects. Past experience of similar investments will be a guide, but future economic conditions might order things differently.

A number of cash forecasts might be produced, each one relating to a particular set of economic circumstances that might affect project cash flows. The likelihood of each of these states occurring could then be ascribed a value between 0 and 1, with the total of these probability factors equalling 1.

For example, the expected one-year cash flows of project X might be as follows:

Forecast economic state	Forecast net cash flow	Probability of occurrence	Weighted value
	1	2	3 = 1 × 2
	£		
Slump	1,000	0.10	100
	2,000	0.20	400
	5,000	0.40	2,000
	8,000	0.20	1,600
Boom	9,000	0.10	900
		1.00 EMV	5,000

By multiplying the value of each estimate by its probability of occurrence and totalling the weighted figures (see column 3), we find the statistical mid-point known as *expected monetary value* (*EMV*), which can be compared with the EMVs of alternative investment proposals. In addition, the investor now has information regarding the likelihood of attaining different values, and also a picture of the variability of possible outcomes around the EMV. He is therefore far more aware of the risk of the project.

The dispersion of a limited number of discrete outcomes can be represented in graphical form as a *histogram*, and Figure 6.2 is the histogram of the forecast cash flows of project *X*, showing the probability of their occurrence. Underneath it is a similar diagram representing the one-year cash flows of project *Y*, which are as follows:

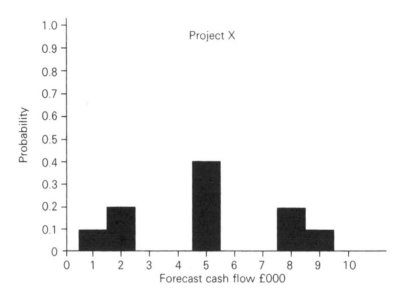

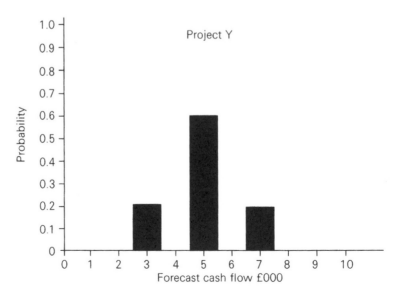

Figure 6.2
Histograms of
project cash flows

Forecast cash flow £	Probability of occurrence	Weighted value £
3,000	0.20	600
5,000	0.60	3,000
7,000	0.20	1,400
	1.00 EMV	5,000

Note that although the average expected cash flows of X and Y are both £5,000, those of X deviate from the EMV more widely than those of Y, making X the riskier of the two projects.

Measuring and analysing risk by using standard deviation

It would be rare for cash flows of investment projects to be limited to a few discrete outcomes as illustrated above. More likely the number would be unlimited and appear as the continuous bell shape shown in Figure 6.3.

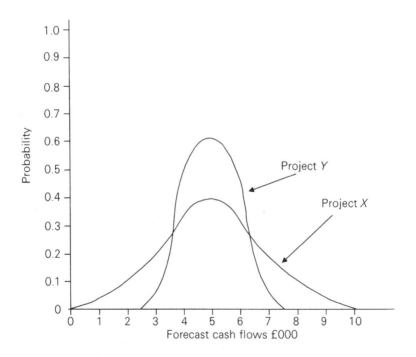

Figure 6.3
Probability distributions of cash flows

The symmetrical bell shape of the continuous probability distribution is known as a *normal curve*. The flatter the curve – the wider the expected outcomes – the higher the risk. Conversely the narrower the bell-shape, the lower the relative risk.

The useful natural property of the normal distribution is that there is a direct correlation between the statistical measure of dispersion, known as *standard deviation* (written σ), and the area under the curve. This relationship is illustrated in

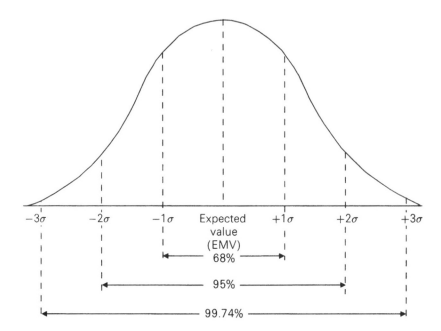

Figure 6.4
Probability and the
normal curve

Figure 6.4, which shows that the area between 1σ *each side* of the expected value covers 68.26% of probable outcomes, 95% between 2σ, and 99.74% between 3σ. More detailed tables are available which give areas between the mean (i.e. the expected value) and any value to its left or right.

If, for example, the expected NPV of a project is £100 and the standard deviation £50, then the probability that the project would have an NPV less than zero would be represented by the area under the curve to the left of zero. In this instance, zero is two standard deviations from the expected value, i.e. (100 – 0) ÷ 50 = 2σ.

Figure 6.4 shows you that, of the 50% of the total outcomes to the left of the mean, 47.5% covers 2σ, therefore there is a 50–47.5% = 2.5% probability that the project will be less than zero.

Readers who have studied statistics will recognise the formula for calculating the standard deviation of a one-year probability distribution of cash flows as:

$$\sigma = \sqrt{\sum_{i=1}^{n} p_i(x_i - \bar{x})^2}$$

where

p_i = the probability of attaining each value
x_i = each of the values in turn
$\bar{x}$ = the average expected value
n = the number of possible values

Derivations of this formula exist to extend the measurement of dispersion to multi-period cash flows, but there is no necessity to demonstrate the resultant calculation of standard deviation in this book. However, readers who have done some statistics might like to calculate the standard deviations of the cash flows of projects X and Y given above.

The answers are £2,608 and £1,265 respectively.

1 Do the given standard deviations of X and Y confirm our previous knowledge as their comparable risks?

2 As regards the cash flows of X, what expected values lie between 1σ either side of the EMV?

1 Yes. X has the higher standard deviation, which confirms the dispersions portrayed by the two histograms. X is therefore the riskier project.

2 The lowest value is £5,000–2,608 = £2,392; and the highest £5,000 + 2,608 = £7,608. There is a 68% probability that the ultimate value will lie between these two figures.

Knowledge of standard deviation provides managers with information of the level of risk attending each proposed project; but it is equally important for them to know how this individual project risk correlates with the total risk already being undertaken on all present projects. This aspect is dealt with in detail in section 6.8 of this chapter where we discuss the question of diversification.

When considering mutually exclusive projects that have the same EMV, the one with the lower standard deviation would be chosen. If the EMVs differ, however, we have a problem. Without considering risk, the highest yielding project is the normal choice, but if total business risk is already high, a lower yielding investment with lower risk might be preferred. This choice can be aided by calculating the *coefficient of variation* (*CV*) of each project, which is simply the standard deviation divided by the expected value of the project.

For example, if project A has an expected value of £6,000, with a standard deviation of £3,000, and project B an expected value of £4,000 with a standard deviation of £1,000, the respective CVs are:

$$\begin{array}{ccc} & A & B \\ \dfrac{\sigma}{EV} & \dfrac{3,000}{6,000} = 0.50 & \dfrac{1,000}{4,000} = 0.25 \end{array}$$

A has the higher standard deviation per £1 of expected value, even though the latter is more attractive than the expected value of B. If management are risk-averse, they might well choose B, whose lower risk is signified by its lower CV.

1 Given the following probabilities and values of sales for the coming year, calculate the expected value of sales for that year.

Probability	Sales value £
0.1	6,000
0.2	10,000
0.4	15,000
0.2	18,000
0.1	20,000

2 State which of the following measures standard deviation:
   a   expected value;
   b   dispersion of expected values around the mean value;
   c   present value;
   d   coefficient of variation.

3 If the expected net present value of a project is £8,000, with a standard deviation of £4,000, what is the probability that the NPV will be greater than £16,000?

(Answers in Appendix E)

6.3 Sensitivity analysis

While the use of standard deviation to measure and analyse risk relates well to utility theory, three difficulties arise in its application to business investment projects:

■ Estimating the probability distribution might be highly *subjective.*
■ Probability distributions are likely to *vary from year to year,* and their dispersions would almost certainly widen with time because of increasing uncertainty.
■ Business investment projects include many *variables,* e.g. sales prices, quantities, capital costs. Overall project risk is therefore a composite of the varying probability distributions attached to each variable.

Many sophisticated mathematical models, involving simulation and sampling techniques, have been developed to overcome these problems, and these are probably worthwhile when applied to projects involving a large commitment of resources. Most businesses look for a simpler approach to risk analysis, however, and *sensitivity analysis* is one such approach.

The technique formalises a question that investors have always asked. If the values of any of the forecast variables change, what difference would each of these changes make to the forecast viability of the investment proposal? Each variable is examined in turn, all other variables being held constant, to ascertain how much that variable could change and still leave the project with a positive NPV or a yield rate higher than the acceptable rate of return.

A business investment with a capital outlay of £48,000 is expected to yield £8,500 annually for ten years. Applying a cost of capital of 10%, calculate whether the project is acceptable. Ignore taxation.

Present value of net cash flows – years 1 to 10:

		£
£8,500 x 6.145*		52,233
less Capital outlay – year 0		48,000
	NPV =	£4,233

*Annuity factor – see Appendix C.

Because the project has a positive NPV it is acceptable.

By how much could the capital outlay in the above project change, before the project becomes unacceptable?

The capital outlay could increase by £4,233, at which point the NPV would be zero. Any further increase would be unacceptable unless accompanied by improvements in other cash flows.

Calculate how much the annual net cash inflow could reduce to before the project fell below zero NPV.

Remember that all other variables remain unchanged.
    Let X equal the lowest annual cash flow to produce a zero NPV; then:

$$X \times 6.145 = 48,000$$
$$X = \frac{48,000}{6.145}$$
$$X = £7,811$$

To ascertain the minimum *life* needed to recover the capital outlay, calculate the annuity factor by dividing £48,000 by the annual cash flow of £8,500 = 5.647. Then look down the 10% column in the Appendix C annuity tables until you find the factor nearest to this figure. Scanning left along the row places the break-even life at about 8¾ years.

EXERCISE 6.7

By how much could the rate of return increase before the project became unacceptable? *Hint:* the procedure here is similar to the life calculation, excepting that we know the life. We are therefore looking for the appropriate column in Appendix C – rather than the row.

The annuity factor is £48,00 ÷ 8.500 = 5.647 (as above).

Looking along the ten-year row in Appendix C, the nearest factor to 5.647 is in the 12% column, i.e. 5.6502. Therefore 12% is the maximum viable rate of return.

All the variables might then be summarised to reveal their comparative sensitivity to change, as follows:

Variable	Original value	Optimum value	Possible absolute change	Possible % change to original value
Capital cost	£48,000	£52,232	+£4,232	8.8
Annual cash flow	£8,500	£7,811	–£689	8.1
Life	10 yrs	8¾ yrs	–1¼ yrs	12.5
Rate of return	10%	12%	+2%	20.0

The practicality of this analysis emerges from a comparison of maximum absolute or percentage changes with possible changes. If none of the variables are likely to change by as much as the values indicated, the project would be given a clean bill of health.

Capital cost would probably be a fixed contract price, and therefore not subject to any change. On the other hand, the annual cash flow is relatively sensitive. A possible reduction of 9% could put the whole project at risk.

A further point is that the net annual cash flow is itself an amalgam of differently behaving variables, and a further breakdown into sales volume, selling price, variable cost and fixed cost could pinpoint a particularly sensitive area.

The major drawback to sensitivity analysis is that each variable is examined in isolation. It is quite possible for any of the elements of an investment decision to change, but also for combinations of them to change simultaneously. Indeed some variables are possibly interdependent. For example, if sales price increases, sales volume could diminish, depending upon the elasticity of product demand.

One can cope with these complications by using a desk-top calculator but the availability of relatively inexpensive and powerful PCs and software now makes the job of analysing multiple changes in variables comparatively easy. Even the smallest of firms can now afford the luxury of a computer to answer its 'what if?' questions – subject of course, to getting professional advice on suitable programmes.

In summary, sensitivity analysis can provide a practical aid to investment decision-making by:

- highlighting the *most sensitive variables* before a decision is made, to enable action to deal with avoidable risk;
- identifying factors requiring *close management control* while the project is proceeding.

QUESTION 6.2

Assume that, in the last activity, the annual cash flow of £8,500 was made up as follows:

		£
Sales 10,000 units at £2 per unit		20,000
less Variable cost @ £1 per unit	10,000	
Fixed costs	1,500	11,500
Net annual cash flow		8,500

Calculate the sensitivity, relative to zero NPV, of sales volume, selling price, variable cost and fixed cost. *Hint*: note from the last activity that a reduction of £689 in the annual cash flow is possible before the NPV of the project falls below zero.

(Answers in Appendix E)

6.4 Payback as a risk-screening device

Payback as a method of investment appraisal was discussed in Chapter 3, and you will recall its major weakness is that it ignores cash flows occurring after the capital break-even point.

Save where a firm is suffering acute cash liquidity problems, the use of a fixed, arbitrary payback period as the sole decision-making technique will almost always discriminate against profitability. To answer this justifiable objection a payback period calculated on *discounted* cash flows is sometimes used, but even this takes no account of (a) cash flows after the payback period, and (b) the range of probable outcomes of *payback* cash flows. The latter may themselves be risky, in which case both the payback and profitability criteria may not be satisfied.

If payback does not consider profitability then it is only being used to screen out *risky* projects, and might be effective in respect of:

- *long-life projects*; because the more delayed cash flows are, the riskier they become;
- *swiftly changing areas of technology*, where early obsolescence has to be protected against, e.g. in microelectronics and communications;
- investments in countries with an *uncertain political future*, e.g. those in which revolutionary or repressive groups are active;
- *brand-new products*, where future demand is completely uncertain.

In general application, when competing projects are equally profitable with similar risk characteristics, payback could be used as the final arbiter of acceptability.

QUESTIONS 6.3

1 'Choosing investment projects on the basis of early payback, takes account of both risk and profitability.' True or false?

2 In which of the following circumstances might payback be used to screen out risky projects?
   a highly profitable investments;
   b projects to be carried out in countries with unstable political regimes;
   c early product obsolescence;
   d investments yielding an acceptable rate of return;
   e new product proposals;
   f long-life project;
   g when capital investment is delayed.

(Answers in Appendix E)

6.5 Risk-adjusted discount rates

When you ask for a motor insurance quotation the insurance company will ask you to provide information on your age, health, accident record and details of the vehicle to be covered. Insurance premiums are adjusted to take account of possible risk, and assessment of risk is based on the information you supply. For example, a bad accident record will almost certainly cost you an additional premium.

The risk premium concept also applies to investors. If you have the choice of putting £100,000 into government securities or into a deep-sea treasure salvage operation, you would not dream of expecting the same return from each of these alternatives.

Government securities can be described as 'risk-free', and they pay an appropriate rate of return. But for you to be attracted to the salvage operation, there would have to be a reasonable expectation that it would return a high premium over the risk-free rate.

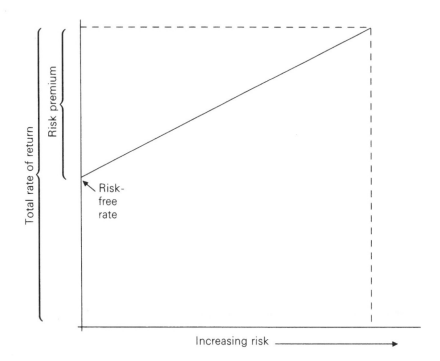

Figure 6.5
The risk/return
relationship

Figure 6.5 shows the intuitive risk/rate-of-return relationship. Further arguments to support this relationship will be discussed at the end of this chapter and in Chapter 15. Investors generally can be said to be indifferent between the various risk/return combinations which lie on the line rising diagonally from the risk-free point on the vertical axis. The increasing risk premium compensates them for accepting more and more risk.

A business has to ensure that its average rate of return on investments is equal to or higher than the cost of capital required by its investors. If its investments are subject to varying degrees of risks, its cost of capital reflects the investors' assessment of the *average* risk attached to the varied operations of the business. Higher-risk projects should therefore be discounted at rates exceeding the cost of capital, and lower-risk proposals at rates equal to or lower than the cost of capital. Differential-risk rates are equally applicable to businesses that engage in only one type of activity, for their plans will include a spectrum of investment proposals from *low-risk* replacement of machinery to high-risk new product introduction.

The choice of rate will be influenced largely by the dispersion of possible cash flow outcomes. For example, a proposal with the promise of extremely high returns, but which might also result in a substantial loss, would be discounted at a rate including a high-risk premium. Projects whose outcomes are less likely to deviate from the expected average return would be discounted at a lower rate.

You will recall that when cash flows are discounted at higher rates, net present values are less. Thus high-risk projects have to yield substantial cash flows to offset the higher discounting, *and* return an acceptable *positive* NPV.

A project is expected to yield a net annual cash flow of £2,000 for eight years, from an investment of £10,400. The firm's cost of capital is 10%. Should the project be accepted?

	£
Present value of £2,000 for 8 yrs @ 10%:	
£2,000 × 5.335	10,670
less Capital outlay	10,400
Net present value	270

Accept the proposal because it yields a positive NPV of £270.

Assume that the same cash flows as in the previous activity, apply to two further proposals – A and B. The former is of above-average risk, and the latter below average. Using risk-adjusted rates of 15% and 8%, respectively, assess whether either of these two investment proposals should proceed.

		£
A – PV of £2,000 for 8 years @ 15%	£2,000 × 4.487 =	8,974
less Capital outlay		10,400
Net present value		(1,426)
B – PV of £2,000 for 8 years @ 8%	£2,000 × 5.747 =	11,494
less Capital outlay		10,400
Net present value		1,094

Accept proposal B, but reject A. Note particularly that, had the company's cost of capital of 10% been applied to A, it would have been marginally acceptable. At the higher 'hurdle' rate of 15% its sensitivity to risk is exposed.

The risk-adjusted discounting method is similar to payback in one respect. It recognises the higher value of *early* cash flows by heavily discounting *later* cash flows. It is superior to payback, however, in that it does take account of cash flows beyond the capital break-even point, and gives more weighting to cash flows within the payback period.

The problem of how to determine the cost of capital, and particularly the risk-adjusted rate, is dealt with in Chapter 15.

Why would it be misleading to apply the average cost of capital as the discounting rate in a company whose investments are subject to varying degrees of risk?

(Answers in Appendix E)

6.6 Risk reduction

In an efficient organisation, the element of risk to be dealt with in the ways suggested in the previous sections of this chapter will be the *unavoidable* part after action has been taken to eliminate or reduce risk. Such action can be summarised under two broad heads:

- *Administrative action* – when appraising, planning and controlling investment projects.
- *Diversification action* – to ensure that total cash flows from all projects are not subject to excessive variations.

Administrative action

Taking out insurance against the risks of accident due to fire, natural hazards, third-party claims, theft and burglary is perhaps the most obvious of management actions designed to minimise possible loss.

Another way of spreading risk is to arrange for particularly large-scale projects to be shared with one or more partners in a *joint-venture* or *consortium* agreement. Each partner contributes capital, takes part in the management and shares profits or losses.

At individual project level, uncertainty can be considerably smoothed out by taking some of the following actions:

- Putting adequate time and resources into *forecasting*.
- Maintaining *checklists of expenditure*, both capital and revenue, to ensure that nothing is overlooked.
- Completing *contracts for supplies and with customers* to ensure continuity and stability of terms of trade.
- Using *'hedging' operations* to cover the risk of loss through changes in currency values and commodity prices. This is effected by buying *options* forward to buy or sell, at predetermined prices. In this way, for example, a manufacturer will know exactly how much he will have to pay for materials in the future and is able, therefore, to quote selling prices with more certainty.
- Arranging for *patent protection* for new inventions and designs.
- Taking over *sources of supply* so that complete control can be maintained over them.

- Maintaining *good industrial relations* with employees through adequate communication and management participation.
- Ensuring that *prescribed time-schedules* for the completion of projects are being met. 'Schedule slippage' can seriously harm profitability, since delayed cash flows will reduce net present value.
- *Frequent cash forecasting* to ensure that adequate funds are available for each project.
- *Continuous monitoring of projects* to see that they are measuring up to expectations.

Diversification

'Don't put all your eggs into one basket' is sound general advice. Drop your basket and all your eggs are smashed!

It is the kind of advice that your friendly bank manager would offer if you asked him how you should invest your Aunt Agatha's legacy. Depending upon your present financial position and future needs, he would probably counsel you to hold your money in a number of investments, which together would form what is referred to as a *portfolio*. Some funds would go into low-risk, fixed-interest, easily liquidated savings accounts or securities, to provide cash for emergencies. The remainder could go into high-income or capital growth securities according to need.

The attraction of sinking all of your funds into one security is that you *may* realise a high return on your investment; but there is also the danger that you may lose all of your money if the security is risky. Even investing in more than one security does not necessarily change this risk, however, if the several investments are in the same or a related industry, and their cash flows react in like manner to general changes in the economy. Such related investments are said to be *positively* correlated, as shown in Figure 6.6, where changes in the cash flows of *B* are seen to be closely related to those in *A*. Clearly no reduction in risk results from combining such investments.

When the cash flows of two investments behave in exactly opposite ways in the same economic climate – so that when the returns on one are rising they are falling on the other – correlation between them is said to be *negative*, and risk is reduced by their combination in a portfolio. Note how in Figure 6.7, equivalent amounts

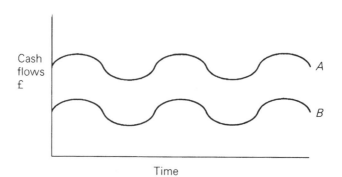

Figure 6.6
Positively correlated investment cash flows

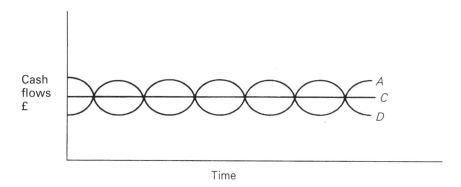

Figure 6.7
Negatively correlated investment cash flows

invested in *A* and *D* result in compensating rising and falling cash flows over time, combining to yield the smoothed-out return *C*.

Most securities and business projects are nearer to positive than to negative correlation, though very rarely being perfectly positively correlated. There will therefore always be some benefit to risk in combining projects of unlike nature.

For example, if an investor has the opportunity to invest equal amounts in two securities *X* and *Y* with expected annual yields of 18% and 12%, and standard deviations of 16% and 10% respectively, the weighted average yield would be (0.5 × 18%) + (0.5 × 12%) = 15%.

It might also be supposed that the standard deviation (i.e. the measure of risk) of the portfolio comprising *A* and *B* is the weighted average of the standard deviations of the two securities, i.e. (0.5 × 16%) + (0.5 × 10%) = 13%. This would only be true, however, if the returns from the two securities vary in exactly the same way over time, i.e. are perfectly positively correlated. If they do not, it can be demonstrated mathematically that the portfolio standard deviation will be less than the weighted average of the deviations on the two securities.

This concept of risk reduction through diversification has encouraged financial researchers to develop theories that have had a profound effect upon analysis related to investment in securities, and this work is having a growing influence upon decisions relating to investment in productive capital assets. The essence of this theory is discussed in the two following sections.

6.7 Selecting an optimal portfolio

EXERCISE 6.10

Figure 6.8 depicts all the possible combinations (portfolios) of *risky* investments available to an investor, plotted according to their portfolio return and risk.

a At a risk level of 6%, which portfolio would you choose?
b If you wished a return of 25%, which portfolio would you choose?
c Explain your choices in **a** and **b** above.

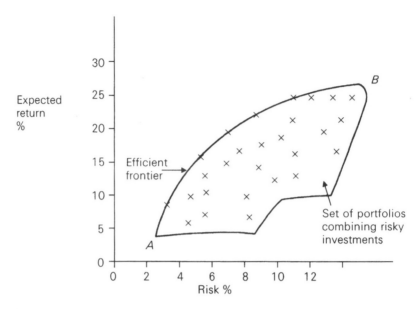

Figure 6.8 The efficient frontier

a The one on the 'efficient frontier' yielding 15%.
b The one on the 'efficient frontier' with a risk level of 12%.
c Of all the portfolios with a risk of 6%, the one chosen yields the highest return; of all the portfolios with a return of 25%, the one chosen has the least risk.

The curve AB in Figure 6.8 is known as the 'efficient frontier' because all the portfolios lying along it are superior to all others within the set. They yield the highest returns at any desired level of risk, and the lowest risk at any desired level of return.

But which is the most efficient portfolio for an individual investor?

The answer can be illustrated by adding 'indifference curves' to the diagram depicting the opportunity set of portfolios – see Figure 6.9.

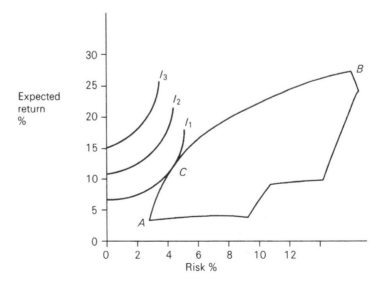

Figure 6.9 An investor's optimal portfolio

,

Indifference curves are derived from Figure 6.1, which depicts a risk-averse investor's utility function. Assuming that such a function can be determined, the indifference curves illustrate that increasing levels of risk have their prices in higher expected returns. The investor to whom the curves relate would be indifferent between any combinations of risk and return lying on each of the indifference curves. Figure 6.9 shows that the optimal risky portfolio for this investor is at point *C* where the lowest indifference curve touches the efficient frontier.

However, investors do not have to restrict themselves to risky investments. *Riskless* securities in the form of, say, government Treasury Bills can be added to their portfolios, and thus reduce total risk.

Figure 6.10 illustrates the effect of making a riskless security available to an investor.

A line drawn from the vertical axis at *Rf* (the risk-free rate of return) at a tangent to the set of risky portfolios at point *M*, now depicts a new efficient frontier *RfMQ*, known as the *capital market line (CML)*.

If we assume:

- that investors have exactly similar expectations regarding the risk and return of each security on the stock market; and
- that the stock market is efficient in that the market value of each security reflects all known information, and is the price that equates supply with the demand for that security

then the 'market portfolio' (*M*) must contain a proportion of every share, and is the only perfectly diversified risky portfolio.

Studies have shown, however, that even the market portfolio cannot completely eliminate risk. Undiversifiable (or systematic) risk still remains after all the risks peculiar to individual securities have been diversified away. This residual risk relates

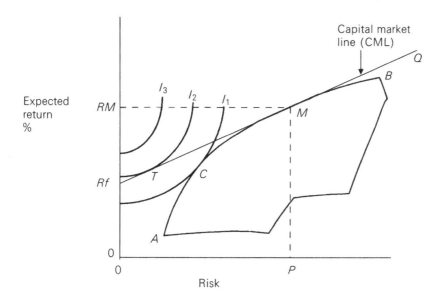

Figure 6.10   The capital market line

to the general global economic and political outlook that affects all business activity. If the outlook changes, so does the expected return and value of the market portfolio. Figure 6.10 reveals that at its current level of systematic risk P, the market portfolio commands a risk premium of $RM - R_f$.

By combining the riskless security with the market portfolio in the proportion of $R_fT{:}TM$ on the capital market line, our investor is able to reach a higher indifference curve at point T, and thereby realise the same return as before, i.e. C, but at lower risk.

Other investors with different risk preferences, whose indifference curves might be placed nearer to M, will invest proportionately more in the risky portfolio M, and consequently less in the riskless security. At M, investors will only hold the market portfolio.

If we assume, rather unrealistically, that investors can borrow at the same rate as they can lend, then where investors' indifference curves are at a tangent to the CML beyond M, they will *borrow* to boost their investment in the market portfolio.

Theoretically, investors should only hold portfolios on the capital market line, all others below it being less efficient as regards return and risk. The CML represents the return/risk relationship of various combinations of the risk-free security and the market portfolio, with risk being a linear function of the proportion invested in the market portfolio. For example, if M comprises 50% of the invested funds, and the standard deviation of M is 10%, the total portfolio risk is $0.5 \times 10\%$ = 5%.

It is unlikely, however, that investors will hold the market portfolio, because of its sheer size; so how practical is the CML in helping them to choose an optimal portfolio?

The answer lies in the realisation that *the slope of the CML represents market risk only*, all other risk being diversified away. It follows therefore that because the *operational* risk of an individual security can be eliminated by combination with other securities in a well-diversified portfolio, investors will only be prepared to pay for the residual, systematic risk, which of course is market related.

Remember that the expected return and value of the market portfolio fluctuate with the underlying general economic and political trend. Likewise each security tends to move in sympathy with this 'market' risk, but not necessarily to the same degree as the market portfolio. A favourable outlook results in a general upward movement in share prices, and vice versa, but some prices will change proportionately more or less than the market portfolio.

Thus, just as the risk premium on a portfolio featured on the CML in Figure 6.10 is a proportionate part of the premium on the market portfolio, so the risk premium on each security is a function of that security's sensitivity to changes in the required return on the market portfolio. This responsiveness to change can be derived statistically from past or forecast data, and is represented by a *beta* (*B*) factor of more than, less than, or equal to 1; with 1 relating to the market portfolio.

6.8 Capital asset pricing model

The *capital asset pricing model (CAPM)* describes the equation for determining the expected return on a security (*RS*), given the current risk-free rate (*i*), knowledge of the expected return on the market portfolio (*RM*) (which is usually proxied by one of the market indices such as the Financial Times Actuaries' Index), and the beta (*B*) of the security as:

$$RS = i + (RM - i)B$$

Here you see that the expected return includes the risk-free rate, plus a premium for risk calculated by applying the beta of the security to the risk premium on the market portfolio (*RM* – *i*).

For example, if a security *X*, has a beta of 1.1, the risk-free rate is 9%, and the expected return on the market portfolio is 15%, the expected return of *X* will be:

$$
\begin{aligned}
RS &= i + (RM - i)B \\
&= 9 + (15 - 9)1.1 \\
&= 15.6\%
\end{aligned}
$$

If underlying economic influences then forced an increase in *RM* to 20%, the return on *X* should increase to 9 + (20 – 9)1.1 = 21.1%. This can be checked by adding to the previous return on *X* of 15.6%, 1.1 times the *increase* in the risk premium of the market portfolio, i.e. 15.6 + 1.1(11 – 6).

Thus, the return on a security with a beta greater than 1 increases or decreases more than proportionately to that of the market portfolio, and is said to be an 'aggressive' investment because of the greater variability (and therefore risk) of its returns. Conversely a security with a beta of less than 1 is a 'defensive' investment because its return is not as volatile as that of the market portfolio, i.e. it is less risky.

We now possess a model that can be applied to the construction of an investor's portfolio, according to his or her specification of required return and risk.

When investments are combined into a portfolio, the expected return is a weighted average of the returns of all the separate securities. Likewise, the risk of the portfolio, *measured by its beta*, is simply a weighted average of the betas of the constituent securities.

If an investor is a risk-taker, he or she will construct a portfolio with a beta greater than 1 (an aggressive portfolio), which should yield a return commensurate with that level of market risk. In so doing, he will assess the risk of an individual security according to the *marginal* effect it has on his diversified portfolio – and not according to its individual standard deviation.

Further discussion on the capital asset pricing model can be found in Chapter 15 in the context of calculating the cost of a company's capital to apply to the appraisal of investments.

QUESTIONS 6.5

1 When the returns on two investments move in sympathy in the same economic environment, are they positively, or negatively correlated?

2 'No risk reduction will result from combining two negatively correlated investments.' True or false?

3 Why will investors only pay for systematic risk?

4 What does the beta of a security measure?

(Answers in Appendix E)

6.9 How best to deal with risk?

'Nothing ventured, nothing gained' – so the saying goes. If it were not for investors willing to take risks there would be little growth in the economy. But risk has to be well managed.

It can be reduced by taking the administrative action discussed earlier in this chapter, or by diversifying into projects whose cash flows are uncorrelated with existing activities. In all cases, however, risk should be analysed. This may be done simply by estimating the cash flows of a project if everything were to go right, and those if everything were to go wrong. If profitable under worst conditions, there is no need for further analysis. If not, a *probability forecast* of the most likely outcome would help the investment decision.

Sensitivity analysis can highlight the variables most critical to the success of a project, e.g. sales demand, whilst *computer models* of each investment can add the ultimate sophistication to investment appraisal.

The final decision will depend upon how much risk management is willing to take, and this is influenced mainly by the extent to which the firm is, or will be, exposed.

TO SUM UP

■ Risk, applied to investment decisions, is the possibility that forecasts of future cash flows may not be realised. If the risks are high, or if investors have a relatively high aversion to risk, this can be dealt with by applying a relatively high risk-adjusted discount rate, which could be calculated by using the capital asset pricing model (see Chapter 15).

■ Another approach is to calculate payback, discounted or not, perhaps in conjunction with another method, because it has the effect of ignoring longer-life, perhaps more risky, cash flows.

■ Sensitivity analysis, which highlights the cash flow variables most critical to the viability of an investment proposal, is perhaps the most practical method of analysing risk.

FURTHER READING

Arnold, G. (2002) *Corporate Financial Management*, Financial Times Pitman, chapters 6–8.
Lumby, S. and C. Jones (1999) *Investment Appraisal and Financial Decisions*, Chapman & Hall, chapters 9–12.
McLaney, E.J. (2000) *Business Finance: Theory and Practice*, Prentice Hall, chapters 6 and 7.
Pike, R. and B. Neale (2003) *Corporate Finance and Investment*, Prentice Hall, chapters 9 and 10.
Samuels, R., F. Wilkes and R. Brayshaw (1999) *Management of Company Finance*, Chapman & Hall, chapters 6, 8–10.

QUESTIONS 6.6

1 Why would an investment A, with a certain return of £5,000, be more attractive to most people than B with a 50/50 chance of earning £8,000 and £2,000 respectively?

2 Show your calculation of the expected value of B in question **1**.

3 What does standard deviation measure?

4 If the returns from a project are normally distributed, with an expected value of £12,000 and a standard deviation of £6,000, what is the probability that the return from the project will be negative?

5 **a** What is the basic question posed by sensitivity?
   b How can sensitivity analysis help in the appraisal of investments?

6 The forecast cash flows of a four-year investment proposal are as follows:

Year 0	1	2	3	4
(£7,000)	£4,000	£2,000	£1,000	£1,000

Calculate whether the project should be accepted under each of the following separate criteria:
   i The cost of capital is 10%;
   ii The required payback period is two years;
   iii This is a low-risk project, warranting only a 7% discounting rate.

7 The following is a table of the % returns for three projects X, Y and Z for each of six years.

▶

Project	Percentage return on investment in year					
	1	2	3	4	5	6
X	10	5	6	8	12	15
Y	8	4	4.8	6.4	9.6	12
Z	5	10	12	10	6	6

a   Which pair combinations of X, Y and Z shows positive correlation? Explain.

b   Which pair combinations of X, Y and Z show negative correlation? Explain.

c   Which combinations will result in risk reduction?

8 If the risk-free rate is 10%, the return on the market portfolio 17% and the beta of a security is 0.9, calculate the expected return on the security.

9 How would you calculate the expected return and risk of a diversified portfolio of securities?

(Answers in Appendix E)

Capital budgeting administration

INTRODUCTION

- The capital budgeting process, embracing both investment and financing decisions, is at the centre of strategic planning, as Figure 1.1 in Chapter 1 revealed, and it is a continuing process.

- How to appraise proposed investments, forecast their cash flows and incorporate risk into the decision-making process were discussed in Chapters 3–6.

- The financing of investment proposals will be considered in Part III. But in this chapter we will examine how businesses may organise and administer their capital budgeting procedures to achieve their objectives more effectively.

LEARNING OBJECTIVES

When you have completed this chapter you should be able to:

1 List and explain the main categories of investments.

2 Discuss the framework within which capital budgeting may be organised.

3 Outline the factors to be considered in the evaluation and authorisation of investment proposals.

4 Describe and illustrate how you may allocate finance to competing projects when capital is rationed.

5 Explain why the implementation of investments should be *monitored*, and subjected to a process of *post-audit*.

7.1 Types of business investment

Though each investment is unique, most of the many and varied industrial and commercial projects can be put into one of the following categories:

■ Replacement of *existing assets*
■ Expansion of *existing products or services*
■ *New* products or services
■ *Research*
■ *Environmental, social* and *welfare.*

Replacement of plant and machinery, buildings and vehicles

This is probably the largest category. Given that the activity for which it is required is still profitable, worn-out machinery has to be replaced. The main problems to solve then are: when to replace, and with what? Whatever our decisions in this respect, they must ultimately rest on the premise that the benefits of replacement must exceed the costs.

Expanding existing products or services

This can simply mean the addition of more capacity to that already existing in a factory; but it may involve the taking over of another business, or opening up a new plant in Britain or overseas. Much more forecast information is required than in replacement decisions.

The development of new products

In a changing and highly competitive market, this is vital to survival. Old products lose market share eventually, and a continuing product development programme is necessary to provide new products to replace the old, and so keep profit stable and growing.

Investment in research

This must be as objective as possible. Products may not be identifiable at this stage, but management should still endeavour to direct resources allocated to research into those areas that they consider offer most potential for development into new products.

Environmental, social and welfare projects

Investment in the environment may be more directly linked with existing or new product development, and should therefore be treated as such. On the other hand, the costs of sports facilities, restaurant and recreational facilities, pensions, medical provision, health and safety, security, and crèches for children of working mothers, may be known, but the benefits are hard to evaluate. Because of this, their costs are more likely to be recovered either by apportionment over revenue-earning projects, or by increasing the rate of return required by all projects.

7.2 Investment guidelines and authorisation

Figure 7.1 illustrates that new investments are born out of *strategic planning*, followed by careful *analysis and evaluation* of alternative proposals.

The size of each business, and the volume and complexity of the investment decisions made, will obviously determine the extent of the organisation for capital budgeting. The sole trader will make his or her own decisions, and the small to medium-sized company will be largely administered by its board of directors. But in the very large conglomerate, or multinational company, a *centralised budgeting committee* may be delegated the task of implementing the investment and financing implications of corporate policy agreed by the board of directors. The staff supporting this committee would include specialists in design, research and development (R&D), production, marketing, finance, taxation, and law; and the guidelines and procedure to be followed to gain project approval, perhaps set out in a *capital budgeting manual*.

The manual would cover:

- Instructions and advice regarding the completion and submission of *standard project approval documentation*.
- *Evaluation criteria* to apply to different types of projects – NPV/payback; target rates of return; assessment of risk; guidance on how to choose between mutually exclusive projects.
- *Availability* and *timing of finance*.
- The *sanctioning of proposals* – perhaps giving dispensation at plant level for proposals below a specified capital cost.

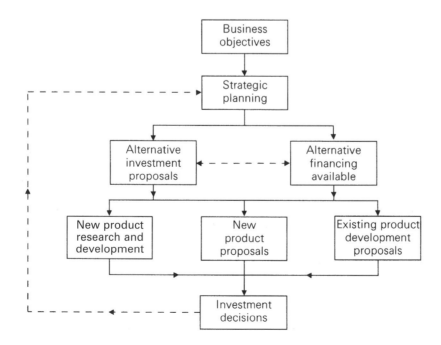

Figure 7.1 The capital budgeting process

■ Appropriate priority to be given to proposals concerned with the *environment, health and safety.*

■ *Accounting and administrative procedures* controlling the acquisition, construction, manufacture and installation of capital resources.

■ A process of *monitoring and post-audit* of projects.

QUESTION 7.1

Indicate which of the following would be included in the guidelines published by a company to assist in the compilation of investment proposals:

1 An organisation chart.
2 Assessment of risk sensitivity.
3 Choosing between mutually exclusive projects.
4 The fixed assets register.
5 Instructions on how to complete proposal forms.
6 Target rates of return.
7 The profit and loss budget for next year.
8 Methods of appraisal.

(Answers in Appendix E)

7.3 Preparing the investment proposal

Investments can be large or small, complicated or simple. For example, the purchase of an additional word processor should not cause too many appraisal problems. The amount of capital required is small, and the benefits derived from its use well known. On the other hand, business expansion requires a much deeper analysis of all the factors influencing the decision. The sophistication of the evaluation of each proposal will clearly depend upon the diversity, type and size of operations, and particularly the impact of advanced technology. For example, some costs and benefits of a comprehensive changeover to computer-aided manufacture (CAM) would be fairly obvious – i.e. labour cost saving; while others, such as the consequences of an improvement in output quality, would not be so obvious.

EXERCISE 7.1

A confectionery manufacturer is considering the introduction of a new product. What information would be required to appraise the proposal?

Hint: the following headings will help you to compile your list; product details; assumptions; capital cost; revenue cash flows; taxation; method of appraisal; risk analysis.

Product details – description; extent of competition; whether new or replacement product; estimated life.

Assumptions – size, growth, and share of the market; home or export sales; expected inflation rate over the project life; selling price.

Capital cost – timing of capital investment, method of financing; cost of capital; buildings and supporting services; machinery and plant; moulds and tools; disposal values of new and existing machinery; additional working capital requirement and when recovered; government grants available; installation costs and time.

Revenue cash flows – sales cash inflows; loss of net revenue from existing products phased out or affected by sales of the new product; additional fixed costs.

Taxation – capital allowances on buildings, plant and machinery; is the company currently paying taxation on its profits?; are there any accumulated tax losses?; what tax rate to apply?

Method of appraisal – NPV, yield rate and payback.

Risk analysis – sensitivity analysis of each variable; perhaps the application of a risk-adjusted discount rate.

A much bigger problem than buying a wordprocessor, as you can see!

The amount of time and effort applied to project appraisal, even within a large firm, will vary. Straightforward machine replacement, save when alternatives have to be considered, will not cause much heart-searching. But commitment of a large capital sum to the expansion of existing productive capacity, or the purchase of another business, has to be given far more attention.

In the early stages, a very brief report outlining a proposal might be submitted, and if it is viewed favourably, the initiator would be requested to submit a formal project sanction document. This would be in a standard form, serially numbered for identification purposes, and outline the purpose and advantages of the proposed capital expenditure. The significant cash flows would be summarised, but supported by more detailed working papers.

In most cases, the cash flow figures submitted would be best estimates, but the effect of possible changes in any of the variables used in the sanction documents would assist the appraising body in their assessment of the risk of the proposal.

Figure 7.2 shows the information that might appear on a capital expenditure proposal summary form.

Reference to schedules refers to the detailed workings needed to produce this summary. Note that the project appears to be only *marginally* profitable and that it is sensitive to risk in many areas. Note also the difference in incidence of *cash flows* compared with *earnings per share* (EPS) – showing clearly that 'profit' is not substantially increased until year 3. Presumably this company will have developed alternative new product proposals, if 'Chocolate Minto' is not thought to show sufficient promise.

Once authorised, the project is included in the capital budget and a timetable drawn up for its implementation.

CAPITAL EXPENDITURE PROPOSAL

Submitted by	P. Nut	No. NP. 4/03
Department	New Product Development	
Date	1.2.2003	Total capital required
Description	Chocolate Minto	£195,000

Justification	NPV @ 15%	+£7573
Replacement for product 9/84	Yield rate:	16.7%
– see report at schedule 7	Payback Period	3 years

Best estimate cash flows

	Schedule				Net Cash Flows	
	1	2	3	4		
Year	Fixed assets	Working capital	Operating cash flows	Taxation	Not discounted	Discounted
0	} −200,000 + 10,000	− 5,000			− 195,000	− 195,000
1			+40,000	–	+ 40,000	+ 34,800
2			+40,000	+ 75,000	+115,000	+ 86,940
3			+50,000	− 20,000	+ 30,000	+ 19,740
4			+80,000	− 25,000	+ 55,000	+ 31,460
5			+70,000	− 40,000	+ 30,000	+ 14,910
6			+60,000	− 35,000	+ 25,000	+ 10,800
7	+ 15,000	+ 5,000	+40,000	− 30,000	+ 30,000	+ 11,280
8				− 22,500	− 22,500	− 7,357
Total					+107,500	+ 7,573

Effect on earnings per share (see schedule 5)

Year	1	2	3	4	5	6	7	8
	+0.005	+0.005	+0.010	+0.025	+0.020	+0.015	+0.005	–

Risk sensitivity:
1 Rate of return
2 Product selling price   } See schedule 6 attached
3 Variable cost-material
4 Taxation rate

Figure 7.2 Capital expenditure proposal

Continuing encouragement should be given to the initiation of investment proposals, whether the initiative lies with a new product development department or with individual production or marketing managers.

Summarise what you would consider to be the nine main aspects covered in the appraisal of a heavy goods vehicle replacement proposal.

(Answer in Appendix E)

7.4 Ranking projects when capital is rationed

Theoretically, a company ought to be able to finance all investment proposals promising a return higher than its cost of capital. This assumes that the providers of capital have full knowledge of the future prospects of the business, and that this is reflected in the costs of their finance, be they shareholders or lenders.

If the business 'smoke signals' indicate either a higher degree of uncertainty in future operations or that the business is already relying too heavily upon *borrowed* funds, the market should react and increase the cost of finance to that company. Even then, the supply of funds should never 'dry up' as long as projects exist which yield higher returns than the cost of capital.

Capital rationing does exist, however, but it appears to be largely self-imposed by businesses for the following reasons:

a Owners of small businesses may rely solely upon retained profit for growth, either because they do not want to relinquish control or because they simply dislike borrowing.
b A policy regarding rate of growth may be related to what is considered to be management's ability to cope with growth.
c A company may defer going to the market for further funds until market conditions are more favourable.
d Companies may plan to keep assets under construction in a period down to a certain level, to prevent a lowering of the rate of return on assets *published in the annual accounts*.

Even though companies plan to restrict their growth for the reasons stated in a, b and c above, the costs of capital will ultimately reflect these policies, and rationing of funds is therefore regulated by the market. All projects yielding positive net present values at the market-adjusted cost of capital should proceed.

If rationing is market-imposed because of overgearing, it ought not to be a continuing restriction, because it will invariably be corrected by the injection of more equity finance into the capital structure of the business.

Priority in allocating capital will be given, first, to essential expenditure on research and development, and to comply with health and safety regulations, with the balance going to those projects which cannot be postponed (e.g. replacement) and finally those which *add most value to the business*.

This implies that those proposals that have the highest net present value per £1 invested should have priority.

The following table lists five proposed investments ranked in order of NPV to capital cost. A cost of capital of 8% is used.

Project	Capital cost £	Life yrs	Net cash flow per annum £	NPV @ 8% £	DCF yield rate %	NPV/ capital £
A	15,000	10	3,912	11,250	23	0.75
B	22,000	10	5,608	15,630	22	0.71
C	14,000	12	3,155	9,780	20	0.70
D	13,000	8	3,741	8.500	23	0.65
E	5,000	5	1,859	2,421	25	0.48
	69,000					

If the amount of finance is restricted to £55,000 and each project is divisible – as with stocks and shares – the NPV to capital invested ranking will apply as follows:

Project	Capital required	NPV
A	15,000	11,250
B	22,000	15,630
C	14,000	9,780
	51,000	36,660
add D 4/13 of £8,500	4,000	2,615
	55,000	39,275

Note that ranking in order of yield rate with finance limited to £55,000 (i.e. E, A, D, B) gives a lower NPV of £37,801. Thus, when projects are divisible the optimum allocation of rationed capital will always follow the NPV to capital-invested ranking.

Most investment proposals in industry are *indivisible* and independent of one another, but still the search is for the highest value given the capital constraint. In these circumstances, different combinations of projects, including those with lower NPV ratings, may prove more valuable.

In our example, A, B and C use £51,000 with a total NPV of £36,660, but if we substitute D and E for C, £55,000 capital invested yields £37,801. That D and E have also got fast paybacks is also in their favour.

Should capital rationing extend for a period longer than one year, more complicated mathematical procedures, such as linear programming, which is beyond the scope of this book, can be applied to the solution of this wealth-maximisation problem.

1 In a single period of capital rationing, divisible projects can be ranked according to:

a the sizes of their net present values;

b their DCF yield rates;

c their ratios of NPV to capital invested.

Which of these will always result in the maximisation of value for the firm?

2 When investment proposals are indivisible, why can you not use the approach indicated in your answer to question 1?

(Answers in Appendix E)

7.5 Monitoring the installation of project facilities

After its sanction, a copy of the capital expenditure proposal documentation will be passed to the accounting department, where appropriate records will be maintained to ensure that authorised capital expenditure is not exceeded. Orders will be placed, either internally or externally, for manufacture of equipment and plant, and expenditure on these will be checked against the approval documents, and charged into a capital work-in-progress account.

Periodic returns should be made to responsible management to indicate progress on each project and, if necessary, additional approval sought if expenditure is forecast to exceed the original approvals. One practical difficulty here is estimating the stage of completion reached on any project at any time, especially in connection with engineering projects. The tasks in relation to buildings is easier, because reliance can be placed upon architect's progress certificates.

When all capital resources of a project are ready to become operational, an accounting transfer of total capital expenditure will be made from the capital work-in-progress account to the appropriate fixed asset accounts, and at the same time records will be opened relating to individual assets.

7.6 Post-audit of capital expenditure

Creative people such as artists and systems and software designers tend to give little thought to their creations once they are completed and accepted. They prefer to move on the next creative challenge. Spenders of business capital tend to adopt the same philosophy, so the learning process of comparing actual with expected project performance is lost. In justification of this attitude, it can be argued that initiators of ideas might be discouraged if they felt that the results of all their approved projects were to be closely scrutinised. The balance between discouragement and motivation is delicate.

It can be strongly argued that reviewing past decisions is part of the continuing role of good management. Periodic management accounting reports can supply a lot of the necessary information, especially when projects are wholly related to identifiable cost, profit or investment centres. Supplementary reports on sales quantities, material usage, labour hours worked, scrap and rectification costs will be especially useful at post-audit stage.

Where projects span more than one department, however, a special study will have to be set up, for unless post-audit is formalised, there is a good chance that review will not take place, especially in a large organisation.

Internal audit staff are probably best qualified to be allocated the role of post-auditors. They are normally independent of any particular department, and are a lot closer than anyone else in the organisation to all the procedural and operational aspects of particular projects. This presumes that they are truly *management* auditors, and not just checking book-keeping entries.

Finally it is important that post-audit, just like any other control system, is cost-effective. The benefits arising out of project review may sometimes only be capable of being assessed subjectively, but they should include:

- An improvement in the quality of *future investment appraisal* arising out of the use of better forecasting methods, assumptions and criteria.
- An improvement in *management performance* through better communication of the results of past decisions.
- The taking of *timely remedial or abortive action*, should an early examination of project performance reveal that it is not living up to its promise; areas of sensitivity highlighted at the appraisal stage should be given priority in the monitoring process.
- The noting of *strengths* (to be encouraged and developed) and *weaknesses* (to be corrected) in project appraisal and performance (the SWOT procedure).

TO SUM UP

- In this chapter we have considered what minimum provision should be made to ensure the effectiveness of the capital budgeting organisation and administration.
- We looked at the administration required to evaluate investment proposals, and how such proposals may be ranked during a period of capital rationing.
- Finally, we discussed the need for an efficient system of post-implementation project monitoring and audit, to check that investments have lived up to their promise.

1 In the 'Chocolate Minto' proposal illustrated in Figure 7.2, what areas of this project would you pay particular attention to in a post-audit?

2 Briefly describe the four steps involved in the organisation and administration of capital budgeting.

3 Five of the following aspects comprise the framework within which a capital budgeting committee operates when considering investment proposals. Name the three that do not directly relate to this framework:
   a Capital rationing.
   b Industrial relations.
   c Recognition of investment priorities.
   d The long-term corporate plan.
   e The budgetary control system.
   f The effect of each project on the profit and loss account.
   g The rate of inflation.
   h Correlation of each project with the portfolio of existing projects.

4 'Project proposals will only include the most probable cash flow forecasts.' Is this statement true or false? Why?

5 Briefly describe the four benefits to be derived from a formalised post-audit of investment projects.

(Answers in Appendix E)

FURTHER READING

Arnold, G. (2002) *Corporate Financial Management*, Financial Times Pitman, chapters 4 and 5.
McLaney, E.J. (2000) *Business Finance: Theory and Practice*, Prentice Hall, chapter 5.
Pike, R. and B. Neale (2003) *Corporate Finance and Investment*, Prentice Hall, chapter 7.
Samuels, R., F. Wilkes and R. Brayshaw (1999) *Management of Company Finance*, Chapman & Hall, chapter 7.

PART

III

Financial Planning

Establishing the need for finance **8**

INTRODUCTION

- Imagine that you have to move to another part of the country to take up a new job. For many reasons, and certainly financially, this could be traumatic. You may not receive your first salary for a month, and until then you and your family have to be fed. With luck you will have some savings for such an emergency, or you might obtain a loan from friends, family or your new employer, to tide you over the lean period.

- However, your problems are only just beginning; whilst you have solved your *short-term* problem of financing daily living expenses, much larger sums of money will be needed to finance the purchase of a house, furniture and perhaps a car.

- The car could perhaps be bought on hire purchase, or by arranging a personal two- or three-year loan through your bank; and a *long-term* housing loan could be arranged with a building society or a bank on the mortgage of your new home.

- Your need for financial assistance arises mainly because you lack *immediate* access to sufficient money of your own. True, your new job will provide salary cash flows, out of which you can repay the instalments on your loans – but in the *future*, not imme- diately. It is this *non-synchronisation* of cash receipts and payments, especially where cash outflows are large if infrequent, that creates the demand for finance – for both private and business purposes. Investment and financing decisions are inextricably linked, investment committing funds to the early acquisition of buildings, machin- ery and working capital, that cannot possibly generate cash inflows in the short term to repay the total amount invested.

  In Part III we examine how business finance needs may be assessed, then matched with sources of finance; and how a decision on the optimum mix of own and borrowed funds might be made.

  In this chapter we look at the four main influences on the types and sources of finance ultimately chosen:

1 The type of organisation requiring the finance.

2 The purpose for which the finance is required.

3 For how long the finance is required.

4 How much finance is required.

When you have completed this chapter you should be able to:

1 Describe the range of business organisations that require finance.

2 Specify the main purposes for which, and for how long, business finance is required.

3 Construct a short-term cash forecast from specified data.

4 Construct a long-term cash flow forecast from specified data.

8.1 Business organisations requiring finance

Businesses are as varied in their sizes as they are in their activities, but there is some relationship between size and the type of activity carried on – certainly in the case of small businesses.

EXERCISE 8.1

From your personal experience, by flipping through the Yellow Pages, or looking at the Yell site online, what types of business do you find are generally operated by one person?

Your list might include plumbers, builders, electricians, dentists, doctors, insurance brokers, shopkeepers, farmers, hairdressers, taxi-drivers and photographers.

Most of these occupations involve *personal service* provided within a limited geographical area. This does not imply that they are only ever one-person operated. However, the sole business owners survive partly because of the lack of growth opportunity in a restricted locality, partly because they value their independence and partly because they are proud of their personal skills.

Where the type of business provides opportunities for growth, e.g. manufacturing or transport, sole ownership restricts the availability of finance, partly because the resources of individuals are limited and partly because the risks have an affect upon the amount that lenders are willing to provide.

The sole ownership constraints can be lifted to some extent by forming partnerships, but again, growth is restricted by available resources, and the legal limits on the size of partnerships (twenty, or fifty in the professions).

Not surprisingly these limitations, and the fact that each partner is *personally* liable for all the debts of the firm, led to the concept of *limited liability* and the legalising of limited partnerships and limited companies.

Company shareholders' liability is limited to the amount that they have agreed to pay for their shares. In the case of *private* limited companies, however, transfer of shares is restricted, and there can be no *public* invitation to subscribe for further shares. These drawbacks can be overcome by conversion to *public limited company* (plc) status which enables large amounts of capital to be channelled into a business from a large group of savers, some of whom may only hold a few shares. Indeed, shareholders are able to reduce their personal total risk by investing in a number of diverse companies.

Thus the limited company, particularly the plc which can make a direct invitation to the public to subscribe for its shares, is an admirable vehicle for growth, as it is able to access a wider range of sources of finance (see Chapter 12).

8.2 Purpose for which finance is required

We have seen that the need for finance in business arises mainly because cash receipts lag behind cash payments.

EXERCISE 8.2

For what purposes would Mary Pike (Chapter 2) have needed finance when she first started her electronics business?

For *fixed assets* – including premises, plant, machinery, tools and presses, vehicles and patent fees.

For *working capital* – to pay wages, purchase materials for stock and production, rent of premises if not owned, product development, production and marketing expenses and services, before receipts from customers self-financed these items. An additional cash buffer might also be required to cover any temporary shortage of funds.

After their initial acquisition, and given that the business continues its existing activities, these assets have to be continually replaced out of earnings to maintain operations at the same level. They therefore represent a *permanent* financial requirement. You will recall from Chapter 2 that Mary was fortunate to be able to call on her family for these *long-term* resources. No doubt she formed a limited company from the start with herself and her family as shareholders.

EXERCISE 8.3

Although permanent assets should be permanently financed, can you think of any circumstances that would call for *temporary* medium- or short-term finance?

1 Short-life investment projects would attract medium-term finance.
2 Short-term *bridging* finance, during a period of temporary cash shortfall, perhaps caused by *seasonal* fluctuations in income, delayed payments by customers, or a period of high inflation before selling prices have time to be adjusted upwards.

After the successful establishment of a business, development should follow, either by way of expanding sales of existing products, by venturing into new ones or both. More fixed and working capital will be needed, and inevitably the growth point will be reached when the amount required exceeds the resources of the existing shareholders and the willingness of lenders. At this stage, help from a venture capital company dealing in risk finance, might be the best way forward (see Chapter 11). But if the company's current performance and growth potential are perceived to be sufficiently attractive by the capital market, a *public* flotation of additional shares might be possible – (see Chapter 12).

Further stages of growth might not only be achieved by expansion of existing and new activities but by acquiring other businesses as going concerns. Here the need for further finance can be obviated by issuing shares in the acquiring business to the owners of the purchased concerns, but only if this is agreed. If a share exchange is not agreed, additional finance must be found to pay off shareholders whose company is taken over.

In summary, a business has to finance:

- a layer of *permanent* fixed and working assets; and
- fluctuating *temporary* cash requirements.

Permanent assets should be provided out of long-term (over ten years) or medium-term (three to ten years) sources of finance to ensure continuing use of these assets. Fluctuating requirements can be met out of short-term sources to reduce the costs of borrowing and provide flexibility in financing arrangements.

QUESTIONS 8.1

1 For what purposes would a hairdresser require finance when she first commences business?

2 Why do farmers sometimes resort to short-term business borrowing?

(Answers in Appendix E)

8.3 How much finance is required?

Finance is the lifeblood of a business. The financial manager of an existing business must, therefore, ensure that finance is available when required. This involves short- and long-term cash forecasting, completed by reference to the overall investment, production and marketing plans of the business.

At the small business start-up stage a potential provider of finance will require the submission of a *business plan* including details of the borrower, forecasts of markets, sales, and profitability, and the fixed and working assets required to meet this plan.

A short-term forecast would help to assess the initial requirement for finance before net cash flow turns positive.

Ken Sharp has set up as a wholesaler supplying the retail baking trade. He has rented a local authority trading estate warehouse at £100 a month, and estimates that he will need permanent stocks of at least £10,000 value. A van, two forklift trucks, and storage racks and pallets will cost him a further £30,000, and his operating expenses are estimated at £2,000 per month.

Ken expects that sales in each of the first two months will be £6,000, rising to £12,000 per month thereafter. He sells to the trade at cost plus 50%, and allows his customers two months' credit. His trade suppliers allow him one month to pay, but all other expenses will be paid in the month in which they are incurred.

Required:

a Prepare a cash forecast covering each of the first six months of Ken's business.

b What is the maximum amount of finance needed in this first six months?

a

Month		1	2	3	4	5	6
Receipts	A			6,000	6,000	12,000	12,000
Payments:							
Stocks – initial			10,000				
– replacement			4,000	4,000	8,000	8,000	8,000
Equipment		30,000					
Operating expenses		2,000	2,000	2,000	2,000	2,000	2,000
Rent		100	100	100	100	100	100
	B	32,100	16,100	6,100	10,100	10,100	10,000
Surplus/(deficit) A–B		(32,100)	(16,100)	(100)	(4,100)	1,900	1,900
Opening balance		–	(32,100)	(48,200)	(48,300)	(52,400)	(50,500)
Closing balance		(32,100)	(48,200)	(48,300)	(52,400)	(50,500)	(48,600)

b Total capital required; £52,400 – see month 4. Note that the total capital required is not just the £40,000 to cover equipment and initial stocks, but also a further £12,400 for operating expenses, rent and supplies. This is due to the two months' delay in receiving payment from customers. The position would, of course, be worsened by the interest payable on any loan negotiated with the bank. Indeed, if Ken has been wildly optimistic regarding sales or costs, or receipts from customers, the capital requirement could be even larger. It might therefore be in Ken's interest to negotiate a slightly larger financial provision to give himself a little more leeway.

The kind of short-term cash forecast illustrated above, if continuously updated at monthly or even, where appropriate, weekly intervals, can provide a useful early warning of expected deficiencies in finance. Action can then be planned in advance to cover the critical period.

QUESTION 8.2

Following on the last activity, by the end of month 4, Ken Sharpe realised that his initial sales forecast had been much too conservative. Actual sales for months 1–4 were £6,000, £12,000, £18,000 and £24,000, respectively, and he now considered that they could be held at £24,000 per month for the foreseeable future.

He continues to sell at cost plus 50%, and credit given to customers and received from suppliers remains the same at two months and one month respectively. Operating expenses and rent are not expected to increase.

Required:

a Prepare a cash forecast for Ken for months 5, 6 and 7.

b Given that his bank overdraft (i.e. the closing balance) at the end of month 4 is £42,000, how long after month 7 will it take to pay off his overdraft?

(Answers in Appendix E)

Long-term cash forecasts are normally prepared as part of the long-term corporate planning process. Scheduled investment in growth, whether by expanding production and marketing facilities, or by acquiring other businesses, has to be synchronised with the availability of finance. Forecast profit and loss accounts and balance sheets will reveal the effects of long-term investment and growth plans, and their consequences for future cash flows.

The cash forecast will not contain all the fine detail of receipts and payments included in the short-term forecast, and will probably be prepared in yearly periods rather than in months. The Cash Flow Statement required by Financial Reporting Standard (FRS) 1 to be produced annually by many companies, is perhaps the best format to use, but prepared as a *planning* statement rather than an historic report. It will incorporate annual cash forecasts of:

- Operating activities
- Returns on investments and servicing of finance
- Tax payable
- Investing activities
- Financing

with the bottom line showing the annual increase or decrease in cash.

The following draft shows some of the items commonly shown by most forecasts:

Long-term Cash Forecast Years 1–5 Year	1	2	3	4	5
Net cash flow from operating activities					
Returns on investments and servicing of finance:					
Interest payable					
Dividends payable					
Taxation:					
Corporation Tax payable					
Investing activities:					
Purchase of tangible fixed assets					
Proceeds from sale of fixed assets					
Net cash (outflow)/inflow before financing					
Financing:					
Issue of Ordinary Share Capital					
Loans received					
Repayment of loans					
Increase/(Decrease) in Cash					

If the last line shows a substantial decrease in funds in one or more years, this might necessitate the arrangement of additional finance to support the plans reflected in the statement. Alternatively, changing circumstances may necessitate a revision of the financial plan.

Ultimately, the raising and management of funds to finance the long- and short-term plans of a business is the responsibility of the treasury manager, who in very large corporations operates as a separate *treasury* department, and whose functions involve close contact with global capital and money markets.

When compiling a cash flow statement it must be noted that *depreciation* is only a profit measurement adjustment in annual financial accounts, and not a cash payment. It has therefore to be added back to the planned operating profit. Likewise, to convert operating profit into net cash flow, increases or decreases in trade debtors, trade creditors and stocks, have to be added back to or deducted from the operating profit in the forecast profit and loss account.

For example, if forecast depreciation for next year is £10,000, debtors are planned to increase by £3,000, and creditors increased by £2,000, the adjustments to a planned operating profit of £50,000 would be:

	£
Planned operating profit	50,000
add back depreciation	10,000
less increase in debtors	(3,000)
add increase in creditors	2,000
Net cash flow from operating activities	59,000

From the following budgeted information, prepare a cash flow forecast for next year:

Profit and Loss Account Budget	
Sales	3,000
Cost of Sales	1,500
Gross Profit	1,500
Depreciation	160
Other Expenses	970
Operating Profit Before Interest	370
Loan Interest	30
Operating Profit After Interest	340
Taxation	119
Dividend	100
Retained Profit	£121

Balance Sheet Budget Last Year		Budget
1,100	Fixed Assets – Cost	1,600
(550)	– Depreciation	(710)
550		890
	Current Assets:	
250	Debtors	300
200	Stock	250
280	Cash	350
	Current Liabilities:	
(100)	Creditors	(150)
(100)	Taxation	(119)
(80)	Dividends	(100)
£1,000		£1,421
800	Share Capital	800
200	Retained Profit	321
–	10% Loan	300
£1,000		1,421

As illustrated above, you will first have to adjust the operating profit of £370 shown in the Budgeted Profit and Loss Account, into net cash flow from operating activities. Depreciation is *added back* because it refers to assets purchased before this year. The increase in debtors relates to sales included in this year's profit, but for which payment has not yet been received. Likewise, the increase in creditors is *added back* to profit, as these purchases have not been paid for. Finally, the increase in stock has had the effect of increasing operating profit, and must therefore be deducted.

	£
Operating profit	370
Add Depreciation	160
Increase in Debtors	(50)
Increase in Stock	(50)
Increase in Creditors	50
Net Cash Flow from Operating Activities	480

Cash Flow Forecast for Next Year

	£
Net Cash Flow from operating activities (see above)	480
Returns on investments and servicing finance:	
Interest paid	(30)
Dividends paid	(80)
Taxation: Corporation Tax paid	(100)
Investing activities:	
Purchase of fixed assets	(500)
Net Cash Outflow before financing	(230)
Financing: Loan	300
Increase in Cash and Cash Equivalents	70

TO SUM UP

- This chapter has emphasised the necessity for scheduled business cash plan-ning. Short-term cash forecasts indicate when temporary shortfalls need to be provided for, while longer term forecasts, incorporating investment plans for growth, highlight when additional longer-term finance should be sought.

- The next stage is for the financial manager to approach the financial markets for the most appropriate form of finance to meet the requirement. This will be dealt with in Chapters 9–13.

QUESTIONS 8.3

1 George Strumpshaw planned to set up a coal distributing business. He had saved £50,000 and estimated that he would need a further £100,000 for vehicles, premises, and initial coal stocks. Would the bank manager agree with George that £100,000 was all the additional finance he needed?

▶

▶

2 Balance Sheets for Fido Dogfood Ltd are shown below. Prepare a forecast from this information to show the net change in cash in the coming year. Use the format given in this section for your forecast, showing in a separate note how you have arrived at the net cash inflow from operating activities.

Balance Sheets – Fido Dogfood Ltd	This year		Forecast for next year	
		£000		
Fixed assets	100		120	
less depreciation	40		52	
		60		68
Current assets:				
Stocks	10		12	
Debtors	12		13	
Cash	3		23	
	25		48	
less Current liabilities:				
Creditors	8		9	
Taxation	2		3	
Dividends	1		3	
		14		33
		74		101
Ordinary share capital		60		60
Retained earnings		14		21
Medium term bank loan (10%)		–		20
		74		101

Notes:
1 There is no planned disposal of assets.
2 Tax and dividends are paid in the year following that in which they arise.
3 A full year's interest on the loan will be *paid* during next year.

3 Why does a public limited company have access to a wider financial market than a company without *public* status?

4 What is *bridging* finance? When might it be needed?

5 Current assets will normally be changed into cash within one year. In what sense therefore are current assets permanent?

▶

▶

6 Which of the following influence the amount of capital required by a business?

   a The number of directors;

   b The amount of tax it pays;

   c The lead time between input of resources and payment of goods by customers;

   d Production methods and techniques;

   e The number of shareholders;

   f Planned output and sales.

7 Referring to Ken Sharp's short-term forecast (p. 117), would it make any difference to the amount of finance required if half the customers who should have paid in month 5 defaulted on their payments?

8 What are the two major differences between the short- and the long-term cash forecasts?

(Answers in Appendix E)

FURTHER READING

Pike, R. and B. Neale (2003) *Corporate Finance and Investment*, Prentice Hall, chapter 15.

9 Financial markets and the business organisation

INTRODUCTION

■ Cash forecasts prepared as described in Chapter 8 will signal the need for additional short- or long-term finance. The financial manager, who should be conversant with the financial markets, will then be responsible for recommending how and when the need should be met.

■ This chapter takes an overview of the sources of finance available to businesses, and how the services of financial intermediaries operating in the financial markets bring together those who have surplus funds with others who require them.

LEARNING OBJECTIVES

When you have completed this chapter you should be able to:

1 Describe the structure and functions of the financial markets.

2 Explain the role of a 'financial intermediary'.

3 Differentiate the functions of the 'money' and the 'capital' markets.

4 List the main sources of short-, medium-, and long-term finance.

5 Identify the major groups of financial institutions associated with sourcing finance.

9.1 Financing by owner's or borrowed funds?

Daisy Bloom is a successful market gardener who a few years ago invested her life savings in her business. It has grown considerably since then, mainly as the result of her 'ploughing back' into the business a large proportion of her profits each year. She now has the opportunity of doubling her operating capacity, but has no cash resource of her own to acquire the necessary fixed and working capital. Her present capital invested is £300,000 and her net profit before tax last year was £45,000. She requires £300,000 additional finance for proposed expansion and estimates that the total profit before tax in the enlarged business will be £105,000.

The improvement in profit will be the result of more efficient operations, and the benefits of bulk buying.

Daisy has two main financing options:

a Invite a friend, Rose Flowers, who has the amount of capital required, to join her in the formation of a limited company; or

b Obtain a loan repayable in ten years' time at an interest rate of 11%. Assuming a tax rate of 40%, calculate the total profit after tax under both options, showing what Daisy's share is in each case.

	Limited company £	Loan £
Trading profit	105,000	105,000
Interest on loan	–	33,000
	105,000	72,000
Taxation	42,000	28,800
	63,000	43,200
Daisy's share	31,500	43,200
Rose's share	31,500	–

Daisy is £11,700 better off under the borrowing than under the company option. This is because the cost of obtaining capital from the new shareholder is her half-share of total profit (i.e. £31,500), whereas the loan only costs £19,800 (interest of £33,000 *less* tax of 40%). It is also worth noting that even under the company option Daisy would be entitled to £4,500 (£31,500–£27,000) more than she previously earned.

This example demonstrates the benefits of borrowing, and explains why businesses are basically financed from two sources:

■ *Use of owners' funds* – such funds are normally permanently invested in the business, only to be repaid if business operations cease.

■ *Use of other people's funds* – to be repaid as agreed, unless they are government grants.

Own funds (equity capital)

These are gleaned from:

a the past and continuing savings of the original owner(s);
b profits earned in the business and retained for reinvestment;
c the savings of people who become part-owners of the business, through partnership or shareholdings including venture capital providers (see Chapter 11).

Once a company has become established and is growing, retained profit provides the bulk of the finance needed but companies will also issue further shares to existing shareholders (i.e. right issues), or to new shareholders.

Other people's funds

These come mainly from:

a loan providers;
b suppliers' credit;
c instalment credit, hire purchase and leasing arrangements:
d grants and loans from central and local government, and the European Union.

It is clearly important for a business to maintain the most cost-efficient mixture of owners' and borrowed funds, as this has a positive effect on investment and earnings, and consequently on the wealth of its owners.

The success of the investment plans of a business will therefore rely heavily on the financial manager keeping in close touch with the financial markets, with the aim of minimising the ongoing cost and risk of the capital mix.

QUESTION 9.1

Which of the following relate **i** to funds provided by the owners of businesses. and **ii** to those made available from other sources?

a Loans.
b Profit retained for reinvestment.
c Making more efficient use of capital already invested.
d Grants and allowances from central and local government.
e Supplier's credit.
f Past and continuing savings of the present owners.
g The savings of newly admitted partners and shareholders (new owners).
h Hire purchase and leasing.

(Answers in Appendix E)

9.2 The financial markets

All markets comprise sellers and buyers who wish to trade; sellers having a *surplus* of a commodity or service, and buyers who are in *deficit*. The more sellers and buyers there are in a market, the more efficient the agreed prices of trades. The financial markets deal in financing, bringing together those who have surplus funds with those who require them. It follows, therefore, that ever-expanding economic activity would result in an increasing demand for finance, and in the evolution of sophisticated markets to bring savers together with investors.

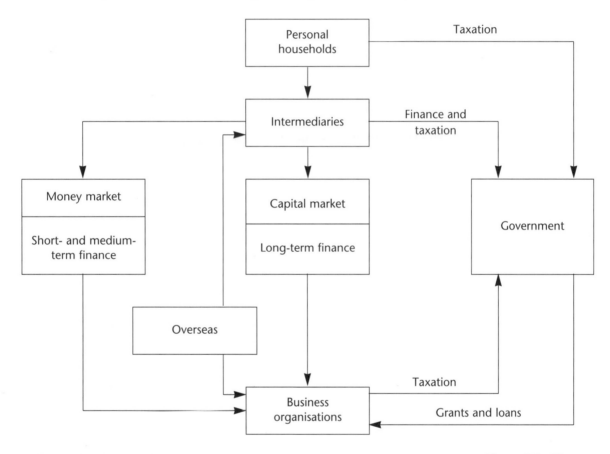

Figure 9.1 Flow of funds to the business sector

Figure 9.1 shows that the government sector obviously has a significant impact on the flow of funds through the economy, by revenue-raising through taxation, and borrowing short-term (using Treasury Bills), and long-term (using government bonds), to meet its public sector expenditure commitments.

However, as we are concerned essentially with the financing decisions of the business sector in this part of the book, Figure 9.1 is drawn to emphasise the flow of financial funding to business organisations. Except for government grants and loans, new business finance largely originates from private individuals and overseas investors. Individuals do invest directly into business firms if invited to do so, but most channel their savings through intermediate specialist institutions known collectively as *financial intermediaries*.

9.3 Financial intermediaries

Leaf through the pages of the *Financial Times* or the financial sections of other newspapers. Note and list the different institutions who advertise to attract the savings of individuals.

You have probably included the commercial banks in your list, building societies and National Savings. But you will also have observed that savings also find their way into insurance companies as premiums; into pension funds to provide future pensions; and into finance houses as savings deposits.

Because they are obliged to pay interest, pensions, or insurance claims, these institutions put those savings to work, with the objective of earning more than they pay to investors. They do so by *re-investing* these funds in company shares and loans, in government securities, in private house loans (building societies and banks), and in hire purchase loans (finance houses).

Other private investments are made through unit trusts; open ended investment companies (OEICs); investment trusts; and venture capital organisations, who offer a diverse range of collective funds based on the share and loan capital of UK and overseas companies and government stocks.

Yet another group of intermediaries advises upon and facilitates the issue of shares and loans by companies. Investors may invest directly with companies, but most issues are made through merchant or investment banking intermediaries (see Chapter 12). This group is usually rewarded by charging commission, and/or management fees for their services.

Thus, a wide-ranging network of intermediate services has developed in the financial markets to enable a more efficient allocation of funds between savers and ultimate business investors than individual investors could make for themselves.

These services are offered through two sub-sets of the financial markets, which are broadly time-related. The *money markets* – providing short- and medium-term finance – and the *capital markets* – lending long term.

9.4 The money markets

The institutions engaged in these markets may provide financial accommodation to service an overnight need, or a five–ten-year loan, though the latter could also be arranged through the capital markets. A summary of the main types of short-

and medium-term finance used by businesses is discussed below, but is the subject of a more expanded analysis in Chapters 10 and 11.

Short-term borrowing

Bank loans are usually for fixed amounts, for specified periods up to, say, three years, at fixed rates of interest, although variable interest governed by changing market rates can be negotiated. Banks normally insist that repayment is secured by the pledging of particular assets – called a fixed charge.

Bank overdrafts are easily arranged and are more flexible than loans because, whilst a top limit of borrowing is specified, the amount of finance required at any particular time may vary, together with interest rates charged, and therefore the average cost of borrowing ought to be lower.

Factoring and invoice discounting involve the selling of debts to a finance house, usually the subsidiary of a clearing bank, which advances about 80% of the debts sold. Capital is thus release to be used on other projects. Factoring also includes a sales ledger management service for customers, with or without the advance of finance. The interest rate charged is above the bank's lending rate, and if sales ledger management is included, there is an additional charge for that.

Bills of exchange are equivalent to postdated cheques. A buyer of goods accepts an undertaking to pay the bill in, say, three months' time, by signing (accepting) it. The supplier is then able to obtain immediate payment by discounting (selling) the bill to a bank or discount house, and has therefore got access to much-needed finance. The discount taken by the bank recompenses them for having to wait for payment from the buyer. Bills are also used to obtain finance not involving the sale of goods, in form of *acceptance credits*.

Trade credit on goods and services   Trade credit is a universal means of financing, especially important to smaller companies which lack access to many credit sources. Taking *extended* credit without agreement of the supplier is often resorted to these days, but might result in the loss of supplier's goodwill as well as endangering the latter's cash flow. Where trade discount is offered for prompt payment, delaying payment may secure more finance, but can be very expensive in loss of discounts. Some suppliers will allow arrangements for customers to pay them by instalments.

Medium-term borrowing

Term loans   These are principally made by banks for from four to ten years to growing companies. They normally cover projects or assets with lives matching those of the loans. Interest may be at a fixed or variable rate, and repayment of the capital can be delayed in the earlier years of the loan if desired. The banks normally insist that term loans be secured on tangible assets, but *unsecured* loans may be negotiated at higher interest rates.

Small firms loan guarantee scheme Government guarantees against default of loans of between £5,000 and £250,000 are made by bankers and other financial institutions to businesses who are unable to obtain a conventional loan.

Hire purchase This is a method of financing now much used by businesses. The agreement prescribes a deposit payment, the repayment being by instalments over a period of usually less than five years, and a final payment whereupon the goods become the possession of the hirer. Tax advantages include capital cost allowance to be set off against profit, and interest charged can be debited against profit of the hirer.

Leasing This is similar to hire purchase, except that the lessee never owns the asset. The lease ensures continuous use of the asset however. Tax capital allowances are passed back to the lessee in lower interest charges, and the lease payments are wholly chargeable as an expense against the profit of the lessee. Leasing was often referred to as 'off-balance sheet' financing, because neither the asset nor the lease liability appeared on the lessee's balance sheet, although this applies only to operating leases (see Chapter 10).

Plant hire This is similar to leasing, but is for shorter daily or weekly periods.

Financial assistance from central and local government and the European Union

Assistance is available from many schemes in the form of grants and loans for promising new businesses.

Investment projects in government designated 'Assisted Areas' which aim to help safeguard or create jobs, may receive government grants if such projects would not proceed without such aid. Grant assistance is also available for research and development projects which might lead to the development of new products and processes (see Chapter 11).

Tax incentives to invest in plant and machinery, and for venture capital providers to invest in small and developing businesses, are also available.

The European Investment Bank (EIB) may make loans for any investment project anywhere in the UK – principally to small and medium-sized businesses (SMEs) (i.e. ones with fewer than 500 employees).

9.5 Financial institutions providing short- and medium-term funds

The commercial banks These are the suppliers of finance known to most people, although they supply little more in total than the insurance companies and pension funds. Natwest Royal Bank of Scotland, Barclays, Lloyds TSB, HBOS, HSBC, and Abbey predominate, traditionally taking short-term deposits from their customers, and lending by way of short-term loans and overdrafts. About an eighth of their total funds is kept in cash or relatively liquid form to meet the demands of depositors, leaving a substantial balance to invest in loans, etc. Increasing competition and criticism of the banks in recent years have moved them to expand their traditional role as short-term lenders, and they are now the principal lenders in the housing market. Medium- and even long-term business loans may now be negotiated, primarily through their merchant banking subsidiaries, who carry out other functions described below under 'merchant banks'.

Banks are also the major operators and intermediaries in the Euro currency loans market (see Chapter 10).

Further short-term finance is provided by the banks' discounting and accepting bills of exchange, particularly in connection with overseas trade.

Discount houses There are ten houses in the London Discount Market Association. Their traditional function is to provide short-term finance by discounting bills of exchange, but they have extended their investing activity to include government Treasury Bills, local authority bonds and certificates of deposit. The latter are negotiable certificates issued by a bank to large corporate depositors of money for fixed periods at fixed rates of interest. The discount houses, together with the commercial banks, the merchant banks which are members of the Accepting Houses Committee and the Bank of England, comprise the three-month short-term *money market.*

Merchant banks These were originally merchants who developed lending businesses.

Hambros, Kleinwort Benson and Morgan Grenfell are well known, but there are many more of similar size, most of whom have been taken over by American and European investment banks. Some smaller independent merchant banks do, however, still remain.

Services rendered by most, but not all, merchant banks are extensive, including:

- providing acceptance credits by discounting bills of exchange;
- advice on export financing; foreign exchange dealing;
- arranging Stock Exchange quotations and new issues of shares and loan stock;
- advice on corporate financial planning; merger advice; leasing financing; hire purchase;
- personal investment advice and management for clients who have over £50,000 to invest;
- venture and development capital for small businesses.

Foreign banks Branches of overseas banks compete with the UK commercial banks in provision of short- and medium-term finance – particularly for overseas trade and investment.

Finance houses These deal mainly in hire purchase and lease financing. Short-term depositors provide most of their funds, although they will accept longer-term deposits and pay a higher rate of interest on them. Though they take the risk of *borrowing* for the short-term and *lending* over medium-term periods, the lending charges are adjusted upwards to absorb this risk, particularly in connection with hire purchase transactions. Finance houses also arrange short- and medium-term loans, and export finance.

Factoring and invoice discounting companies   Although independent companies, many are subsidiaries of the commercial banks. They provide short-term finance by purchasing business debts. Factoring companies, as we saw above, also offer debtor's ledger management services for an additional charge.

Leasing companies   The majority are subsidiaries of commercial banks, merchant banks and finance houses, though some are independents in the Finance and Leasing Association. They specialise in lease finance.

9.6 The capital markets

When companies plan to invest in long-term assets, they turn to the capital markets for long-term finance (i.e. 10 years or more). This may be to borrow, or to issue more shares.

Borrowing creates a liability that has to be repaid by the company, according to the terms of the loan, and may be arranged in one of the ways discussed below.

Mortgage loans are normally made by insurance companies and pension funds for periods of more than twenty years at fixed rates of interest. They are mainly secured by deposit of the title deeds of the property mortgaged. The main recipients are large companies to finance long-term assets, but smaller companies are increasingly being accommodated by mortgage loans from other institutions, such as building societies.

Term loans are similar to medium-term loans, but for longer periods and at higher interest rates. They are usually secured on fixed assets.

Debentures and loan stocks are transferable securities, normally secured on specific assets or by a 'floating charge' on *all* the assets of the business giving the holder priority in repayment of the debt over the claims of other creditors. The interest rate is fixed, and the securities are repayable on or between certain dates. Unsecured debentures may also be issued, but at higher interest rates.

Convertible loan stock has the added feature of giving the holders the *option* to convert their loan securities into shares on or between specified dates at predetermined prices.

Sale and leaseback is not strictly long-term borrowing but is a method of releasing capital for investment by realising 100% of the value of property by selling it, mainly to insurance companies and pension funds, but retaining use of it by leasing it back for a long period. The rent is reviewed every five years or so, which can make this a very expensive method of financing, as well as giving up any possible future increases in the value of the property.

An issue of shares to existing (a rights issue – see Chapter 13) or new shareholders (see Chapter 12) increases a company's *permanent* capital.

Investment and merchant banks are the primary financial institutions who advise upon and arrange the issue, with the largest proportion taken up by some of the institutions described below.

9.7 Financial institutions providing long-term finance

The London Stock Exchange Although the institutions described in this section are the main investors in the capital market (see Chapter 12), individual shareholders own about 20% of *quoted* equity shares. In recent years, personal equity investment has been encouraged through privatisation issues, and the introduction of 'free of tax' private equity plans (PEPS) and Individual Savings Accounts (ISAs).

Insurance companies and pension funds Both types of institution invest in long-term assets because their liabilities to policy-holders and pensioners respectively are essentially long-term too. As there is a continuous stream of premium and pension contribution cash, immediate liabilities for insurance claims or pensions are met out of current income, the surplus being available for longer-term investment. Both have to plan investments with an eye on *stability* of income and capital, so loans, mortgages, property, sale and lease back, government and local authority stocks are preferred. In recent years, inflation has forced them to invest in the shares of limited companies to maintain the capital value of their funds. However, despite their long-term leanings, insurance companies will now entertain applications for capital from smaller companies.

Unit trusts Money received from investors seeking income or capital growth, or both, is added to a fund invested in securities appropriate to the wishes of investors. The fund is divided into units, each representing a share of the fund. Some funds specialise in particular industries, e.g. oil-related or biotechnology companies, others have a wide spread of investments to reduce risk further. Many trusts now specialise in overseas investments. The trusts also invest in *new issues* of securities through the Stock Exchange.

A unit trust is called an 'open-ended' fund, as new cash is continually being received and paid out. Units can be bought and sold through the unit trust managers at offer and bid prices, respectively, quoted daily.

Investment trust companies These are limited companies specialising in the shares and loan stocks of other companies. They obtain capital by issuing their shares, which are traded on the Stock Exchange, and by borrowing. Note that a unit trust is unable to borrow.

If approached by smaller companies they will be unwilling to invest directly in their shares, subject to a minimum investment of about £25,000.

Open-ended investment companies (OEICs)   These are investment vehicles for both individual and institutional investors, and are a cross between unit and investment trusts, They are open-ended funds like unit trusts, but are corporations rather than trusts. They issue shares – not units – at single rather than dual prices. Their greater flexibility and wider appeal to investors in Europe and further afield will continue to encourage their establishment, and the conversion of existing unit trusts to OEICs status.

Building societies   These specialise predominantly in lending to individuals to enable them to purchase their homes. Funds are borrowed on short-term from savers, and loaned for the long-term to borrowers, the risk in doing this being smoothed out to some extent by the variability of interest rates charged to borrowers, assistance is also given to small businesses to purchase premises.

Other financial institutions

3i Group plc   This is the holding company for various UK and overseas subsidiary and associated companies. It was founded in 1945 by the clearing banks, but went public in 1994. It operates largely in the UK, and its main business is the provision of equity and loan capital and management expertise to small and medium-sized businesses that do not have ready access to the capital markets.

Venture and development capital   While 3i is one of the largest institutions in its field, there are many other venture capital companies, private individuals, government and EU agencies who offer financial assistance to new commercial ventures ripe for exploitation, and to small and medium-sized businesses that require capital for development but are too small to appeal to the public (see Chapter 11).

The British Venture Capital Association (BVCA) represents most sources of venture capital in the UK.

Investment banks offer corporate finance advice, particularly in the areas of initial public offerings (IPOs) of shares, mergers and takeovers, treasury advice.

TO SUM UP

- Most investment finance is channelled into businesses through a network of financial intermediaries participating in the financial markets.
- In this chapter we have examined the nature of financial intermediaries, and the different forms they take. We have seen that they operate through the money and capital markets to filter the aggregated surplus funds of the personal and other sectors of the economy into the business sector.
- The different types of short-, medium- and long-term finance summarised in this chapter will be examined in more detail in Chapters 10–13.

1 What is the difference between a bank loan and an overdraft?

2 Do companies who deal in invoice discounting also offer a sales ledger management service?

3 How does convertible loan stock differ from ordinary loan stock?

4 'Hire purchase and leasing are two ways of purchasing assets by instalments.' True or false?

(Answers in Appendix E)

1 Why do commercial banks mainly supply short-term finance, and insurance companies and pension funds long-term finance?

2 Unit trusts and investment trusts both invest in company shares and loan stocks. How, then, do these two institutions differ?

3 Study the following balance sheet, then answer the questions relating to it that follow.

Leisure Clothing Limited – balance sheet at 31 December 2000

ASSETS EMPLOYED			
Fixed assets:			£
Land and buildings (cost *less* depreciation)			212,000
Plant and machinery (cost *less* depreciation)			362,000
			574,000
Current assets:			
Stocks		35,000	
Debtors		40,000	
Cash		1,000	
		76,000	
less **Current liabilities**:			
Trade creditors	30,000		
Hire purchase contracts	3,000		
Bank overdraft	5,000	38,000	38,000
			612,000
FINANCED BY			
Ordinary share capital			250,000
Retained earnings			250,000
Shareholders' interest			500,000
Long-term liabilities:			
12% Debentures (2009)		50,000	
14% Mortgage loan (2013)		50,000	
10% Loan (2003)		12,000	112,000
			612,000

Notes:
1 There is a contingent liability for bills of exchange discounted of £2,000.
2 The present value of least contracts outstanding is £20,000.

▶

1 Briefly indicate which funds are supplied by the owners of the company and which by other sources.

2 Which of the sources of funds are short-term, which medium-term and which long-term?

3 Which institutions are likely to have provided the various funds in question 2?

4 How can **a** land buildings and **b** debtors be the basis for further financing?

(Answers in Appendix E)

FURTHER READING

Arnold, G. (2002) *Corporate Financial Investment*, Financial Times Pitman, chapters 1 and 9.

Pike, R. and B. Neale (2003) *Corporate Finance and Investment*, Prentice Hall, chapter 2.

Samuels, R., F. Wilkes and R. Brayshaw (1999) *Management of Company Finance*, Chapman & Hall, chapter 2, 11 and 12.

Short- and medium-term finance

- Short-term finance could describe any liability repayable within three years, though most sources are repayable within one year.

- Medium-term provision is usually arranged to match the lives of projects from four to ten years.

- Beyond ten years, finance is usually in the form of equity capital and long-term loans. The problems that small and medium-sized businesses have in accessing long-term finance are discussed in Chapter 11, while the long-term securities markets open to larger companies are described in Chapters 12 and 13.

- In this chapter we discuss more fully the types of short- and medium-term finance which were summarised in Chapter 9.

When you have completed this chapter you should be able to:

1 List and describe the different types of short-term finance, their advantages and risks.

2 Describe the circumstances most appropriate for arranging a term loan, and specify the conditions most likely to appear in the loan agreement.

3 List the different kinds of Eurocurrency loans.

4 Explain the nature of hire purchase finance and its advantages and risks.

5 Explain the difference between financial and operating leases, and list the advantages of lease finance.

6 Show the necessity of comparing the cost of leasing an asset with alternative methods of financing, before appraising the project in connection with which the asset is required.

10.1 Types and sources of short-term finance

Except for Sterling commercial paper, the following types of finance are available to most businesses

Trade credit   Most suppliers would cease trading if they did not grant customers time to pay. Trade credit and accrued expenses are a spontaneous and constant source of finance, therefore, upon which all businesses, but especially small ones, depend for many short-term needs.

Sometimes cash discounts are offered by suppliers to encourage early payment of outstanding accounts. Ignoring this discount can be expensive. For example, a supplier offering 2½% if invoices are paid within 10 days might otherwise expect payment within 30 days. The cost of ignoring the prompt payment discount and paying at the end of 30 days would amount to an annual rate of interest of (2.5 ÷ 97.5) × (365 ÷ 20) = 47% (approx.). Note that the extended period of credit is 20 days, i.e. 30 less 10, and that the amount of *additional* finance is not 100 but 97.5.

EXERCISE 10.1

What would the annual interest rate be in the above example if the buyer takes extended credit of 60 days from the date of the invoice?

$$(2.5 \div 97.5) \times (365 \div 50) = 18.7\%$$

The cost of taking extended credit from suppliers decreases dramatically with time, but apart from comparing this with the cost of alternative finance, the risk that supplies will be stopped, and credit-rating damaged, acts as a brake.

Bank overdrafts   This is a much-used facility for businesses to draw cheques up to an agreed credit limit and is largely arranged to cover seasonal cash shortages, and as *bridging* finance for the purchase of property and machinery. Subject to the credit standing of customers, overdrafts are generally renewable and are used as 'permanent' finance by some businesses although they can be called in at short notice by the bank.

Interest is charged on the outstanding balance each day, at bank base rate plus an additional lending premium related to the credit standing of the customer. The advantages of an overdraft are:

- It is the *cheapest* form of short-term finance.
- It is *easily and quickly negotiated*, and easily *renewed*.
- *Security may not be required*, although about 50% of all overdrafts are secured on assets by fixed or floating charge or by personal guarantee.
- It offers the *flexibility* of sums being repayable or drawn without notice.

The major drawbacks are that overdrafts are generally repayable on demand, though banks normally allow notice of six to twelve months; and that short-term interest rates may be increased whereas long-term rates are fixed.

When considering an application for an overdraft, a bank will require information on current and past trading and financial performance of the applicant, together with cash and sales forecasts. The current and acid test ratios we met in Chapter 2 will be of particular interest to the bank.

Bank loans   Short-term loans negotiated with banks and other financial institutions differ from overdrafts as they are arranged for a specific amount, for a specific period and are subject to specific repayment terms. They only flexibility may be in the interest rate, which may be fixed or variable. Security is normally required for a loan, and assessment of the applicant's credit status is more exacting than for an overdraft.

Sterling commercial paper   These are promissory notes issued by very large companies for borrowings of at least £500,000. They are issued to other large companies or financial institutions at relatively low interest rates for periods of a few months.

Bill financing   As stated in Chapter 9, a bill of exchange is similar to a postdated cheque in that the person signing (accepting) it agrees to pay it some 60 to 180 days later. Meanwhile the person receiving it can sell it to a bank or discount house at a discount, thus providing needed funds. The discount rate is quite low because of the integrity of the acceptor – usually about 1% above bank base rate, which may be lower than the cost of an overdraft to some businesses.

When used in connection with purchase and sale of goods, bills of exchange are known as *trade bills*, and provide a facility for a vendor to receive immediate payment for goods sold, and for the purchaser time to sell the goods before the acceptance is due for payment.

A *bank bill* is used to provide short-term finance for any purpose. It is drawn by the person requiring the finance, accepted by a bank or an acceptance house (which charges an acceptance fee) and discounted by the drawer at a bank or discount house. The drawer thus acquires low-cost short-term finance for the period stated in the bill, at the end of which he will have to reimburse the acceptance house, which will already have paid the bill when it was presented for payment by the discount house or bank.

The main advantages of bill finance are that it is as cheap as, if not cheaper than, overdrafts, and extends the volume of short-term finance available.

Factoring involves the sale of book debts to a factoring company on a continuing basis, the factor administering the sales ledger of the client and providing credit control and an optional without recourse insurance against non-payment of debts. It is, therefore, a management and financing service with financing being optional, though usually taken up. Agreements are normally drawn up for an initial period of twelve months, continuing thereafter indefinitely until notice (of about six months) is given. The main factoring service providers are subsidiaries of the clearing banks.

The cost of factoring includes:

- a *factoring fee* based upon the work involved in servicing the client's sales ledger; this is usually between 0.5 and 3% of *gross turnover*, depending upon the size and rate of turnover, and the average value of invoices;
- a *financing charge* on the amount drawn by the client on a day-to-day basis, at between 1½ and 5% over base rate;
- *collection charges* such as legal fees incurred in collecting older debts.

Factoring is thus more expensive than bank borrowing, but provides additional management services that more than compensate for the difference in cost, especially in the case of growing small and medium-sized companies who lack credit control expertise.

The mechanics of factoring are that the client sends his invoices to the factor at, say, weekly intervals, from which the factoring fee is deducted and the balance placed to the client's account. The factor sends the invoices to the client's customer, requiring payment to be made to the factor.

Meanwhile the client may draw upon up to 80% of the balance of his account, according to need, and will receive the balance of each invoice when it is paid by his customer to the factor.

The main advantages of factoring are:

- *Capital is released* immediately from accounts receivable, thus providing additional finance for business expansion, particularly when a lack of security prevents other forms of borrowing, and lessening the risk of overtrading.
- *Cash flows* are more predictable, and credit insurance lowers the cost of bad debts.
- *Savings* in accounts receivable, administration and credit control.
- The provision of an expert, specialised *credit control service*.
- *Better terms* can be negotiated with suppliers, and cash discounts on supplies taken advantage of.

Factoring for export business is dealt with in Chapter 23.

Invoice discounting is solely a means of raising cash, by selling book debts to an invoice discounting company. The client company, however, continues to administer its own sales ledger in the normal way but, in addition, sends the discounting company copies of the invoices agreed under the arrangement.

The discounting company makes an initial payment of up to 75% to the client, who, acting as agent for the discounting company, collects the debts from customers in the normal way and pays all monies so received direct to the discounting company's collection account. The discounting company finally accounts to the client for the balance of the invoiced amount due. It is a financing method more suited to the large, well-established, company.

The costs of invoice discounting include a *financing charge* of up to 5% above bank base rate, plus a service charge of between ¼% and 1% of each invoiced amount.

There has been a huge growth in factoring and invoice discounting in recent years, but particularly the latter, probably attributable to the growing late payment behaviour of debtors over the same period.

Unpaid taxation and dividends   Delays in payment of taxation of up to twelve months can provide a valuable line of credit, as can dividends which may be delayed for up to six months.

QUESTIONS 10.1

1 What might be the result of taking extended credit from suppliers when cash discount is not normally allowed?

2 A bank that 'accepts' a bill on behalf of a client is doing so in connection with **a** the bill of costs connected with factoring, **b** an invoice sent by a supplier, **c** a bank overdraft, **d** a bill of exchange, **e** a short-term loan. Indicate which is the most appropriate of the alternatives.

3 In connection with factoring, which of the following is incorrect?
   a Customers are not allowed cash discount if the supplier has factored his or her debts.
   b The factor services the customer's sales ledger.
   c A factoring arrangement always includes the provision of finance.

4 Simon Poacher's Pie and Paté Company is experiencing a rapid expansion in sales, and requires approximately £50,000 additional working capital. Although the company has not yet reached its bank overdraft limit, it wishes to retain this facility to cover any cash flow emergencies. The two immediate financing alternatives are:
   a to extend the credit received from suppliers by forgoing cash discounts; payment terms are currently 2% if accounts are paid within 10 days, net in 40 days; and purchases are running at £52,500 per month;
   b to sell accounts receivable of £70,000 per month to a factor, who will charge a service fee of 2% on accounts purchased. The factor will make available to Simon 75% of the receivables, after deduction of a service fee of 12% per annum on total turnover. It is estimated that Simon will save £840 per month on sales ledger administration and bad debts if he chooses factoring.

Required:
a Calculate the cost per cent of each alternative.
b Which method of financing would you choose?

(Answers in Appendix E)

10.2 Types and sources of medium-term finance

Medium-term financing has grown considerably in the last twenty years to fill the gap which has widened between short- and long-term facilities. Among the reasons for this gap are:

- Reluctance of *borrowers* to commit themselves to long-term loans at high interest rates during a period of economic uncertainty, and with the possibility that interest rates might fall during the term of the loan.
- Conversely, *lenders* have been reluctant to lend at other than high interest rates, given the level of inflation and general uncertainty.
- Borrowing medium-term offers more *stability* as regards term, interest and amount than short-term borrowing.
- In the face of *political and competitive pressure*, clearing banks have been more willing to lend medium-term.
- Competition from *overseas banks*, particularly branches of US banks, who are able to lend at keener interest rates because of their lower overhead costs in this country.
- Growth of *leasing* to help overcome the liquidity problems of companies.
- Growth of the *Eurocurrency market*, making it possible to borrow European and other international currencies for medium terms, at competitive interest rates.

10.3 Term loans

Whilst the clearing banks are the largest providers of term loans, they operate in a highly competitive market. Branches and subsidiaries of foreign banks, insurance companies, merchant banks and finance houses are all willing to consider applications for term loans. Even the government, under its selective assistance scheme, offers medium-term loans at concessionary rates (see Chapter 11).

Negotiations for a medium-term loan will cover the following:

- The lender will have to be satisfied about the *commercial standing* of the applicant, the efficacy of its management, and the forecast adequacy of future cash flows to service the loan repayments.
- *Security* for a loan is infrequently required, but this will be entirely dependent upon the credit status of the applicant.
- *Terms* of between five and seven years are predominant.
- The *interest rate* on term loans is usually 1%–4% over the interbank rate depending upon the customer's standing, security and loan agreement covenants. Rates are normally variable, being adjusted every six months on average. If a fixed interest rate is agreed, there may be provision for the borrower to renegotiate the rate, although a penalty clause may deter him from doing so.
- *Repayment terms* can be extremely flexible. Loans can be paid back in a lump sum at the end of the loan period, but more frequently the arrangement is repayment

by instalments. An agreed delay before repayment commences will give a business time to generate cash flows.

■ The lender charges an *arrangement fee* to cover the costs of credit status investigation and administrative and legal costs.

Negotiations for medium-term loans are smoother than for long-term ones. The period of negotiation is shorter; it is easier to deal with one lender than hundreds of security holders; terms can be renegotiated informally.

Term loans are particularly useful for:

■ assets whose lives can be matched with the term of the loan, such as plant and machinery; swiftly changing technology may now render long-term finance unsuitable for such purposes;
■ financing additional working capital for a self-liquidating project;
■ funding short-term overdrafts that have virtually become hardcore borrowing;
■ periods when market conditions do not favour the issue of long-term debt;
■ providing flexibility in financing when future needs are uncertain;
■ small to medium-sized companies, for whom long-term funds are not available.

EXERCISE 10.2

If a term loan of £50,000 has to be repaid by equal annual instalments over four years we are in effect paying the lender an annuity. Appendix C gives the present value of an annuity of £1 for different periods, at different rates of interest. Using the table in Appendix C, and assuming an interest rate of 10%, calculate the annual repayment instalment on the £50,000 loan.

Loan ÷ PV annuity factor = 50,000 ÷ 3.1699 = £15,773

QUESTIONS 10.2

'The trouble with medium-term loans is that they can be called in at any time at the whim of the lender.' True or false? Explain.

(Answer in Appendix E)

10.4 Eurocurrency loans

These originated in the mid-1960s when there were large deposits of US dollars (known as Eurodollars) in European banks – partly the result of a US trade surplus. It was more profitable for companies to hold deposits in Europe when US interest rates were low, and also because the US Federal authorities had placed exchange control restrictions on the movement of dollars overseas.

Since the 1960s, however, the expansion of multi-national operations by commercial companies, banks and other financial institutions, and the resultant increased demand for finance, has led to the 'globalisation' of the financial markets. This has been greatly facilitated by a continuing advance in computer and communications technology available to the main financial centres, led by London, New York and Tokyo. International financial operations can now be speedily completed across computer screens in different parts of the world.

Eurocurrency deposits are not only denominated in dollars. They may be in any currency deposited with a bank outside the country of the currency's origin, e.g. oil revenues from the Middle East deposited in Europe, but are still generally referred to as Eurocurrency. The market is mainly European and centred on London, but operates internationally in any currency.

The short-term Eurocurrency *money market* is largely used for interbank transactions, but also by very large companies.

The *capital market* includes issues of Eurocommercial paper (ECP), Euronotes and Eurobonds.

Eurocommercial paper up to an agreed limit, is issued in tranches by very large companies to syndicated banks who place it with lenders. It has short-term maturity dates chosen by the issuing company, with market-related interest rates.

Medium-term unsecured Euronotes with maturities of between three and ten years, are also issued to syndicated banks up to an agreed borrowing limit. Periodic placings up to this limit with institutional lenders are made at variable interest rates determined by the banks. Governments, large companies, and financial institutions are the main borrowers. The amounts borrowed are large, and rarely less than £500,000.

Long-term ten–fifteen-year secured Eurobond issues largely by multinational companies, are sold simultaneously in more than one country, with one bank acting for a consortium of banks, taking the lead in the arrangements. Interest rates may be fixed or variable. Issue costs are high, but because loans tend to be over £10 million, the size of the loan can easily absorb them.

The major problem with borrowing or lending international currencies is the risk of exchange rate losses. Loans must normally be repaid in the currency originally borrowed, so if (say) sterling depreciates against the borrowed currency, the cost of both interest and repayment of the loan could be very high. Companies operating in the country whose currency has been borrowed can overcome this problem by using cash flows and assets in that country to meet their liabilities.

QUESTIONS 10.3

1 'A Eurocurrency loan is one arranged in a European country.' True or false?

2 What is the difference between Euronotes and Eurobonds?

(Answers in Appendix E)

10.5 Hire purchase

For the small to medium-sized business unable to negotiate further bank credit, this is a second line of finance offering use of productive assets upon payment of a relatively small initial down payment, followed by an agreed number of instalments which include both interest and capital repayment.

The assets do not become the possessions of the hirer until the final instalment is paid.

Finance houses are the usual suppliers of credit, either acting through the supplier or, more likely, dealing direct with the hirer following investigation of his credit status.

Agreements are commonly between one and five years but may be longer. They will always be shorter than the life of the asset, with asset disposal value greater than outstanding instalments at any time.

The required deposit is dependent upon current government credit regulations, but instalment repayments can be arranged to match the hirer's cash flows.

The rates of interest charged, commonly between 20% and 40%, are relatively high, to compensate finance houses for the risks of borrowing short-term from the banks and the money market, whilst being committed to longer-term lending. Variable rates of interest may be adopted for long-term agreements.

Advantages of hire purchase are:

- *Capital is released* for alternative investment.
- It is *readily available, easily negotiated finance*, when other credit is restricted.
- The most *up-to-date equipment* can be utilised to increase profit out of which instalments can be paid.
- *VAT is recoverable in full* against outputs at the time of payment of the initial deposit.
- The *real* cost of instalments will be reduced in times of high inflation.
- *After-sales service* is often more forthcoming when instalments are still outstanding than if an asset is owned and fully paid for.

The major drawback of hire purchase finance is that it commits the hirer to a contractual payment that he may find difficult to meet.

Hire purchase is now referred to as 'lease purchase', presenting a more respectable image in the financial markets.

QUESTION 10.4

If you buy an asset on hire purchase, can you offer it as security for another loan?

(Answer in Appendix E)

10.6 Leasing

Nature of leasing

Term loans and hire purchase give businesses the chance to use equipment and other assets, even though they may not have the necessary finance to pay for them immediately. *Leasing* is yet another way of financing the use of an asset without having to pay its full cost immediately. Unlike borrowing and hire purchase, however, the leased asset does not normally become the property of the lessee; this should not be seen as a disadvantage for it is the use not the *ownership* of the asset that is important.

Leasing is generally less expensive than hire purchase but is highly competitive with term loan borrowing and buying.

Most people think of leasing in connection with property, and up to about 1960 this was so. Since then, there has been a significant growth in the provision of lease financing for plant and machinery, computers, business cars, agricultural machinery, ships, aircraft, telecommunication and hospital equipment.

Statistics produced by the Finance and Leasing Association show that a substantial proportion of capital assets installed in the UK is financed by leasing.

This growth is attributed to three main influences:

- It affords a means of financing *when further borrowing is impossible*; though this should be considered in the context of gearing, which is subject to further discussion below.
- *Capital allowances* granted to the lessor in respect of the equipment are substantially passed on to the lessee in the form of lower rentals.
- From the capital provider's viewpoint, there is *less risk* in leasing than lending as it is much easier to repossess a leased asset than one used as security for a loan; operationally risky firms will therefore be more attractive to a lessor than to a lender.

A lease is a contract between the owner of an asset, the *lessor*, and the user, the *lessee*, for the hire by the latter of a specific asset selected by the lessee from a manufacturer or vendor of such assets. The lessee has possession and use of the asset on payment of specified rentals over an agreed period but ownership remains with the lessor.

Leasing is similar to borrowing in that it imposes a continuing financial obligation on the lessee.

Types of lease

Lease financing is mainly offered by subsidiary companies of clearing banks, finance houses, merchant banks, and independent specialist leasing firms. It is a competitive business so terms of leasing are comparatively very similar.

What main points would you expect a lease agreement to cover?

The essential aspects will be the period of hire, the periodic amount payable, the frequency of the payment, insurance and maintenance. But they will vary depending upon whether the lease is a *financial* or an *operating one*.

A financial lease is a non-cancellable contract providing for payment of specified rentals over an obligatory *primary* period, aimed at repaying the capital outlay of the lessor and to give him or her a margin of profit. The lessee is responsible for maintenance and insurance of the equipment.

This arrangement is, therefore, a way of financing use of an asset over its useful life. Five-year contracts are typical of this type of lease but 10–15 year leases for assets such as aircraft are not unknown.

Rentals are commonly payable quarterly in advance during the primary period but can be timed to match the lessee's cash flows arising from using the asset. At the end of the primary period, the lessee has the option to renew the lease for a *secondary* period at a reduced rental, and if the asset is sold, the lessee and lessor generally share the proceeds, with the major part going to the lessee. Some leases do provide for cancellation before expiry of the obligatory period upon payment of an onerous penalty by the lessee.

An operating lease refers to contracts for assets, whereby the total rentals payable during the period of the lease do not fully repay the capital outlay of the lessor. The latter relies upon higher rentals, further lease contracts in respect of the same asset or a high residual value after the initial contract to enable him to recover his costs and realise a profit.

Operating leases are cancellable upon the lessee giving a short period of notice, which makes the arrangement attractive to users who anticipate rapid technological change, or who may cease to require the asset. The lessor is responsible for maintenance and insurance.

Taxation and leasing

One reason for growth in lease financing has been the facility it affords to companies and public bodies which are in a temporary or permanent non-taxpaying position to take advantage of the capital allowances claimable by the lessor. Trading losses may eliminate taxable profit. Insurance companies, building societies and some public bodies whose liability to corporation tax is relatively low or non-existent are in a similar position of being unable to take full advantage of the capital allowances available on the purchase of industrial plant and equipment. Leasing makes these allowances available through reduced rentals.

Even if taxable profit does exist, and thus weakens the advantage of leasing over purchasing, the fact that rentals are chargeable against profits for tax purposes gives a further advantage to leasing.

Choice between leasing, borrowing and buying

Lease rentals are known with *certainty* when the lease contract is written, so the risk that rental payments will vary is almost nil. The natural alternative to leasing is borrowing and buying; therefore the net of tax *borrowing* rate of interest is both the opportunity and the risk discounting rate to apply to the appraisal of the leasing cash flows, when comparing leasing with borrowing and buying.

EXERCISE 10.4

Simon Poacher's Pie and Paté Company need to replace a machine which is part of the paté production line. Without it the line would grind to a halt. A suitable replacement has a cash cost of £80,000, with no residual value at the end of its useful life of five years.

It could be leased for £19,000 per annum over five years, each rental being payable in advance. Show whether the company should borrow £80,000 from its bank on a five-year term loan at 10% interest or opt for the alternative of leasing.

The machine attracts a 25% tax writing down allowance on the reducing annual balance. Assume corporation tax at 40%, with a tax payment/receipt time-lag of one year. The company is currently earning sufficient taxable profits to absorb capital allowances and lease payments.

Hints:

1 Because the company is currently paying tax, the net of tax discounting rate to apply to the cash flows is 10% – (0.40 ×10%) = 6%.

2 The loan interest on the instalments to repay a bank loan is allowed as an expense for tax purposes. If the resulting net repayments, after the interest tax relief, are discounted at 6%, this will give a present value (PV) approximately equal to the amount borrowed of £80,000. In your appraisal of the term loan, therefore, you need only show £80,000 as the purchase price of the machine at the commencement of year 1, rather than a schedule of instalment repayments.

a Borrowing

Five-year term loan	Purchase price £	Tax savings 40% £	PV factor @ 6%	Present value £
Year 0	−80,000		1.000	−80,000
1				
2		+8,000	0.890	+7,120
3		+6,000	0.840	+5,040
4		+4,500	0.792	+3,564
5		+3,375	0.747	+2,521
6		+10,125	0.705	+7,138
Net present value				−54,617

b *Leasing*

Year	Lease rental £	Tax saved £	Net cash flow £	PV factor @ 6%	Present value £
0	−19,000		−19,000	1.000	−19,000
1	−19,000		−19,000	0.943	−17,917
2	−19,000	+7,600	−11,400	0.890	−10,146
3	−19,000	+7,600	−11,400	0.840	−9,576
4	−19,000	+7,600	−11,400	0.792	−9,029
5		+7,600	+7,600	0.747	+5,677
6		+7,600	+7,600	0.705	+5,358
Net present value					−54,633

Notes:

1 Borrowing and buying has the lower NPV cost, and is therefore preferred.

2 If the lease agreement had been extended beyond the primary period to include secondary period rentals, leasing would have been comparatively even more expensive, although secondary period rentals are usually very low.

3 A residual value for the machine would probably have had the same effect on both alternatives.

If we assume that the company will be in a non-taxpaying position over the life of the asset, we must discount the pre-tax rate of 10%.

EXERCISE 10.5

Now compare the alternative methods of financing, ignoring taxation, and discounting the cash flows at 10%.

a *Five-year term loan*
   Purchase price – present value . . . £80,000

b *Leasing*

Year	Lease rentals £	PV factor @ 10%	Present value £
0	−19,000	1.000	−19,000
1–4	−19,000	3.170	−60,230
			−79,230

The decision is now reversed, and leasing is preferred to borrowing and purchasing. Further, even if the delayed tax allowances applicable to the alternatives of £32,000 and £30,400 respectively, are brought into account in the fifth year, the decision is not affected.

This activity illustrates that the combined effect on rentals reduced by passed-on capital allowances, and delay in taxation allowances, favours leasing. When a company has ample taxable profit, however, the borrow-and-buy alternative is a serious competitor to leasing.

The above illustrations relate purely to the *financing* decision. The investment decision is presumed to have been pre-empted by the *necessity* to replace the machine as being an essential part of a whole production line. In other cases the investment decision may be forced, for example, for health or safety reasons.

When the investment decision is not pre-empted by circumstances, however, *it must take account of how the investment is to be financed.*

The investment decision and leasing

Investment and financing decisions are always inextricably linked, for the decision to proceed with a project will depend not only on the benefits arising but also on the discounting rate applied to the cash flows. As stated in the last section, the cash outflows connected with leasing are known with certainty and the same applies to borrow and buy, and hire purchase financing. But the *project* net revenues or cost savings will be riskier cash flows, and should therefore be discounted at an appropriately higher rate.

EXERCISE 10.6

Pike Electronics were considering the purchase of a machine that would yield cost savings of £11,000 per annum for the next five years. The machine could be leased at an annual rental of £9,000 for 5 years, all rentals payable in advance.

Assuming a corporation tax rate of 40%, an overall cost of capital for Pike of 12% and a five-year life for the machine, show whether the project should proceed.

Operational cash flows					
Year	Cost savings £	less Tax £	Net cash flow £	PV factor @ 12%	Present value £
1	+11,000		+11,000	0.893	+9,823
2	+11,000	−4,400	+6,600	0.797	+5,260
3	+11,000	−4,400	+6,600	0.712	+4,699
4	+11,000	−4,400	+6,600	0.636	+4,198
5	+11,000	−4,400	+6,600	0.567	+3,742
6		−4,400	−4,400	0.507	−2,231
Net present value					+25,491

Lease rentals

Year	Rentals £	Tax saving £	Net cash flows £	PV factor @ 12%	Present value £
0	−9,000		−9,000	1.000	−9,000
1	−9,000		−9,000	0.893	−8,037
2	−9,000	+3,600	−5,400	0.797	−4,304
3	−9,000	+3,600	−5,400	0.712	−3,845
4	−9,000	+3,600	−5,400	0.636	−3,434
5		+3,600	+3,600	0.567	+2,041
6		+3,600	+3,600	0.507	+1,825
Net present value					−24,754

Note that, the present value cost of the lease is less than the present value of the cost savings. Based upon this data, the project would proceed.

EXERCISE 10.7

Now discount the lease cash flows at a net of tax borrowing rate of 5%, which is appropriate to its more certain cash flows.

Year	0	1	2	3	4	5	6
Net cash flows	−9,000	−9,000	−5,400	−5,400	−5,400	+3,600	+3,600
PV factor @ 5%	1.000	0.952	0.907	0.864	0.823	0.784	0.746
	−9,000	−8,568	−4,898	−4,666	−4,444	+2,822	+2,686
Net present value	−26,068						

The present value cost of leasing, discounted at 5%, is now revealed to be more than the present value of the cost savings. The project should therefore not go ahead, subject to analysing the sensitivity to change of the operational cash flows.

This activity shows how important it is:

- to link the *financing and investment decisions*, because the way a project is financed will directly affect its viability;
- to apply appropriate risk rates to *operational* as distinct from *financing* cash flows;
- to *appraise financing alternatives separately*, with the objective of choosing the lowest cost alternative to compare with the present value of the operational cash flow benefit.

Summary of advantages of leasing to the lessee

■ *Additional credit* is obtained above normal debt capacity, although this is nullified to the extent that leasing liabilities have to be disclosed in the lessee's balance sheet.

■ *No capital outlay is required*, which enables a company to obtain the use of up-to-date equipment in times of tight credit restrictions.

■ *Grants* payable to firms in assisted areas are claimable by the lessor and are invariably passed on to the lessee, in the form of either a lump sum or reduced rentals. These do not affect the taxation capital allowances.

■ *Availability* of certain assets may be possible only through leasing, which may be easier to arrange than a loan, because the property in the leased asset remains with the lessor, giving him greater security.

■ *Tax allowances* – capital allowances are included in the rentals, which themselves can be written off against profits for tax purposes.

■ *Inflation* – rentals are normally fixed, which provides a hedge against rising prices.

■ *Fixed contract* – unlike an overdraft, the financial lease contract cannot be withdrawn.

TO SUM UP

■ Established business owners should be aware of the types, advantages and risks of the variety of short- and medium-term finance discussed in this chapter. The difficulties encountered by SMEs, particularly start-up firms, in obtaining finance, are examined in Chapter 11.

QUESTION 10.5

Norfolk Mushrooms plc decided to replace one of their spawning machines, the current new cash price of which is £100,000. The new machine should have at least a five-year life, but because of its specialised construction, will have a negligible residual value at the end of that time.

The company is considering three alternative ways of financing the replacement:

a A *£100,000 term loan* arranged with their bank, to be paid off by equal annual instalments over five years. The bank lending rate is 12% gross.

b A *hire purchase contract*, requiring an initial deposit of £30,000, followed by five equal annual instalments of £22,000, paid at the end of each of the years 1–5. The interest included in the five annual instalments is respectively £12,000, £11,000, £9,000, £6,000 and £2,800.

c *Leasing* the machine by paying five annual rentals of £23,000 at the commencement of each year.

▶

If purchased, the machine will attract a 25% tax writing down allowance on the reducing annual balance. Corporation tax is to be taken as 50%, and it can be assumed that there is a one year time-lag in paying corporation tax. Which financial alternative will be preferred? Show your workings.

(Answers in Appendix E)

FURTHER READING

Arnold, G. (2002) *Corporate Financial Management*, Financial Times Pitman, chapter 12.

McLaney, E.J. (2000) *Business Finance: Theory and Practice*, Prentice Hall, chapter 8.

Pike, R. and B. Neale (2003) *Corporate Finance and Investment*, Prentice Hall, chapter 16.

Samuels, R., F. Wilkes and R. Brayshaw (1999) *Management of Company Finance*, Chapman & Hall, chapter 16.

11 Finance for small and developing businesses

INTRODUCTION

■ In this chapter we look at the particular financing difficulties of small businesses.

■ We then discuss the various sources and kinds of finance that may be available to these businesses from private individuals, government and other bodies, at the start-up stage, and then at further stages in their development.

LEARNING OBJECTIVES

When you have completed this chapter you should be able to:

1 Discuss the financial management difficulties faced by small businesses.

2 Describe the sources of venture equity capital available to small businesses.

3 Identify and discuss the sources of loan capital and government grants which may be accessed by small start-up businesses.

4 Advise upon the availability of equity and loan capital to growing and expanding small businesses.

5 Describe the nature and financing of management buyouts and buyins.

11.1 The financial problems of being 'small'

In the context of financial need, a small business is an enterprise with special problems at all stages in its development. The Bolton Committee on Small Firms decreed a business having 50 to 200 employees to be 'small' but size of turnover must also be a factor. For instance, a business with up to £1 million sales per annum in a non-labour intensive industry, such as wholesaling, could be classified as small. The European Union defines small and medium-sized firms (SMEs) as being those with fewer than 250 employees with an annual turnover of less than £25 million.

Since the Macmillan Committee Report (1931), various committees have investigated the efficiency of the financial markets, particularly their accessibility to small firms; and after each report action was taken to improve the situation. One of the earliest initiatives to provide long-term finance to small firms was the formation in 1945 of the Industrial and Commercial Finance Corporation (ICFC), which still operates successfully as part of Investors in Industry plc (3i).

In 1971, the *Bolton Report* identified some of the difficulties of small firms:

- they may have little or no *past business record* on which to base an application for finance;
- *management* may be inexperienced or incompetent, and have little knowledge of sources of finance;
- *interest rates* asked are higher than for larger, established firms because of the perceived higher risks, and security for loans may be inadequate given the stringent demands of lenders;
- *sources of capital* are fewer, because some institutions will deal only with larger firms;
- *financial management* is often not given the attention it warrants, production and sales being deemed all-important;
- *large customers* tend to treat small suppliers badly, by delaying payment of their debts, thus aggravating the small firm's financial problems;
- *lenders* are reluctant to lend to firms with no obvious management succession plans, and where risk of insolvency is greater because of their size.

The *Wilson Committee* reported in 1979 on the workings of the financial institutions, and found that small firms were still at a disadvantage not only as regards accessibility of finance but also in relation to the cost and security impositions placed on them. Consequently many schemes, both private and public, have since been introduced to ease the difficulties of small businesses.

Since 1979, the pressure to assist small businesses has also quickened because governments and the European Union recognised the need to develop new types of business activity to fill the vacuum caused by the decline of older, traditional industries. The high unemployment caused by this decline, by the introduction of new less labour-intensive technology, and by competition from overseas, may be alleviated by the development of small businesses.

A Small Business Service has more recently been set up by the government to address the problems of SMEs, working together with the Business Links Network which provides independent advice to businesses in England.

11.2 Three stages in business development

There are three stages in business development:

- Start-up
- Early growth
- Expansion.

Additional sources of equity, loan and subsidised finance (see below) become available at the second and third stages, as the confidence of investors in the potential of a business grows.

Start-up

Traditionally, founders of new businesses have relied on their own or family savings for finance. This tradition continues, and is the equity catalyst that persuades suppliers to grant credit facilities, and lenders to loan capital. However, the influence of the Wilson Committee, together with government and European Union measures to create new employment, has led to the provision of many new sources since 1980.

Start-up businesses requiring 'seedcorn' finance include (a) those that require finance for research and development costs of a product or service, and (b) those who are about to produce and market their product/service.

Clearly, the levels of risk, volumes of capital required, and prospective profitability of both types of business will vary, and the sources of 'seedcorn' finance will be fewer than for developed and profitable businesses. If a bank loan is not available, then equity *venture* capital must be sought.

Venture capital   The capital subscribed by the owners of a business is known as the 'equity'. Its holders take the greatest risks, because their rights are deferred to those of lenders and other prior charges. In new small firms these risks will obviously be greater than in an established business. In recent years, however, many organisations have become willing to make risk capital available to small businesses.

For relatively small amounts up to £100,000 private investors known as 'Business Angels' are the largest source. They may be accessed through local Business Link networks, which are local partnerships of Training and Enterprise Councils (TECs), Chambers of Commerce, Enterprise Agencies, Local Authorities, and other local providers of business support; or the British Venture Capital Association (BVCA) who represent not only 'Business Angels', but also other major sources of venture capital.

Individual or groups of investors have combined in many areas to offer start-up equity funding. They have been encouraged by the government Enterprise Investment Scheme (EIS), which allows individuals not previously connected with a company to invest in it up to £150,000 in any one tax year. Income tax relief is allowed on the amount of the investment at the lower rate of tax (currently 20%), and Capital Gains tax relief on disposal if the investor holds the shares for at least five years.

Where over £100,000 is required by a start-up company, specialist independent venture capital firms, who are largely members of BVCA (e.g. 3i), and subsidiaries of banks and other financial institutions, will be interested. In addition, since 1995 many quoted Venture Capital Trusts (VCTs) have been set up to invest in unquoted trading companies, and to provide EIS tax relief to their investors.

When considering an application for venture capital potential investors will look for a sound business plan, a committed management team, continuing 'hands-on' control of their investment, a good financial return, and, the promise of a rewarding way of eventually realising their investment. In the main, they do not expect to have a controlling equity interest in the business.

Loan capital   The clearing banks have always granted overdraft and loan facilities secured on private or business assets or personal guarantees, if they can be satisfied that the resulting forecast cash flows will be sufficient to pay interest, and ultimately to repay the advance.

Since 1981, however, bank lending has been boosted by the government's Small Firms' Loan Guarantee Scheme, which is aimed at helping those businesses unable to obtain a conventional loan. Between £5,000 and £250,000 may be loaned, 85% of which is guaranteed by the government. In inner city areas the lending floor is £500.

All loan guarantees must be approved by the DTI, excepting loans of up to £30,000 which lenders may grant without *prior* approval of that government department. The loans are secured by business assets and are normally repayable between two and seven years. Normal business lending criteria should be applied when assessing a loan proposal, but experience to date reveals a high level of bad debts in connection with these loans – possibly because the banks are cushioned by the government guarantee.

A relatively low premium of 2.00% (from April 2003) on the full amount of the loan is payable by the borrower to the government in addition to the commercial interest rate charge by the lender.

Since 1994 the European Investment Fund (EIF) has also supplied loan guarantees to SMEs at an appropriate commercial fee.

Other sources of start-up loans include:

- *The Phoenix Fund*, set up by the government in November 1999 to encourage entrepreneurship in disadvantaged areas. The objective is to create jobs, and help to regenerate these areas.
- *Smart Grants* are made by the Small Business Service to SMEs to make better use of technology, and to develop technologically innovative products and processes.
- *Local Authorities* may help small businesses, particularly in inner urban areas, by providing loans, sometimes interest-free, to purchase property, plant and working capital.
- *Development Agencies* in Scotland, Wales and Northern Ireland aim to further the growth of economic activity in their areas. They provide finance to encourage small firms to start new enterprises.
- *EU* loans of between £15,000 and £250,000, may be negotiated through some commercial banks, the 3i Group and regional development agencies (RDAs) with the European Investment Bank (EIB).
- *The Prince's Youth Business Trust* is a charity set up to assist young people aged between 18 and 29, who have a good business idea, but are unable to raise all

the necessary funding from any other source. It has so far been very effective in helping start-up businesses.

Grants and subsidies   These are made by local government and EU agencies, and have been developed to help fill some of the gaps that exist in the normal market provision. They are aimed mostly to assist areas of high unemployment and economic dereliction, and to encourage research, development and innovation.

Government grants in Assisted Areas   These are areas of industrial decline which consequently experience the highest rates of unemployment. They are designated as either 'development areas' or 'intermediate areas' and the objective of the financial assistance is to create or safeguard jobs and encourage enterprise. Assistance is by way of *Regional Selective Assistance, Enterprise Grants* and *Regional Innovation Grants*.

Regional Selective Assistance   Grants ranging from 5% to 15% of an investment project's fixed asset costs, e.g. plant and machinery, over £500,000 may be made to manufacturing and service industries in assisted areas, which benefit both the regional and national economy, and create or safeguard jobs. Grants are taxable.

Most of the finance for each project must come from private or other sources, and it must be shown that without this assistance the project would not go ahead in the Assisted Area, or would go ahead on a smaller scale or with fewer quality features.

The company should be viable and the project have good prospects of being self-sustaining within a few years.

The grant is usually paid in three or more annual instalments, but there is a simplified procedure for grants of £25,000 or less, which are generally made in one instalment.

Enterprise grants of 15% of fixed asset expenditure up to £500,000, with a maximum of £75,000 are available to high-growth SMEs in Assisted Areas of England, seeking to maximise value added projects with quality. It is not essential that jobs be created, but important that the project would not go ahead without a grant.

Regional innovation grants of 50% of agreed project costs up to a maximum of £25,000 may be available to businesses with up to 50 employees in areas of industrial decline or urban decay, for innovative research and development directed at new products or processes.

A first approach for any of the above grants can be made either to a regional Government Office or to an area Business Link.

Enterprise zones   These are areas designated for ten years by the government in areas of economic decay. The objective is to increase industrial and commercial activity by offering favourable taxation, local rating, and planning treatment. This scheme is additional to other regional schemes, and is administered by the Regional Government Offices.

Government regeneration programmes aim to improve the quality of life through the regeneration of urban and rural areas, including support for new and existing businesses. Local partnership of local authorities, TEC's and other parties interested in local regeneration, submit schemes through regional Government Offices for approval. Finance may be provided jointly by the government's Single Regeneration Budget, private sources of finance, and European Structural Funding.

Early growth

Equity capital   Having surmounted start-up financing problems and established a growing market for their products or services, most businesses will undoubtedly require injections of additional permanent capital to finance growth. Their long-term plans should, of course, have anticipated the need, and advance negotiations should have taken place with potential financiers so that the capital is available when required.

Retained profit will be the natural source of some of the requirement, but if the owners have no other personal resources they will have to seek the help of outsiders for more equity capital. It is at this growth stage that venture capital houses, some of them financed by EIS funds, show most interest. Their subscribers are essentially risk-takers, and are willing to support developing businesses with high profit potential. Their aim is to realise a profit on the sale of their shares after five years.

This venture capital may be forthcoming from 'Business Angels' who have supported the start-up stage, but a new approach to a larger venture capital provider, such as 3i, is more likely. Their business judgement and experience will be invaluable at this stage, and they may take a longer than five-year view of their investment by providing a package of equity and loan finance which allows a breathing space to the business free of short-term debt pressures. However, most of them would expect at least a non-executive representation on the board of directors of the company they support, even though their equity interest may be a minor one. Sums provided may be between £100,000 and £5 million, but could be greater.

Loan capital   Given that a business has a sound layer of equity finance, all the clearing banks have schemes to help it with medium- to long-term loans of between one and twenty years, for the purchase of additional fixed assets and working capital, or to convert existing short-term into medium-term borrowing. This facility was discussed in Chapter 10.

Loans of up to £20 million may also be negotiated as discussed in the previous section on start-up finance, with the EIB. Assistance is offered to SMEs with fewer than 500 employees and net assets of less than £60 million, anywhere in the UK, for investment projects in most industrial sectors.

A growing business will sensibly take advantage of normal suppliers' credit, and may also use hire purchase or lease finance, factoring or invoice discounting, if bank credit is currently restricted.

Grants and subsidies   Most of the government assistance schemes applicable to start-up firms continue to be available to growing and expanding businesses. In particular, venture capital providers will encourage SMEs to apply for government development funding through regional government offices, to work alongside venture capital funding.

The *European Union* has made £120 billion of Structural Funding available (1994–9), to address the socio-economic disparities between regions. Single Programming Documents (SPDs) agreed by the European Commission, set out the funding available to individual regions, and its purposes and objectives. These include stimulating areas lagging behind, areas of industrial decline, unemployment, adaptation of workers to industrial change, and promoting rural development. Grants to SMEs (for this purpose those with less than 200 employees) may be made available as start-up or growth finance, particularly where this creates or safeguards jobs, and involves exporting outside the region, or developing new and advanced production sectors.

The EU Structural Fund does not fully finance projects, but works in partnership with public and private finance. SMEs seeking funding apply to an area Business Link, or a regional government office.

Expansion

A successful firm may reach a stage when its retained earnings are not sufficient to finance expansion, and when its gearing is already high, but it is still too small and relatively unknown to sell shares to the public. The amount of capital required for expansion might be substantial, but if a high yield is promised the business should be able to attract the necessary funds.

Equity finance   Institutional investors, merchant banks and venture capital houses, perhaps acting in syndicate, will be interested at this stage. They will be looking for a record of business growth with high potential exit value that can be realised within a reasonable period. Realisation might be by way of (a) a public flotation of shares (see Chapter 12), (b) a management buyout or buyin (see following section), or (c) a trade sale to a large business. A good example of the latter was Waterstone's Booksellers who had been supported by venture capital in its early days, and eventually sold out to W.H. Smith in the late 1980s.

Loan capital   Further tranches of loan capital can be negotiated with clearing, merchant, and foreign banks, subject to any limit that may be put upon borrowing (see Chapter 10).

In particular, loans above £20 million can be negotiated direct with the EIB for periods of between eight and ten years, at fixed or floating interest rates.

Sectors eligible for these large EIB loans include advanced technology, environmental protection, transport, telecommunications and energy. Loans may be for up to half the project costs, and are paid in one or several instalments.

11.3 Financing management buyouts and buyins

Buyouts

A management buyout is the purchase of a part or the whole of a business by its managers and/or employees. As with most corporate restructuring, the management buyout originated in the USA in the 1960s, and has grown apace since then both in America and in the UK.

In the UK, buyouts were boosted in the late 1970s and early 1980s, and in the early 1990s by the efforts of employees of firms trying to salvage the viable elements of ailing businesses put into receivership. Since then, the number of buyouts has grown phenomenally.

As well as buying the assets of ailing businesses, management acquisitions arise in three main situations:

- When *conglomerates or very large companies decide to sell the non-core* parts of their business, in order to concentrate on their mainstream activities in markets that have become aggressively competitive. The proceeds from the buyout helps to finance their revised business objective.
- When *family private companies* decide to sell out, perhaps because the main shareholder is retiring.
- When *venture capitalists* who have financed a business through its growth and expansion stages wish to realise their investment.

From management's point of view, freedom from centralised direction, and a financial stake in their business, motivates them to higher performance. Many buyout managers have become millionaires in recent years.

As always, the need gives rise to the provision, and specialist institutions (e.g. 3i), sometimes acting in syndicates, have developed to assist or act for managers in buyout negotiations. They advise on valuation of the assets to be bought, and negotiate the package of finance to support the buyout.

The managers are expected to contribute a reasonable proportion of the equity capital, the remainder coming mainly from venture and development capital houses. However, loan finance is normally a high proportion of the capital of these restructured companies (known as 'leveraged buyouts' in the USA). Consequently high interest charges are a heavy burden on subsequent operations, and the first priority of financial management is to reduce the high level of gearing.

Buyins

These relate to the process where entrepreneurs/managers actively search for businesses which are for sale, badly managed, or have succession problems, with a view to buying and managing their assets. Venture capitalists who are experienced in buyins work in tandem with the buyin managers to advise on the suitability of target businesses, and to provide a significant proportion of the loan and other finance required for the purchase.

TO SUM UP

- Just as 'mighty oaks from tiny acorns grow' so thriving large enterprises emerge from small beginnings. Most have initial, if not continuing, financial problems, and this chapter summarises the governmental, institutional, and EU efforts to open up equity, loan, and grant finance to encourage SMEs.

- In this chapter we have examined the various sources available at the start-up, growth and expansionary stages of SMEs' development.

  In Chapter 12 we will be looking at how successful SMEs can tap the greater financial resources of the wider capital markets.

QUESTIONS 11.1

1 Give four reasons for a small firm being at a disadvantage in obtaining additional business finance.

2 What assistance is provided by the Government to help rejuvenate areas of economic decay in the UK?

(Answers in Appendix E)

FURTHER READING

McLaney, E.J. (2000) *Business Finance: Theory and Practice*, Prentice Hall, chapter 16.
Samuels, R., F. Wilkes and R. Brayshaw (1999) *Management of Company Finance*, Chapman & Hall, chapter 27.

'Going public' and the securities market

CHAPTER

INTRODUCTION

- The financial markets bring together those who require short, medium, and long-term funds, and suppliers of those funds.
- In this chapter and Chapter 13 we are concerned with the market for long-term finance.

LEARNING OBJECTIVES

When you have completed this chapter you should be able to:

1 Recall and discuss the advantages and disadvantages of converting a private into a public limited company.

2 Describe the features of the different types of shares a company can issue.

3 Discuss the role of the Stock Exchange in the capital markets.

4 Explain the role of the Alternative Investment Market (AIM).

5 List the different ways in which a company may issue shares, and describe the circumstances under which each method may be used.

6 Describe the procedure for making an issue of securities and obtaining a Stock Exchange quotation.

7 Define the term 'derivatives', and give examples of future and options.

12.1 'Going public'

Mary Pike, chairperson and managing director of Pike Electronics Ltd, was discussing with her Business Investment Adviser, James Thorburn, her company's need for a large injection of additional capital. Latest accounts of the company showed it had a net asset value of £3 million, and that pre-tax profit last year was about £1 million.

'Most private companies that experience the rapid growth that your company has achieved over the last five years have reached the stage when existing shareholders' private resources are exhausted, and retained profit is insufficient to cope with the rate of expansion,' James began. 'Further borrowing on top of your current £1 million of loans will probably be resisted by lenders until you have a more substantial layer of equity capital.

'One solution to your financial problem,' James continued, 'is to retain the services of a financial intermediary – usually a merchant bank – to find a few private individuals or a financial institution such as an insurance company or an investment trust that is willing to subscribe more capital. This is known a *private placing*.'

'Isn't such a method expensive?' queried Mary.

'Well, the administrative costs would not be too onerous,' James replied 'but the *private* nature of the arrangement, which renders the investment less liquid, and the inherent uncertainty associated with a relatively unknown business, will cause the investor to look for a higher than normal rate of return. In addition, the subscribing institutional shareholders might insist upon representation on your board of directors, and would probably expect the company to convert to *public* status and apply for a Stock Exchange listing within two or three years, in order to provide a wider market for the sale of their investment.'

'How would going public affect our company?' questioned Mary.

'You would first have to register Pike Electronics as a *public limited company* (plc) with the Registrar of Companies. You simply add that you are a public limited company to your memorandum of association which sets out your constitution. That you already have the required minimum issued capital of £50,000, leaves the way open for you to advertise your shares for sale publicly.'

James handed Mary a memorandum he had drawn up in anticipation of their discussion, listing the advantages and disadvantages of going public.

Advantages

- *Access to the capital market and to larger amounts of finance* becomes possible by having shares quoted on the Stock Exchange.
- Institutions are more likely to invest in a public listed company, and *additional borrowing* becomes possible.
- *A market price* for the company's shares is established, providing a recognised value for sale purposes, and for inheritance tax valuation.
- Shareholders will find it easier to *sell their shares* in a wider market.
- The *purchase of other companies* is made easier by being able to offer the vendors shares instead of cash.
- The company attains a *higher financial standing*.
- It provides an opportunity for public companies to introduce *tax-efficient employee share option schemes*.

Disadvantages

- *Costs* of a public flotation of shares are high – as much as 4%–10% of the value of the issue.

- Because outside shareholders are admitted, some *control may be lost* over the business.
- Publicly quoted companies are subject to *more scrutiny* than private.
- The risk of being *taken over* is introduced by making it easier for the company's shares to be purchased on the Stock Exchange.
- As the Stock Market tends to be influenced more by the *short- than long-term strategy* of its listed companies, a company committed to a long-term plan may find its stock market performance disappointing.

'What chances do we have of obtaining a quotation for our shares?' asked Mary.

'In my opinion, an excellent chance', replied James, 'You will be required to reveal your last five years' trading record; have a minimum market capitalisation of £500,000; make at least 25% of your equity shares available to the public; and sign a Stock Exchange *listing* agreement which binds you to disclose specified information about your company in future.'

QUESTIONS 12.1

1 Give two advantages each accruing to **a** an individual shareholder, **b** the company, when a company 'goes public' and obtains a Stock Exchange quotation.

2 Why does a public quotation increase the risk of a company being taken over?

3 What additional pressures are created for a company when it goes public?

(Answers in Appendix E)

12.2 Types of shares

Presuming that a public quotation could allow more flexibility into her company's capital structure, Mary wanted to know a little more about the different types of shares that can be issued by a company.

'The two main classes of shares are *ordinary* and *preference*,' said James Thorburn. '*Ordinary shares* (sometimes referred to as the "equity" shares) are those held by the highest risk-takers in the company. This implies that the holder's claims upon profit – for dividend, and assets – if the company is liquidated, are deferred to the prior rights of creditors and other security holders. However, the capital liability of ordinary shareholders is limited to the amount they have agreed to subscribe on their shares; therefore they cannot be called upon to meet any further deficiency that the company may incur.

'In your company the ordinary shares are the voting, controlling shares, but in some companies, when a significant proportion of the shares is held by the directors, and the remainder are widely held by a large number of small shareholders, the directors may effectively control the company.

'*Preference shares*', also part of the equity ownership, are attractive to risk-averse investors because of their fixed rate of dividend, which normally must be at a higher level than the rate of interest paid to lenders, because of the relatively greater risk of non-payment of dividend. Whilst they are part of the share capital, the holders are not normally entitled to a vote, unless the terms of issue specify otherwise, and even then votes are usually only exercisable when dividends are in arrears.

'Preference shareholders have a prior right to dividend before ordinary shareholders, but it may be withheld if the directors consider there are insufficient resources to meet it. There is an implied right to accumulation of dividends if they are unpaid, unless the shares are stated to be non-cumulative. Payment of such arrears has priority over future ordinary dividends.

'If the company goes into liquidation, preference shareholders are not entitled to payment of dividend arrears or of capital before ordinary shareholders, unless their terms of issue provide otherwise, which they usually do.

'Three varieties of preference shares have been issued by companies from time to time, to confer special rights, these are redeemable preference shares, participating preference shares and convertible preference shares.

'*Redeemable preference shares* are similar to loan capital in that they are repayable, but they lack the advantage enjoyed by *loan* interest of being able to charge dividend against profit for taxation purposes. *Participating preference shares* enjoy the right to a further share in the profits beyond their fixed dividend, normally after the ordinary shareholders have received up to a stated percentage on their capital. *Convertible preference shares* give the option to holders to convert their shares into ordinary shares at a specified price over a specified period of time.'

Mary interrupted: 'Why is it that preference shares seem to be so unpopular nowadays?'

'There are four main reasons,' James replied. 'First, their dividends are not chargeable against profits for taxation purposes; second, the dividends can be passed over in years of poor profitability; third, their fixed return is subject to the ravages of inflation from the investors' point of view; and fourth, holders take greater risks than debenture holders but do not enjoy the higher returns and voting control of ordinary shareholders. The previous permanence of preference share capital (excepting for redeemable shares) may also have deterred investors, but this is no longer the case as the Companies Act 1985 permits the repayment of any class of shares – subject to specified conditions.'

QUESTIONS 12.2

1 'The difference between loans and all shares is that the return to investors on the former is fixed, but on shares it is not.' True or false? Explain.

2 'Only ordinary shareholders are entitled to vote at meetings.' True or false? Explain.

3 Why have there been fewer preference share issues in recent years?

(Answers in Appendix E)

12.3 The Stock Exchange and the capital market

'You stated earlier, James, that a Stock Exchange listing provides access to a wider capital market. Can you please tell me something about the functions of the Stock Exchange?' queried Mary.

'The capital markets embrace all the activities of financial institutions engaged in:

- the *raising of long-term finance* for private and public bodies whether situated in the UK or overseas (i.e. the primary market);
- *trading in the securities and other financial instruments* created by the activity above (i.e. the secondary market),' began Thorburn.

'The Stock Exchange plays a central role in this international market. It provides the primary facility for marketing new issues of shares and other securities, and also a well-regulated secondary market in shares. British government and local authority stocks, industrial and commercial loan stocks, and many overseas stocks, that are included in its Official List. Without this assured market facility, buyers would not be so willing to subscribe to new issues of securities, as it would then be more difficult to dispose of them.

'The Stock Exchange, now called the London Stock Exchange Ltd, is an independent company with a Board of Directors drawn from the Exchange's executive, and from its customer and user base. The Board of the Exchange:

- *consider applications* for the listing of securities;
- *decide on the admission of new members*, or expulsion of existing members;
- supervise the *solvency requirements* of membership;
- *enforce the rules* imposed by the Financial Services Authority (FSA) (see below);
- enforce the *general rules and discipline* of membership.

'It derives its income from listing and membership fees, settlement operations, and the provision of investment information throughout the investment world.

'The main participants on the Stock Exchange are Retail Service Providers (RSPs) and stockbrokers. The function of RSPs is to provide a market in securities which they have nominated, and to maintain two-way prices, i.e. a lower price at which they are prepared to buy and a higher price at which they will sell.

'Some *stockbrokers* act for clients as agents only, when purchasing or selling securities on their behalf, in which case they deal with RSPs. As *dual capacity* stockbrokers/dealers, however, they will buy and sell shares on their own account, and may act as both agent and principal in carrying out clients' "buy" and "sell" instructions.

'Unfortunately the integration of the broking and dealing functions within the same financial grouping can give rise to conflicts of interest, and this has made it essential to create a protective regulatory framework both within and between financial institutions.

'The larger institutions avoid internal conflicts of interest by separating the broking and RSP functions into different subsidiary companies or divisions. These separate entities operate at arm's length, acting according to the instructions, and in the best interests of their clients. The current trading prices of the shares of large companies are displayed publicly on the electronic 'order book' by the Stock Exchange Electronic Trading Service (SETS), and those of other companies on the Stock Exchange Automated Quotations (SEAQ) computer system. Settlement of agreed transactions is then recorded through the 'Crest' electronic system. Stock Exchange dealings are thus highly transparent.

'The Financial Services Act 1986 provided the initial framework for the protection of investors, its provisions being administered by the Securities and Investments Board (SIB). In 1997, however, the Financial Services Authority (FSA) took over the functions of the SIB. The FSA is an independent non-governmental body given statutory powers by the Financial Services and Markets Act 2000. It is financed by the financial services industry, and HM Treasury appoints its Board of Directors. The equivalent regulatory body, *as regards the securities industry*, in the USA is the Securities and Exchange Commission (SEC). In addition to the investment authorities previously supervised by the SIB, the FSA will also regulate and supervise banking, building and friendly societies, and insurance companies.'

Mary interrupted: 'I understand that some companies are not suitable for full Stock Exchange listing. Would the Alternative Investment Market (AIM) be a more suitable vehicle through which to launch our company onto the stock market?'

'It is certainly a cheaper way than a full listing to establish a market for your shares, but your requirements for a *large* amount of finance, and the fact that your reputation is already established in the industry, points the way to a full listing.

'The AIM was set up by the Stock Exchange in 1995 to assist small to medium-sized young and growing companies to obtain finance and a market regulated by the London Stock Exchange, for all their securities.

It enables relatively unknown and risky companies with short track records to retain substantial control over their destinies without the immediate expense of a full listing. Its main features are:

- companies must register a *nominated adviser and a stockbroker* with the Stock Exchange;
- *no formal lower limit on company size*; though a capitalisation value of at least £500,000 is expected (full listing £3–£5 million);
- companies need have *no minimum trading record* (full listing five years), though relevant details should appear in the prospectus;
- a *'placing'* is the normal method of marketing shares (see below);
- the *prospectus and advertisements* giving details of the share issue need only be in abridged form, but must comply with the admission requirements of the AIM;
- companies must undertake to keep the *shareholders and the market regularly informed*;
- *no entry fee* is required, but an annual listing fee of £2,500 in year 1, rising to £4,000 in year 3 is payable.'

12.4 New public issues of securities

Turning to the question of going public, James handed Mary another memorandum on various ways in which a company can make new issues of shares; and including a brief note on the use of share options.

Stock Exchange introduction

1 This method is used when all that is needed is a stock market quotation by a public company whose shares are already widely held, to create a market and thus value for the company's shares. Valuation might be required for inheritance tax purposes, or to facilitate a sale.

2 The company has to be of substantial size, and will supply market-makers with sufficient shares to create a free market in them.

3 No new capital is required but a *prospectus* is prepared and advertised for information purposes only. A prospectus is the document issued by a company to persuade investors to buy the company's shares. It contains details of the securities to be issued, past trading record, and future prospects, and has to comply with the Companies Act and Stock Exchange regulations.

Stock Exchange placing

1 A small, not very well-known company with a capital of about £1 million, which wishes to obtain a market quotation *and* capital of up to £500,000, would use this method. It is a combination of an introduction and a private placing. The placing letter will contain the same information as a prospectus, and the issue will be advertised.

2 A proportion of the shares is made available to the public through RSPs and brokers, the remainder probably going to institutional investors. Any issue larger than £500,000 would have to be dealt with as a direct public issue (see below), as the Stock Exchange discourages the restrictions on marketability associated with placing. A placing is the cheapest way of issuing securities.

Public issue by prospectus

1 A relatively low percentage of funds is raised in this way by public companies, only the largest issues, by well-known companies, being able to justify the high issue costs.

2 Companies advertise in the press, inviting offers at a price intended to attract sufficient investors to absorb the whole issue in one day. Timing of the issue is therefore of utmost importance, and the price fixed so as to secure the whole of the finance required with the issue of the least number of shares.

3 The prospectus and procedure of issue must comply with the stringent requirements of the Companies Acts and the Stock Exchange.

4 To ensure that all shares issued are taken up, one or more financial institutions *'underwrite'* the issue, i.e. agree to purchase all, or a proportion of, the shares not taken up by the public. For this service they receive a commission of about 1.25% of the value of the issue.

5 Issues are sometimes grossly oversubscribed, in which case the company has to scale down applications. This is usually effected by allotment to the widest spread of subscribers possible. When an issue is undersubscribed, shares not taken up by the public are allotted to the underwriters.

6 Oversubscribed issues are caused by 'stags', i.e. applicants who consider that the issue is underpriced and whose intention is to sell their shares at a profit immediately after allotment. The share price of an oversubscribed issue will usually go to a considerable premium, and this helps 'stags' in their operations.

Offers for sale

1 This method enables the shareholders or the company to obtain immediate cash for their existing or new shares, respectively.

2 An issuing house will act as the principal rather than as agent, by purchasing all the shares from the company at an agreed price, and then offering them to the public by advertisement at the same price or at a slightly higher price. The remuneration of the issuing house is either by way of a fee or the difference (or 'turn') between the buying and selling prices of the shares.

3 Smaller issues, by lesser-known companies, tend to be dealt with in this way. Otherwise, the procedure is the same as for an issue by prospectus.

Offers for sale by tender

1 Shares are offered to the public by a company or issuing house at a minimum price, applicants stating how many shares they are willing to take up and at what price. Allotments may then be made at a price which will just clear all the shares. This method is used when the issuing house finds it difficult to predetermine an issue price, because the company has no equivalent on the stock market, because its operations are unique, or because the market does not appear sympathetic towards the proposed issue.

2 As the Stock Exchange requires there to be an adequate market in the shares, and the company normally desires a good spread of shareholdings, the 'striking price' at which the shares are eventually allotted may be less than the price at which all shares offered can be cleared.

3 If there is heavy demand for the shares, the company takes advantage of the premium resulting from this, and 'stags' are discouraged by the unknown striking price.

4 This method has been used by public companies since 1961, especially by companies in whose shares public demand is uncertain.

Bonus share issue

These are not issues of shares through the market, but are made directly to existing shareholders. Also called 'capitalisation issues', they are made by companies whose share prices are largely comprised of accumulated reserves, and may therefore be disproportionately high relative to their nominal values. The shareholders are not called upon to pay any more money, but receive an additional allocation of shares proportionate to the number they already hold, e.g. one new share for every two already held.

The effect of the issue is to reduce the market value of each share, because the number of shares has increased, whereas the total market value of the company has remained unchanged. The bonus issue helps to make the shares more marketable because of their lower price.

12.5 Procedure for an issue of securities

The broker of Pike Electronics advised that an offer for sale would be the most suitable vehicle for the company to raise additional equity finance and to obtain a Stock Exchange quotation. All the arrangements would be made by an Issuing House which specialises in this work.

The procedure would be broadly as follows:

- an evaluation by the Issuing House of the company's *financial standing* and future prospects;
- an assessment of the *finance required*, and advice regarding the most appropriate package of finance to meet the need;
- advice on the *timing* of the issue;
- agreement with the Stock Exchange on the *method of issue*;
- completion on an *underwriting agreement*;
- preparation of a *prospectus and other documents* required by the Stock Exchange in the initial application for a quotation;
- *advertising* the offer for sale and publication of the prospectus;
- *arrangements with bankers* to receive the amounts payable;
- the *issue price of the share* to be agreed at a level to ensure the success of the issue;
- *final application* for a Stock Exchange quotation, and signing of the listing agreement, which binds the company to maintain a regular supply of information to the Stock Exchange and shareholders.

12.6 Who are the investors in shares?

Mary asked James Thorburn who the major investors were. James replied:
'Currently, about 65% of equity shares are held by the institutions, which include insurance companies, pension funds, investment and unit trusts.'

'Does that mean that the institutions will be the dominant applicants for our shares?' queried Mary.

'Not necessarily. Although individuals have found it more tax-efficient and secure to invest their savings *indirectly* through pension fund contributions and unit trusts, more encouragement has been given in recent years for them to invest directly in companies. The privatisation issues of the 1980s and 1990s, the introduction of personal equity plans (PEPS), and ISAS, the inflation-indexed capital gains tax allowance and the conversion of a number of building and insurance societies to plc status in the 1990s, have all helped in this.

'In any case, when shares are allotted, the issuing house will probably advise a policy of allotting *in full* to individuals, and scaling down those to institutions. This would strengthen your controlling interest, as shares would be more widely held. It would not, of course, prevent institutions from buying your shares on the stock market in the future.'

This reminder of the secondary market in share dealing prompted a further question from Mary.

'When I had discussions the other day with the broker handling our share issue, he mentioned futures and options. What are futures and options? Will they affect the value of, and dealings in, our shares?'

'Financial products such as futures and options are known as *derivatives*. They are *derived* from other existing financial products, e.g. equity futures and options are derived from equities in the share market. Their price movements are derived from the price movements of their underlying securities. 'Dealings in futures and options do not provide additional finance for your company, but they do offer an additional market service to investors in general which improves the liquidity of their investments,' replied James, 'because of this the stock market is more efficient, and people are encouraged to invest.'

He then promised to send Mary a short memorandum describing futures and options.

12.7 Equity share futures and options

These are traded at the London International Financial Futures and Options Exchange (LIFFE) which was established in 1982, but taken over by Euronext in 2002.

Other products dealt in on the exchange are interest rates swaps, certain Government bonds and commodities (e.g. cocoa).

Both futures and options are used by investors for:

- *hedging* i.e. protecting against future capital loss in their investments;
- *speculation* i.e. gambling on forecasts of favourable movements in future Stock Market prices.

The main difference between futures and options is that futures contracts are *binding obligations* to buy or sell assets, whereas options convey rights to buy or sell assets, but not obligations. Futures are agreed, whereas options are purchased.

Equity share futures

A range of *equity* futures is dealt in on LIFFE including those based on the FTSE 100 and Mid 250 Stock Indices

Futures contracts may be used to protect an expected rise in the market before funds are available to an investor. For example, an investor expecting a large cash sum in three months' time, could protect his position by buying FTSE 100 Index futures contracts now, and selling futures for a higher sum when the market rises. The profit made on the futures position would then compensate him for the higher price he has to pay for his investments when the expected cash sum arrives.

Share options

An option is the right to buy or sell something at an agreed price (the exercise price) within a stated period of time. As applied to shares, a payment (a premium) is made through or to a stockbroker for a *call option*, which gives the *right to buy* shares by a future date; or for a *put option*, which gives the *right to sell* shares by a future date. Note that the option gives a *right* to its holder to either buy or sell, but does not impose an *obligation* to do so. The holder may exercise the option, or let it lapse.

However, the giver (the 'writer') of the option, i.e. the dealer to whom the premium has been paid, is obliged to deliver or buy the shares respectively, if the option holder exercises his right.

Traditional options have been dealt in for over 200 years, and are usually written for a date three months hence, when either the shares are exchanged, or the option lapses. The disadvantage of the traditional option is that it cannot be traded before the exercise date, and it was because of this inflexibility that the *traded options market* was created in the UK in 1978.

Equity options were first traded on LIFFE in 1992, and currently (2003), options are available on most of the shares in the FTSE 100 index.

Because traded options cost much less than the underlying shares, an investor is able to back an investment opinion without risking too much money. For example, supposing an investor with insufficient resources at present, wishes to purchase a share which is traded on the options market and whose value is expected to rise in the near future. He could buy a standard call contract for 1,000 shares at, say, 20 pence per share, the contract being exercisable three, six, or nine months hence. At the time the contract is written the price of the share is £2.80, and the agreed exercise (buying) price is £2.95.

If the market price of the share goes above £3.15 (i.e. £2.95 + £0.20) the option holder can take a profit. If he waits until expiry date to exercise the option, and if by this time the price of the share has moved up to £3.50, he will realise a profit of £3.50 – £3.15 = £0.35 per share.

However, the option holder does not have to wait until expiry date, for he can sell his call option at any time. If the share price increased to £3.30 before expiry date, the price of the option should increase to approximately £3.30 – £2.95 = 35 pence, giving him a profit of 35 – 20 = 15 pence per share, or £150 on the contract.

This represents a return of 75% on his original outlay of £200. Conversely, if the price of the share went down, the option would not be exercised.

Thus, the risk of loss can be hedged by the investor because it is limited to the amount paid for the option contract, whilst the profit on trading in options can be substantially more than trading in the underlying shares, because more options than shares can be bought with a given sum of money.

TO SUM UP

- In this chapter we have looked at the advantages and disadvantages of making a public issue of shares, and characteristics of ordinary and preference shares.

- The Stock Exchange plays a pivotal role in regulating the issue and marketing of shares, and we examined the various ways in which a company may make a new share issue, and the procedure involved.

- Expanding companies requiring additional finance usually appeal to existing shareholders in the first place, by way of a 'rights issue', or they may resort to long-term borrowing. We examine the implications of both in Chapter 13.

QUESTIONS 12.3

1 What are the main functions of the Stock Exchange?

2 Briefly differentiate between the functions of stockbrokers and Retail Service Providers (RSPs).

3 What are the implications of RSPs' prices reading 89p–94p?

4 'A Stock Exchange introduction is a method used by small companies to obtain further capital.' True or false? Explain.

5 When investors state the price that they are willing to pay for a share this relates to:
   a a placing;
   b an offer for sale;
   c an offer for sale by tender;
   d a public issue by prospectus.

Which is the appropriate method?

6 Explain **a** Stock Exchange listing agreement; **b** share issue prospects.

7 'Preference shares, along with ordinary shares, are part of the permanent capital of a company.' Is this statement true or untrue?

▶

8 Which of the following is retained by a company to guide it through the process of going public?

a Stock Exchange;

b Merchant bank;

c Issuing house;

d Stockbroker;

e Registrar of Companies;

f Finance house.

9 What is the function of AIM?

(Answers in Appendix E)

FURTHER READING

Arnold, G. (2002) *Corporate Financial Management*, Financial Times Pitman, chapters 1 and 9.

McLaney, E.J. (2000) *Business Finance: Theory and Practice*, Prentice Hall, chapters 8 and 9.

Pike, R. and B. Neale (2003) *Corporate Finance and Investment*, Prentice Hall, chapters 2 and 13.

Samuels, R., F. Wilkes and R. Brayshaw (1999) *Management of Company Finance*, Chapman & Hall, chapters 2, 11 and 12.

13 Long-term finance for expansion

INTRODUCTION

■ To rapidly expanding companies such as Pike Electronics, 'going public' opens up many new sources of finance. This is largely because a public company is subject to more public scrutiny than a private company, through the rigorous statutory and Stock Exchange disclosure requirements. As a result, suppliers of finance are able to apply more informed judgement to their investment decisions.

■ From the company's viewpoint, although the improved availability of finance will be welcome, financial planning still has to take account of the following four factors:

1 Availability of *internally generated profit for reinvestment* within the company; about two-thirds of new sources of finance in industrial and commercial companies comes from retained earnings, which of course increases that proportion of equity capital.

2 Injection of *additional debt capital* when required and when borrowing capacity permits.

3 The need to keep an acceptable balance between *borrowed* and *equity capital* (see Chapter 14).

4 Whether existing shareholders will be willing to dip into their pockets for further finance when retained earnings and borrowing capital are insufficient to finance expansion. This is done by way of a *'rights' issue*.

LEARNING OBJECTIVES

When you have completed this chapter you should be able to:

1 Explain the nature of a rights issue of shares, and the circumstances under which it would be made.

2 Calculate the theoretical *ex rights* price of a share in a rights issue, and the value of rights.

3 Describe the actions open to a shareholder in respect of a rights issue.

4 Discuss the general features of long-term debt capital.

5 Describe debentures, and calculate their market value and yield to redemption.

6 Discuss the nature of, and advantages of, convertible securities, and demonstrate how they are valued.

7 Explain why sale and leaseback may be an attractive alternative to other forms of borrowing.

13.1 Rights issue of shares

A 'rights issue' is an offer to existing shareholders enabling them to subscribe for additional shares in the company in proportion to their current holdings. For example, a 1-for-4 offer made to a shareholder of 1,000 shares would entitle him or her to subscribe for a further 250 shares. Both the Companies Act 1985 and Stock Exchange listing regulations require companies to offer new issues of shares to *existing* shareholders before offering them to the public, although a company may suspend this requirement by passing a special resolution. It is the main method of making new share issues.

The attractions of making a 'rights' over a public issue are:

- The *proportionate ownership rights of existing shareholders* are preserved, and therefore their control over the company.
- The issue is more likely to be successful because it is being offered to *committed shareholders*;
- *Costs of issue* are much less than for a public issue; underwriting is not normally required, but if it is, it will cost less because there is more certainty of the issue succeeding, no prospectus is required, and administration costs are less;
- A *broader equity capital base* provides further scope for borrowing.

A rights issue is made in the following circumstances:

- To *finance further investment*;
- To replace *short-term debt capital* that has caused the company to become overgeared;
- To take advantage of *favourable market conditions* to obtain equity finance; fewer shares will have to be issued when share prices are buoyant and there is a greater chance the issue will be taken up fully.

When the issue is agreed, each shareholder is sent a 'rights' letter outlining her entitlement to new shares. She may then accept the offer, or renounce the privilege and sell the 'rights' through a broker or to the company. A renounceable allotment letter is enclosed with the offer to the shareholder, and a time limit is placed upon the receipt of acceptances.

Even if the share price is depressed, existing shareholders may be willing to subscribe for the issue because they will retain their same proportionate holdings.

Subscription price

One of the main features of a 'rights' issue is its price. This is usually substantially below the current market price of the share and is kept as low as possible to ensure the success of the issue.

Obviously, if the market price of the share, subsequent to the issue, were to fall below the rights subscription price, the issue would fail. A discount of between 15% and 30% on the current market price has been made on past issues.

EXERCISE 13.1

Alpha Printing plc has 400,0000 £1 ordinary shares in issue. The current market price of the share is £3. The company is to raise further capital of £250,000 by a rights issue. If the issue price is fixed at £2.50:

a How many shares would have to be issued?

b How many shares does a shareholder have to hold currently to have the right to subscribe for a further share?

---

a £250,000 ÷ £2.50 = 100,000 shares.

b A shareholder has to hold 400,000 ÷ 100,000 = 4 shares to subscribe for one new share.

Note that the rights share is priced at a discount of 16.6% of the current market price, which will result in there being more shares relative to capital value than there are at present, and consequently a reduction in earnings per share (EPS). In theory a lower EPS should not really matter as long as the new capital earns the same return as existing capital.

EXERCISE 13.2

Alpha Printing currently earns 20% on the market value of its shares, and this rate is expected on the new capital. Calculate:

a EPS on the existing capital;

b EPS after the rights issue.

---

a EPS = equity earnings ÷ number of equity shares = (0.20 × £1.2 million) ÷ £400,000 = 60 pence.

b EPS = equity earnings ÷ number of equity shares = (0.20 × £1.45 million) ÷ 500,000 = 58 pence.

The EPS of Alpha is reduced even though the return on capital is still 20%. This may have a depressive effect on market price, which, however, could be countered by maintaining the original dividend per share.

Valuing rights

There is a *natural* fall in market price of a share after a rights issue because of the relatively low subscription price; the fall occurs at a time shortly before the final closing of the rights offer. Up to that time a buyer of the shares is entitled to the rights, and the share price (*cum rights*) paid by him reflects this; subsequently, a seller of the shares keeps the rights to sell or to exercise, and the share price falls to its *ex rights* value.

EXERCISE 13.3

Given that a holder of four shares in Alpha exercises his right to apply for a further share at a price of £2.50, what should the *ex rights* price of the share be?

		£
Value of shares held previously	4 @ £3 =	12.00
add rights share	1 @ £2.50 =	2.50
		14.50
Theoretical ex rights price £14.50 ÷ 5	=	2.90

The shareholder now holds five shares at £2.90, instead of four shares @ £3 and cash of £2.50. His *total* wealth has therefore not changed as a result of exercising his right.

What if a shareholder does not want to subscribe for further shares? Does this mean that his shareholding after the rights issue is worth only 4 × £2.90 = £11.60 – a loss of 40 pence? As indicated earlier, this apparent loss can be offset by the shareholder renouncing and selling his rights to further shares. An Alpha shareholder ought to be able to sell his right for 40 pence, because when the buyer exercises it he will have paid a total of £0.40 + £2.50 = £2.90, which, as you have already seen, is the *ex rights* value of the share. Thus the seller is compensated for the 40 pence fall in the value of his share. However, if the holder of a right does not exercise it, he will not lose value, as the Stock Exchange require companies to sell rights not taken up by the acceptance date, and compensate the shareholders concerned.

The *theoretical value of a right in each share* is the difference between the cum rights share value and the theoretical *ex rights* value, i.e. £3 *less* £2.90 = 10 pence in Alpha's case. This is sometimes expressed as the nil *paid value of a right to take up another share*, and is the difference between the theoretical *ex rights price* and the *subscription price*. For Alpha, this is £2.90 *less* £2.50 = 40 pence, and is simply the 10 pence right in each of four shares.

Of course, should the market not be very enthusiastic about the purpose of the issue, the share price could fall and affect the value of a right.

A shareholder with sufficient cash should subscribe for rights shares if he or she believes that the expected return on the additional investment makes it worthwhile. In making the decision, she will compare alternative investment opportunities, and the composition of the present portfolio. Investors do not always act rationally, however, and misconceived loyalty may persuade the shareholder to take up the rights instead of diversifying.

QUESTIONS 13.1

Trident Hire Cars plc are expanding their operations and require additional capital of £200,000. A 1-for-3 rights issue is offered to shareholders at £2.00 per share. The current market price of the share is £2.80. Calculate:

a the theoretical *ex rights* price of each Trident share;

b the value of a right in *each* existing share;

c the nil paid value of a right to take up a further share.

(Answers in Appendix E)

13.2 The characteristics of long-term debt capital

'Long-term' in this context is over ten years but rarely longer than thirty years. Companies try to match financing terms with the lives of their assets, those having long lives tending to be financed with long-term capital, to ensure that vital operating capacity is undisturbed, with property attracting *mortgage loans* of twenty–twenty-five years' duration, and plant and machinery and permanent working capital, loans of between ten and twenty years.

The general features of long-term debt capital are as follows:

- Lenders are *creditors* whose debts are subject to specific repayment dates.
- Lenders have *no control over borrowers* other than is provided for in the loan agreement covenants.
- Loan agreements can include onerous conditions to *protect the lender*, including restrictions on further borrowing and pledging of assets; restrictions on dividends; the right of a lender to appoint a director to the company's board; disclosure of financial information by the borrower to the lender; and an obligation to consult the lender regarding exceptional transactions such as acquiring, or merging with, other companies.
- A *fixed rate of interest* is normally payable, although variable rates can be negotiated.
- Interest is a prior charge profits before any dividends are payable and is treated as an expense for corporation tax purposes; loans are usually *secured* either by a

fixed charge on a specified asset, or a *floating charge* on all the company's assets, or both, giving the lender priority in repayment of his or her debt in a liquidation of the company, over other creditors.

- Loan stocks may include a *call* feature which enables the company to repay the debt before its maturity date at a specified price. The call would be exercised if interest rates fell and the company wished to renegotiate the loan to take advantage of the lower rates.
- *Capital is committed to a project for a long period* during which circumstances could change (e.g. interest rates) to the advantage or detriment of the borrower.

Since the mid-1960s conditions have militated against long-term borrowing and it is now a lower proportion of total financing. The greatest influences in this respect have been:

- a *deteriorating economic position* both at home and abroad, resulting in lower profits, unable to support a high level of interest payment;
- a consequent *reduction in industrial capital investment*, particularly in property, which has traditionally been financed long-term;
- the *traumatic reduction in property values* in the mid-1970s and the early 1990s, with a consequent reduction in security for loans;
- *high inflation*, causing interest rates to reach their highest levels for years, rates that borrowers are not prepared to commit themselves to pay when economic conditions and financial markets are so uncertain, given that insolvency is the penalty for overborrowing;
- lenders are unwilling to lend long-term knowing that the *real* values of their loans diminish with inflation;
- the *willingness of banks to continue lending* for short and medium terms.

The main factor governing borrowing is the rate of interest. There is little doubt that, if interest rates in general are low, there is more long-term borrowing and consequently a higher level of economic activity.

However, inflation is not the only factor causing high interest rates. Government borrowing, caused by high government spending, can push interest rates higher, and because investment in gilt-edged securities (government, local authority and Commonwealth bonds) is risk-free, investors prefer them as safer homes for their savings.

Interest rates on industrial long-term securities take their cue from similarly dated gilt-edged securities but with the addition of risk premiums to compensate for the higher operational risks and restrictive covenants.

QUESTION 13.2

Read through the previous section again. Now summarise the conditions that encourage borrowing long-term.

(Answer in Appendix E)

In Chapter 9 a brief description was given of the various types of loan capital. They fall broadly into three categories:

- Loans arranged with one or a small consortia of lenders, including *mortgage* and *term loans*.
- Loan stocks issued as *securities* that are readily saleable on the market, including debentures, unsecured loan stock, Eurocurrency loans and convertible loan stock, also known collectively as *corporate bonds*.
- *Sale* and *leaseback*.

Mortgage loans

This is finance obtained on the security of specific property, and is usually negotiated through a merchant bank with an insurance company or a pension fund. These institutions follow a policy of matching their long-term insurance and pension commitments with stable, long-term income, and will lend mainly to large established companies on the security of specific property. As much as two-thirds of the lender's valuation of the property will be advanced, for up to thirty-five years on *commercial* property (because of their rentable value), with a review of interest rates after twenty years; and up to twenty years for industrial assets.

The agreement is normally to repay the loan by instalments at a fixed rate of interest, although variable rates are increasingly used because of the uncertainty of inflation. The borrower also normally pays the lender an arrangement fee of about 2% of the loan.

Finally a trustee is usually appointed to watch over the rights of each lender, to foreclose upon and sell the property should anything go wrong and repay lenders out of the proceeds. Trustees are often banks or insurance companies.

Term loans

For periods of over ten years, loans can be negotiated with commercial banks, investment trusts, insurance companies and pension funds, on the security of fixed assets. The rate of interest is normally fixed, and is determined by reference to an appropriate gilt-edged security of equal life.

Information on the past financial and operating performance of the prospective borrower has to be supplied to the lender, who charges to the borrower the costs of the investigation and arrangement of the loan.

Debentures (or loan stock)

A debenture is a bond under seal issued to a lender acknowledging a debt. It states the interest payable, the nature of the security (if any), the restrictive covenants and the timing and circumstances lending to repayment of the loan. Only large, established companies can issue debentures; the institutions being the chief investors. They may be listed on the Stock Exchange.

Secured debentures are charged either on specific assets (a fixed charge), or upon all the assets, where there are predominantly current assets (a floating charge).

Trustees are appointed to represent the interests of the debenture-holders. Should the terms of the trust deed not be met, or the company go into liquidation, the debenture-holders would be entitled to repayment of their debt out of the sale proceeds of the security before any other class of creditor is paid.

Unsecured debentures are mere promises to repay a loan, and therefore have no prior right to repayment over other classes of creditors. Only extremely credit-worthy companies are in a position to issue unsecured debentures, which will probably carry a higher rate of interest to compensate for the lack of security.

Debentures may be *repayable* at the end of their stated life, by instalments over the period of their issue or after a specified period; by conversion into some other form of security – usually equity shares (see convertible securities, section 13.4); or purchase by the issuing company on the open market where this right has been reserved, usually to take advantage of falling interest rates.

Subordinated debentures (also known as Mezzanine finance) are issues whose rights as to interest and capital repayment are deferred to those of other debenture-holders and, very often, to unsecured creditors as well. This kind of security is often used in takeovers and management buyouts.

As with all loans, inflation erodes the real value of the amount repayable at maturity, and although the rate of interest includes a provision for expected inflation over the life of the debenture, this obviously will not cover unanticipated inflation.

Debentures commonly have nominal values of £100, although they may be issued at a lower price to make them attractive to investors. The rate of interest charged (known as the *coupon* rate), will be the yield currently being earned on securities of similar risk.

Valuation of debentures   If a £100 debenture is redeemable in 20 years at £100 (par) value, then provided general interest rates and the level of risk associated with the debenture do not change, its market value at any time should remain at £100. If, for example, a £100 10% debenture matures in three years' time, its present value can be shown to be:

$$D_0 = \frac{I}{1 + r} + \frac{I}{(1 + r)^2} + \frac{I}{(1 + r)^3} + \frac{100}{(1 + r)^3}$$

where

D_0 = present market value of the debenture
I = interest payable per annum
r = current expected yield on this class of debenture
      (assumed to be 10%)

then

$$D_0 = \frac{10}{1.10} + \frac{10}{(1.10)^2} + \frac{10}{(1.10)^3} + \frac{100}{(1.10)^3}$$

$$= (10 \times 2.4868) + (100 \times 0.7513)$$

$$D_0 = £100$$

If interest rates or risk change, however, the *expected yield* on this debenture will also change, and the market value of the security will increase or decrease accordingly.

EXERCISE 13.4

If the expected yield on the above debenture increased to 12% because market interest rates have increased, what would its current market value be with only three years to run to maturity?

$$D_0 = \frac{10}{1.12} + \frac{10}{(1.12)^2} + \frac{10}{(1.12)^3} + \frac{100}{(1.12)^3}$$

$$= (10 \times 2.4018) + (100 \times 0.7118)$$

$$D_0 = £95.20$$

The lower market value indicates that investors are only willing to pay £95.20 for a 10% debenture, for which they now require a 12% yield.

The market value of *all* fixed interest securities moves up or down with changes in expected yields. Given that the market value and the coupon rate of a debenture are known, its expected market yield can be ascertained by calculating the rate of return (using the 'trial and error' method illustrated in Chapter 3 or relevant computer program), that discounts future interest payments plus capital repayment to the current market value of the debenture. In the last activity, £95.20 is the current market value, and 12% would be the yield rate derived by trial and error.

The rate derived in this way is known as the *yield to redemption*.

Eurobonds

These are bonds issued on the international Eurocurrency markets by large corporations, and were described in Chapter 10 in section 10.4 on 'Eurocurrency loans'.

13.3 Convertible securities

Norfolk Agrimek plc, agricultural engineers, have 400,000 ordinary shares in issue, market price currently £3.50, and their present gearing ratio is in line with the company's target.

The company is expanding and requires £500,000 additional long-term capital. The directors are considering the alternatives of a 'rights' issue of ordinary shares, or a secured loan.

The company's finance director Tom Payne has given the following information regarding the current state of the financial markets:

- *The company's share price is depressed* – partly the result of the economic recession and in line with other shares, but also, in this opinion, because the market is undervaluing the company's earnings growth potential.
- *The company's profit forecast promises substantial growth* – especially taking expansion into account, but this growth will not materialise for three or four years because of delays in building construction.
- *Interest rates are currently very high* – which is another reason for low share prices.

Tom explained to the board that if a rights issue were made, more shares would have to be issued at present low prices than later when profits and share prices would be higher. As a consequence, EPS would be considerably diluted during the next two or three years, and this could depress share prices even further.

On the other hand, high interest rates do not encourage more long-term loan capital.

Tom suggested the current situation was conducive to the issue of *convertible securities*, and went on to explain that these were fixed-interest loan stock or preference shares giving an option to the holders to convert them into ordinary shares on or between predetermined dates, at predetermined prices. Convertibles are therefore loans with delayed equity options and, because of this option, can be issued at lower interest rates than ordinary debentures. Should the option to change the loan stock for ordinary shares not be exercised within the prescribed time, the stock reverts to being a pure loan, redeemable on a specified date.

The present yield on a straight fifteen-year debenture is 14½%, but Norfolk Agrimek could issue 5,000 13% convertible debentures of £100 each, giving the holders the option to convert each debenture into 25 ordinary shares in four years' time. The option could be held open for, say, four years, after which the debentures would be ordinary debt repayable fifteen years from the date of issue.

The *conversion ratio* of 25 shares for each £100 debenture implies a *conversion price* of £4 per share. To be of advantage to the company this price has to be higher than the current share market price of £3.50, but has also to be realistically attainable before the date of conversion, to encourage investors to convert.

The *conversion value* of the convertible debenture on its date of issue is $25 \times £3.50$ = £87.50, indicating that each £100 convertible is issued at a *conversion premium* of £12.50 or ($12\frac{1}{2}/87\frac{1}{2} \times 100 = 14\%$).

By issuing convertibles the company obtains the advantage of low-cost debt capital (remember the corporation tax advantage of interest) and is able to issue ordinary shares, via conversion, at a price larger than the present one. Investors have the surety of a *fixed* income initially, with the prospect of higher equity earnings later. They also have some protection against capital loss because the convertible will never fall below the market value of straight debentures of the same risk.

As a consequence of this, and the possibility of high equity gain, a convertible may have a market value higher than its conversion value.

Assume that there are three more years to run before expiry of Norfolk's conversion option. The market price of the ordinary share is now £3.70, and the present yield on a non-convertible debenture is 15%. Calculate:

a the market value of the convertible debenture as equity, i.e. calculate its conversion value;

b the value of a £100 convertible as a non-convertible debenture (ignore taxation).

Hint: there are ten years remaining before redemption, and therefore ten years' interest of £13 plus £100 at the end of ten years.

a Conversion value: £3.70 × 25 = 92.50.

b Value as a simple debenture, discounted at 15%:

$$D_0 = \frac{13}{1.15} + \frac{13}{(1.15)^2} + \frac{13}{(1.15)^3} \ldots \frac{13}{(1.15)^{10}} + \frac{100}{(1.15)^{10}}$$

$$= (13 \times 5.0188) + (100 \times 0.2472)$$

$$= £65.2444 + 24.72$$

$$= £89.96$$

Although the conversion value of £92.50 is higher than the straight debt value of £89.96, a holder of the convertible might be wiser to hold than to convert, especially if interest rates are expected to remain high. The share value has grown from £3.50 to £3.70 (1.5% per annum) in five years, and even if the growth only continued at 1% p.a. during the next three years, conversion value would remain higher than debenture value.

13.4 Warrants

A warrant is an option to purchase a stated number of shares at a specified price (the exercise price), usually within a specified time. They are normally attached to debt or equity issues to make these securities more attractive to investors, or to lower the interest rate payable on debt capital. If the company succeeds in its operations and its share price goes ahead of the warrant exercise price, holders will either apply for shares at the exercise price or sell their options. In these circumstances, the value of an option will be the difference between the share market price and the exercise price. Warrants may be sold separately from their parent securities but provide additional capital for a company only if they are exercised.

13.5 Sale and leaseback

A company owning property may sell it to an insurance company, pension fund or other leasing finance company, and simultaneously arrange to lease it back for a substantially long period, subject to periodic rent reviews – usually every five years. The company thus continues in occupation and releases capital for investment.

The obvious alternative finance, utilising the same property, is a mortgage loan, which is cheaper, ensures that the company retains property which may increase in value, and will continue to provide security for further loans. The drawback to a mortgage loan is that only between 50% and 60% of the value of the property may be borrowed.

Properties suitable for sale and leaseback are shops and offices in prime areas which will generate a steady and inflation-proofed rental income to institutions which require stable, certain revenue.

When a company requires a large amount of capital and is unable to obtain it any other way, sale and leaseback offers a convenient way of obtaining it.

TO SUM UP

- In Chapters 10–13 we have examined the whole spectrum of finance available to companies for the short, medium, and long term. This chapter considered how the needs of expanding companies could be met either by a rights issue of shares, or by long-term borrowing.

- In Chapter 14 we look at the factors that influence the financing mix decision at any stage in the development of a business.

QUESTIONS 13.3

1 Phoenix Holidays plc has 500,00 ordinary shares in issue, the current market price of each share being £2.60. The company requires £400,000 of new capital and it proposes to make a rights issue of one new share for every five shares currently held, at a price of £2 per share. Calculate or explain:

   a how many shares would be issued;

   b the theoretical *ex rights* value of the share;

   c the value of the right in each share;

   d if the actual *ex rights* value of the share before expiry of the rights offer was £2.30, the nil paid value of a right to take up another share;

   e why the *ex rights* price of the share has fallen below its theoretical level calculated in **b**.

▶

▶

2 a Instead of the rights issue, Phoenix Holidays issued 13% convertible debentures of £100 each, with the option to convert each debenture into 30 ordinary shares commencing in two years' time. At the date of issue what would be: **i** the conversion ratio, **ii** the conversion price, **iii** the conversion value and **iv** the conversion premium?

b What advantages do convertible securities confer to a holder over ordinary loan stock?

3 'The options conferred by both warrants and convertibles are the same in that cash is subscribed for further shares in both cases.' True or false?

4 Both mortgage loans and sale and leaseback arrangements result in annual payments being made by the company arranging the finance. What is the nature of the payment in each case, and why might the amounts differ?

5 An 8% debenture (par value £100) issued by Digital Solutions Ltd in 2002 is due for redemption at par at the end of three years. The current market rate of interest for stock of this risk is 6%.

What is the current theoretical value of each debenture?

(Answers in Appendix E)

FURTHER READING

Arnold, G. (2002) *Corporate Financial Management*, Financial Times Pitman, chapters 10, 11 and 21.

McLaney, E.J. (2000) *Business Finance: Theory and Practice*, Prentice Hall, chapter 8,

Pike, R. and B. Neale (2003) *Corporate Finance and Investment*, Prentice Hall, chapter 18.

Samuels, R., F. Wilkes and R. Brayshaw (1999) *Management of Company Finance*, Chapman & Hall, chapters 12 and 14.

The financing decision

INTRODUCTION

■ Chapters 9–13 have been concerned with the range of business finance available in the financial markets, and the features of each type that might favour it as the most appropriate choice of finance in particular circumstances.

■ In this chapter we look at the main factors influencing the business financing decision.

LEARNING OBJECTIVES

When you have completed this chapter you should be able to:

1 Define capital gearing, and discuss its benefits and drawbacks.

2 Explain and illustrate the financial risk to a business, of capital gearing.

3 Describe and illustrate how borrowing capacity ratios and EBIT/EPS analysis could assist in determining the financing mix.

4 Discuss the factors other than gearing that may influence the choice of finance.

14.1 Gearing

Daisy Bloom's market garden at the start of Chapter 9 showed how borrowing can be of great value to a business, so long as the return earned on the borrowed money is greater than its cost. Borrowing is referred to as 'gearing' (or 'leverage' in the USA), because changes in trading profit in a geared company have a greater effect on shareholders' return than in an ungeared company.

Gearing is a two-edged sword, however, for whilst it can increase the owner's income, it also adds a further element of *financial* risk to the operating risk of a business.

The capital structures of Sparks Ltd and Fire Ltd are as follows:

	Sparks Ltd £	Fire Ltd £
Shares of £1 each	50,000	25,000
10% debentures	–	25,000
	50,000	50,000

It is estimated that in the coming year each company has a 50% chance of earning profit of £10,000 and a 50% chance of £2,500.

Ignoring taxation, calculate the earnings per share (EPS) resulting from each of the possible outcomes, for each company, and the expected value of EPS for each of them in that year. Which company's shareholders fare best? Which company's shareholders' earnings are the more risky? State why in each case.

	Sparks Ltd 50%	Sparks Ltd 50%	Fire Ltd 50%	Fire Ltd 50%
Estimated profit	10,000	2,500	10,000	2,500
less Interest	–	–	2,500	2,500
	10,000	2,500	7,500	–
Number of shares	50,000	50,000	25,000	25,000
Earnings per share	0.20	0.05	0.30	0
Expected value of EPS	0.125		0.15	

Notes:

1 If £10,000 profit is realised, EPS is increased by the gearing of Fire Ltd from 0.20 to 0.30.

2 There is a higher expected value of EPS in Fire Ltd.

3 On the other hand, if profit is only £2,500, gearing reduces the EPS of Fire from 0.5 to zero.

4 The *operating* risk represented by the range of estimated profits is the same in both cases, i.e. £2,500–£10,000. It is only after deduction of interest that the gap between probable EPS of Fire appears wider than Sparks': a range of zero–0.30 compared with 0.05–0.20 respectively.

5 The *wider dispersion*, which you remember could be compared by calculating standard deviations, illustrates that the possibility of additional net income through gearing has its price in additional financial risk in the case of Fire Ltd.

Lenders take lower risk. They get a fixed return on their capital, leaving it to the business owners to accept possible volatility in *their* earnings. In compensation for taking this higher risk, owners expect a higher return, although they do receive the benefit of tax relief on the interest paid on loans, and this takes the edge off the financial risk to some extent.

Apart from fluctuating net profit, the main risks attending borrowing are:

- the obligation to *repay or renew the loan* – the long-term risk;
- the commitment to *pay interest on the loan* – the short-term risk.

Firms will consequently take on an amount of borrowing that will not evidence too high a reliance on repayable funds, and whose interest charges can be adequately covered by expected future cash flows.

You will recall the borrowing capacity ratios in Chapter 2. The long-term debt to net assets ratio measures a firm's dependence upon capital that has to be repaid; and the interest cover ratio, the number of times that earnings before interest covers interest payable. In calculating both these ratios we must take account of other forms of *continuing* debt such as renewable overdrafts and lease contracts, which increase the capital to be repaid, and the fixed charges to be met out of profit.

EXERCISE 14.2

Advice: before working the following, refer to Chapter 2 and the ratios in section 2.6. 'Has the business overborrowed?'

Yachting Supplies Ltd expect turnover, and therefore net assets, to treble in the next two years. Net assets are currently valued at £50,000, financed by 25,000 £1 (nominal) shares. Given the expansion in assets, what *value* of capital could be borrowed at 10% interest if the owners require a long-term debt to net assets ratio of 1:3?

What minimum annual profit before interest and tax will have to be realised to meet an interest cover ratio of 6?

Capital to be borrowed: (£50,000 × 3) ÷ 3 = £50,000

Profit before interest and tax: (10% × £50,000) ÷ 6 = £30,000

The weakness of using ratios to decide borrowing capacity is that they have to be subjectively assessed, or gleaned from somebody else's experience, and this is not very satisfactory.

Unfortunately, there is no exact way of deciding what amount of money a company can borrow. Patently, the essence of the decision is the same as that applying to private borrowing – an assessment of the risks of having to repay the loan, and to pay interest in the meantime.

One way for a company is to analyse the effect on EPS of obtaining additional capital by borrowing or issuing further shares. If interest has to be paid, then profit has to be at least sufficient to cover that interest before shareholders start to gain. Once interest is covered by profit, any additional profit generated by the loan capital belongs to shareholders, and this will increase the EPS on the shares they already hold.

Using the Yachting Supplies data in the last activity which shows a requirement for additional finance of £100,000, assume that the company has the financing alternatives of:

a issuing 50,000 shares at £2 each; or

b issuing 25,000 shares at £2 each, and £50,000 10% loan stock.

Calculate the EPS under both alternatives if earnings before interest and tax (EBIT) is £50,000. Assume corporation tax at 50%.

	All shares £	Shares and loan stock £
EBIT	50,000	50,000
less Interest	–	5,000
	50,000	45,000
Corporation tax	25,000	22,500
	25,000	22,500
Number of shares	75,000	50,000
EPS	33p	45p

Note the much higher EPS under the loan stock issue.

From the above information we can now construct a chart to show EPS at different levels of EBIT, and this is shown in Figure 14.1.

Obtain a sheet of graph paper, read the following information and draw the EBIT/EPS chart yourself.

The vertical axis shows EPS and the horizontal EBIT. First plot the coordinate for EPS 33p at £50,000 EBIT for the share option; then draw a line from the origin through this point. The line represents EPS at all levels of EBIT if an all-share issue is made.

Now plot the EPS for the mixed capital option at £50,000 EBIT, i.e. 45p. Draw a further line through this coordinate, but this time commencing at a point of £5,000 along the EBIT axis. Recall that interest of £5,000 has to be paid first before EPS commences.

Observe the crossover point at £15,000 EBIT, where EPS of 10p is the same under both options. Below that level of EBIT the share option shows the higher EPS; above it, the mixed capital option is superior.

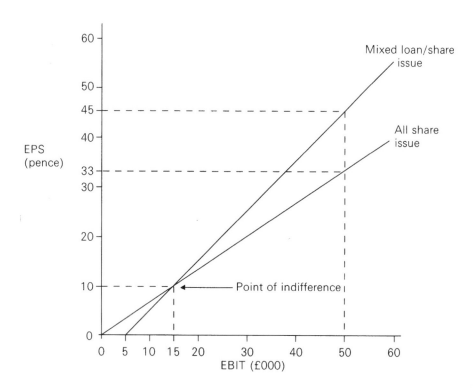

Figure 14.1
EBIT/EPS analysis chart

This point of indifference between either financing option can also be calculated algebraically by using the following simple equation:

$$\frac{X(1-T)}{\text{total number of shares if only shares issued}} = \frac{(X-I)(1-T)}{\text{total number of shares if mixed capital issued}}$$

where

X = EBIT at the indifference point
T = corporation tax rate
I = interest payable on loan

The left-hand function represents the EPS for an all-share issue, the right-hand one for a loan and share issue. At the indifference point they should be equal – hence the equation.

Applied to the above example we have:

$$\frac{X(1-T)}{75,000} = \frac{(X-5,000)(1-T)}{50,000}$$

$$\frac{X}{75,000} = \frac{X-5,000}{50,000}$$

$$50,000\ X = 75,000\ X - 375,000,000$$

$$25,000\ X = 375,000,000$$

$$X = 15,000$$

This can also be checked by calculating EPS at £15,000 EBIT:

	All shares	Shares and loan stock
	£	£
EBIT	15,000	15,000
less Interest	–	5,000
	15,000	10,000
Corporation tax	7,500	5,000
	7,500	5,000
Number of shares	75,000	50,000
EPS	10p	10p

The next step is to estimate the probability that EBIT will be in excess of £15,000 in most future years. If it is estimated to be so, then the mixed issue is preferable; if it is not, the all share issue should be made.

In this example it is fairly clear that a mix of share and loan finance is the better option given that the break-even EBIT of £15,000 represents a modest 10% return on £150,000 capital.

QUESTIONS 14.1

The following data relates to two companies of equal size in the same line of business, Aqua Ltd and Foam Ltd.

	Aqua Ltd	Foam Ltd
Capital structure	£	£
Ordinary shares of 25p each	50,000	25,000
Retained earnings	150,000	115,000
10% debentures	20,000	80,000
	220,000	220,000
EBIT	40,000	40,000

Required:

1 Calculate the long-term debt to net assets and interest cover ratios of both companies.

2 Which company is more highly geared?

▶

▶

3 Assuming a corporation tax rate of 50%, calculate the present shareholders' EPS.

4 What would shareholders' EPS be if earnings **a** trebled and **b** fell to £10,000?

5 If Aqua Ltd needed £50,000 additional capital, at what level of EBIT would shareholders be indifferent between issuing shares at £2 each, and further 10% debentures?

6 How would you use your answer in question **5** to make your financing decision?

(Answers in Appendix E)

14.2 Further factors influencing the choice of finance

If you were to visit your bank and ask for a personal loan, you would be asked what you wanted the money for, how much you wanted and for how long. There would be other questions, of course, including your present borrowing commitments. Your bank deals with businessmen and women in much the same way, and the work you did in Chapter 7 on how business finance requirements might be determined, and the first section of this chapter on gearing, would help you to present your case. There are, however, at least four other factors that greatly influence the financing decision. These are:

- *cost*
- *flexibility*
- *accessibility*
- *control*.

We will examine each of these in turn.

Cost

The expected profitability of an investment project can be ascertained by comparing its yield with the company's cost of capital, as shown in Chapter 3. It follows that the cost of capital is the minimum rate of return a business must earn on investments to satisfy the requirements of the capital providers, whether lenders or shareholders. In Chapter 15 we will examine how a company's overall cost of capital might be determined; but it will help at this stage to consider the economic and other influences bearing on the costs of individual types of finance. These include:

- The *term-structure of interest rates*, which relates interest to the length of the borrowing period; traditionally short-term loans carry a lower rate of interest than long-term ones because of the promise of earlier liquidity, and lower risk of non-repayment.

■ *Forecast rates of inflation* – the rates at which money is loaned must include some compensation for the expected fall in its purchasing power when it is eventually repaid. If inflation is expected to fall, then long-term rates of interest may be temporarily below short-term rates.

■ *Government policy* – e.g. a higher borrowing requirement by the government will add to the demand for money and tend to raise interest rates.

■ *Rates of interest* – if overseas rates of interest are high, then UK rates may have to follow suit, otherwise the value of sterling may be affected by the flight of money abroad.

■ The *cost of money to the lender* – e.g. a finance house must charge its borrowers rates of interest on their hire purchase contracts that more than cover the deposit account interest paid by them.

■ *Risk* – the higher the project risk to which the finance is exposed, the higher the rate of return expected.

■ *Taxation* – if there is an interest element in the cost, this is chargeable against profit for tax purposes, effectively reducing the cost of such finance.

■ The *costs of arranging the finance* – these can be as high as 8% of the value of a share issue.

■ The *security offered for loans* – e.g. saleable tangible assets would be more acceptable than intangible assets.

Financing policy must be directed at reducing capital costs.

Flexibility

Flexibility in financing means 'keeping one's options open' in relation to borrowing and lending.

EXERCISE 14.5

How do building societies build flexibility into their various savings schemes?

By offering progressively higher rates of interest to depositors who are willing to lock their funds away for lengthening periods of time. Depositors can thus keep as much 'instant' cash as they need in the easily accessible ordinary savings account, and as long as they match their requirements for cash at longer intervals with giving the required notice of withdrawal, can earn higher interest in longer-term deposit accounts. Withdrawals can even be made from the latter but with some interest penalty imposed. Further, building society interest rates are not fixed; they vary with market rates, adding more flexibility to their schemes.

If a business becomes locked in by *long-term* borrowing at a fixed rate of high interest, it suffers two disadvantages:

■ It will have to *pay interest on all the finance*, even if there are surplus funds from time to time.

- It will be obliged to *continue to pay the same high rate of interest*, even though interest rates generally may be falling.

The above factors can discourage long-term borrowing therefore, as will lenders' reticence to commit themselves to long-term lending contracts during periods of high uncertainty and inflation. In addition, the introduction into borrowing arrangements of interest rates that *vary* in sympathy with the general level of rates has made short- and medium-term financing more attractive than long-term.

Building more flexibility into financing should therefore make it cheaper in the long run, since:

- borrowing only as much capital as required in the short-term is *cheaper* than paying for surplus funds;
- borrowing short-term is generally *cheaper than long-term*;
- *borrowing short-term at high rates of interest*, when interest rates are expected to continue to fall, may be worthwhile to take advantage of lower long-term rates in the future;
- *borrowing over short or medium periods* perhaps at variable interest rates, or leasing, or hire purchasing, to match fast obsolescing plant or machinery, could be more sensible than borrowing expensive fixed-interest long-term funds.

As you would expect, however, there are risks associated with flexibility of short-term borrowing since:

- *loans can be called in by the lender at fairly short notice*; which could put the security charged against the loan in jeopardy;
- *loans may not be renewable* at a time when finance is tight;
- *loans are subject to more volatile interest rate changes* than long-term borrowing, making cash planning difficult;
- if interest rates fall considerably, *long-term borrowing becomes more attractive*; more especially if inflation is forecast to rise in the medium- to long-term.

Large companies' flexibility to manage the risk of interest rate changes has been considerably advanced in recent years by the facilities offered by banking intermediaries to:

- *swap* interest rate obligations between two companies, one of which may be able to borrow at a lower *fixed* rate of interest, and the other at a lower *variable* rate, to the mutual advantage of both companies;
- *agree in advance* with a borrower, the higher and/or lower limits to which *variable* rate loans will be allowed to rise or fall.

Accessibility

Accessibility of finance does not worry the large, well-established companies, which can probably rely on internally generated funds for most needs.

It is the small- to medium-sized growing companies which find their way blocked to the full range of financing available to larger companies. Paradoxically sole trader and partnership businesses may find it easier than limited companies to obtain finance, as the *personal* assets of the owners underpin any borrowing. Shareholders' liability by comparison is limited.

Generally, smaller firms find finance for expansion not only harder to access but also comparatively dearer than larger companies, since the latter are reckoned lower risks.

Reasons for their difficulties were discussed in Chapter 10, as were the various sources of finance developed in recent years to help them.

Control

Imagine you started a business five years ago, which you have nursed through good years and bad, to a healthy and still-growing state. Considerable further growth may now be possible but is beyond the earning or borrowing capacity of the firm. You are presented therefore with the alternatives of stagnating, but keeping complete control over your company, or 'going public', that is becoming a plc, and advertising publicly for more finance through an ordinary share issue.

You will inevitably lose some control, depending upon the amount of capital required, but to retain a majority interest (at least 50%), and continue to see your dreams of growth being realised, may be more acceptable than retaining complete control.

Obviously, if there is borrowing capacity left, this will be used to maintain control. Preference shares are another financing alternative. They are normally non-voting shares, which help to retain control, but the dividend cost will be relatively high to compensate for this. More to the point, preference dividend is not chargeable as an expense against profit, as is interest, which makes it comparatively even more expensive.

QUESTIONS 14.2

1 What are the benefits and risks attending flexible financing arrangements?

2 'All business firms have equal accessibility to the capital market.' True or false?

3 'The need for more finance may lead to some loss of control by the present owners.' Explain this statement. How might this be avoided?

(Answers in Appendix E)

14.3 The financing decision

No universal model may be applied to all financing problems. Businesses differ in size and activity, and a particular choice of finance at one time may not be appropriate at another (see Figure 14.2).

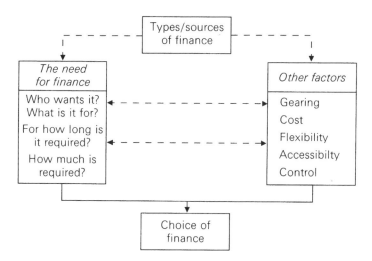

Figure 14.2
The financing
decision

■ In this chapter we have discussed the various factors influencing the business financing decision. We took the 'Daisy Bloom' illustration (see Chapter 9) of the advantages of borrowing a step further by emphasising the *financial risk* associated with gearing. You also saw how ratio and EBIT/EPS analysis might be used to analyse gearing.

■ The possible effect of gearing on the share price and consequently the wealth of the shareholder is examined in Chapter 15.

QUESTION 14.3

The Rainyday Garment Co. Ltd was expanding rapidly after four years' existence, and required further finance. One new machine costing £60,000 was needed immediately. The balance sheet and profit and loss account for the company for the year just ended are shown below:

Balance sheet	£		£
Share capital	60,000	Land and buildings (net)	
			156,000
Retained earnings	136,000	Plant and machinery (net)	
			58,000
	196,000	Vehicles (net)	12,000
Term loan	70,000		226,000
Trade creditors	26,000	Stock	58,000
Bank overdraft	2,000	Debtors	40,000
Dividend	10,000		
Tax payable	20,000		
	324,000		324,000

▶

▶

Profit and loss account	£
Sales	240,000
Cost of sales (including depreciation £12,000)	150,000
	90,000
Taxation	20,000
	70,000
Dividend payable	10,000
Retained profit for the year	60,000

Additional information:

1 As a result of the additional investment, turnover is expected to increase by one-third next year, with further growth in future years.

2 Average stock turnover in the industry based on sales is six times, and average debtors outstanding 45 days.

3 The eight-year term loan which is secured on the property was arranged with the company's bank one year ago. The balance is repayable by equal instalments over the next seven years with interest at 12% per annum on the outstanding balance at the beginning of each year. Last year's interest of £9,600 is included in cost of sales.

4 It can be assumed that cost of sales (excluding depreciation and interest), as a percentage of sales, will be the same next year as this.

5 It is planned to maintain dividends at the same amount next year.

Required:

a Calculate and comment on the current, acid test, stock, debtors and gearing ratios of the company.

b Suggest how Rainyday might finance their expansion, assuming more efficient management of working capital.

Hint: A funds flow forecast for next year will help you in making your decision.

(Answers in Appendix E)

FURTHER READING

Arnold, G. (2002) *Corporate Financial Management*, Financial Times Pitman, chapter 18.

McLaney, E.J. (2000) *Business Finance: Theory and Practice*, Prentice Hall, chapter 11.

Pike, R and B. Neale (2003) *Corporate Finance and Investment*, Prentice Hall, chapter 20.

Samuels, R., F. Wilkes and R. Brayshaw (1999) *Management of Company Finance*, Chapman & Hall, chapter 18.

Cost of capital

INTRODUCTION

- You will recall that when we were discussing *investment decisions* in Part 2, the acceptability of a proposed project was dependent, not only on its forecast cash flows, but also on the proposal meeting the *required rate of return* of the business.

- Part III has largely been concerned with the *financing decision*, and the different types, sources and costs of available finance.

- It follows that, as the different types of finance comprising the financial structure of a business, have varying costs, then its overall cost of capital will be a function of its particular mix of finance.

- In this chapter we consider how the cost of capital (or required rate of return) of a business may be determined.

LEARNING OBJECTIVES

When you have completed this chapter you should be able to:

1 Explain the concept of opportunity cost as applied to the cost capital.

2 Calculate the traditional weighted average cost of capital (WACC).

3 Explain and illustrate why the Modigliani and Miller view of cost of capital differs from the traditional view – with and without taxes.

4 Demonstrate how to calculate the cost of loan and preference capital.

5 Explain and illustrate the cost of equity capital, applying the dividend valuation model.

6 Explain and illustrate the cost of equity capital, applying the capital asset pricing model (CAPM).

15.1 Minimum acceptable rate of return

When appraising investments we need to know the investor's *required rate of return* (see Chapter 3). This is the discounting rate applied to cash flows to ascertain their *net present value* (NPV). If NPV is positive, a project is deemed to be acceptable because it will add to the value of the business; if negative, it would normally be rejected. Alternatively a project should not proceed unless its discounted cashflow (DCF) yield rate is higher than the required rate of return.

This 'cut-off' point, below which proposed investments should be rejected, is the minimum acceptable to investors. It is their *cost of capital*.

Sanjeev Patel has surplus cash which he wishes to invest in an easily accessible savings account. He is a non-taxpayer. He ascertains that the rates of interest of three savings institutions are 7½% net of tax, 8½% net of tax and 12% gross of tax respectively. In his continuing search for a better return, which of the above rates would he consider as his 'cost of capital'?

Sanjeev does not pay tax, therefore the gross yield of 12% would be the yardstick guiding his search. It is the best opportunity discovered to date, the one that he would call his *opportunity cost*.

The concept of opportunity cost applies to all investors. The *owner of a small business* would not continue trading indefinitely if his profit did not measure up to that obtainable on an investment of similar risk. A *lender* expects a rate of interest equivalent to that obtainable on an alternative investment of similar risk. Likewise a *shareholder*, acting rationally, would sell his or her shares if the combined dividend and capital growth on them was less than he or she could obtain on another share of equivalent risk.

15.2 The effect of gearing on the cost of capital

Traditional view – weighted average cost

In Chapters 9 and 14 we discussed the benefits to a business of borrowing. Most firms adopt a 'geared' capital structure, using borrowed as well as own funds but rarely take borrowing to an extreme point. This is because they fear that a high burden of interest, and capital that has to be repaid, puts at risk not only the interest and capital of lenders but also the income and capital of its owners. Further, the more variable its operating income, the higher this risk will be.

If a company employs various types of finance, the required rate of return on investments will be a mix of their various costs, weighted in proportion to the amount of each in the total pool of funds.

For example, if a company is financed with £1,500 ordinary shares, and £500 loan stock, the after-tax costs of each being 16% and 8% respectively, its weighted average cost of capital (WACC) is:

	Capital proportion		Cost %		Weighted cost %
£1,500 ordinary shares	0.75	×	16	=	12
£500 loan stock	0.25	×	8	=	2
					14

Assuming that capital is maintained in these proportions, and that their costs remain the same in future then, provided investment projects yield a return at least equal to the weighted average cost of capital of 14%, shareholders' and lenders' costs of capital will be satisfied.

On the supply side, shareholders who sense that the risks inherent in high gearing are greater than the extra income derived from using loan capital will sell their holdings and cause share prices to fall. This automatically forces up the rate of return required by investors in those shares. Likewise lenders will charge more for excessive borrowing and will eventually refuse to supply more finance because of the risk of loss through bankruptcy of the borrower.

EXERCISE 15.2

1 Complete the weighted average cost column in the following schedule by adding together the proportionate costs of share and loan capital for each of the five capital mixes.

2 What is the optimum level of gearing?

Share capital		Loan capital		Weighted average
Cost £	Proportion %	Cost £	Proportion %	cost £
9	90	5	10	
9	80	5	20	
9	70	5½	30	
10	60	6	40	
12	50	8	50	

1 8.6; 8.2; 7.95; 8.4; 10.0.
2 At the lowest cost point, i.e. 70:30 share to loan capital.

The above schedule illustrates the traditional and most widely held view that the weighted average cost of capital of a company will fall with increased borrowing until a point is reached when the higher costs of share and loan capital force the average up. The optimum gearing ratio is achieved when the weighted average cost of capital (*WACC*) is at its lowest point.

The WACC can be expressed in the following formula:

$$WACC = K_e \left(\frac{E}{E + D} \right) + K_d \left(\frac{D}{E + D} \right)$$

where

K_e = the cost of equity capital
K_d = the cost of debt (loan) capital
E = the total market value of equity capital
D = the total market value of debt capital

and applied to the 'optimum' capital structure given above:

$$WACC = 9(70) + 5.5(30)$$
$$= 7.95\%$$

The Modigliani and Miller view

In a research paper published in 1958, Modigliani and Miller (hereafter, MM) argued that the cost of capital of a company is not affected by the way it is financed. They agreed that *capital gearing adds financial risk to a company's normal operating risk* and thereby forces up the return required by investors in shares, but they claimed that this increased rate is *exactly* compensated by the additional income accruing to shareholders as a result of the gearing. They concluded, therefore, that there is no difference in the costs of capital, nor the values, of a geared and an ungeared company of equal operating risks.

To illustrate the MM theory let us examine two companies, *A* and *B*. *A* is all-share-financed, and *B* has a mixed share/loan capital structure. Both companies' shares are valued by the market at £2 each, and both make a trading profit of £20,000. The capital structures and profit and loss accounts of both companies are shown below. Taxation has been ignored at this stage.

	A		**B**
Share capital 100,000 shares		50,000 shares	
@ £2 each	200,000	@ £2 each	100,000
Loan capital 5%	–		100,000
	£200,000		£200,000
Net operating profit	20,000		20,000
less Interest	–		5,000
Shareholders' profit	£20,000		£15,000

Note that the return required on the shares of A is 20,000 ÷ 200,000 = 10%; and in B it is 15,000 ÷ 100,000 = 15%; although the share prices are both the same at £2 each.

B's share holds its value despite the risk of gearing, because of the additional £5,000 income accruing to B's shareholders from the use of the loan capital (i.e. ½ × £20,000 *less* interest of £5,000 = £5,000).

The *weighted average* costs of capital are the same as shown below:

	A			B
20,000 - 200,000	= 10%	Shares 0.5 × 15%	=	7½
		Loan 0.5 × 5%	=	2½
				10%

MM supported their arguments by showing that if the share prices of two similar operating risk companies drift apart, investors will see the chance of making money by switching investment from the high-priced share in one company to the low-priced share in the other. This process of switching is called *arbitrage*.

For example, if B's share price increased to £2.40 because of market imperfections, a holder of, say, 2% of the shares in B would realise that company A is making the same profit as B, but on a smaller capital value. She would therefore:

- sell 1,000 shares for £2,400;
- create own gearing by borrowing an amount equal to the previous proportionate shareholding × B's loan capital, i.e. 2% of £100,000 = £2,000;
- buy 2% of the shares of A for £4,000.

A comparison of this investor's income *after* these transactions, with what she previously received, shows:

	£
Share of profit from A on 2,000 shares (2% of 320,000) =	400
less Interest on loan 5% × £2,000 =	100
Net income (the same as the previous income from B, i.e. 2% of £15,000)	£300

Therefore the investor's income remains unchanged, but she realises a *capital gain* of £400 comprising:

	£
Sale of shares in *B*	2,400
Amount borrowed	2,000
	4,400
less Invested in *A*	4,000
	400

Investors will continue the arbitrage process until both shares have the same value and both companies the same WACC.

However, the MM hypothesis was based on the assumption that capital markets are perfect.

- They ignored the impact of *taxes on interest paid*.
- They assumed that individuals and companies can borrow at the same rates of interest, *regardless of differing credit ratings*.
- They assumed that investors are *perfectly informed* and that they always act rationally.
- They ignored *companies' fears of bankruptcy costs* at high levels of gearing.
- They ignored the costs connected with *share transactions*.

MM later (1963) relented on the effects of interest being allowed as a charge against taxation, and agreed that this effective Inland Revenue subsidy does reduce a firm's WACC, and increase its value by the tax shield. They stand firm on their basic theory, however.

The WACC given in section 15.2 must therefore be amended to:

$$WACC = K_e\left(\frac{E}{E + D}\right) + K_d(1 - t)\left(\frac{D}{E + D}\right)$$

where t = the corporation tax rate.

Controversy continues over the effect of gearing on cost of capital and valuation but the traditional view of an optimum capital structure for each company prevails, fear and costs of bankruptcy appearing to be the limiting factors on the extent of borrowing.

QUESTIONS 15.1

1 The investment 'cut-off' rate of a company is **a** the highest rate of return on investment projects, **b** the planned level of capital expenditure, **c** the investor's cost of capital, **d** the dividend yield. Which of these statements is correct?

2 What is the opportunity cost of funds supplied by ordinary shareholders?

▶

▶

3 'The weighted average cost of capital is less than the cost of a geared company's equity capital.' True or false?

4 The yield rate of a project is 9%. The company's weighted average cost of capital is 12%. If the project goes ahead, **a** will the suppliers of the company's loan capital be satisfied and **b** will the ordinary shareholders be satisfied?

5 Jerome Ltd is currently financed wholly by share capital, and its shareholders' required rate of return is 14%. If it obtained a 9% loan, its cost of share capital would increase to 15%, and the loan to equity ratio would be 1:2. What would be the company's cost of capital after obtaining the loan, **a** taking the traditional view of the effects of gearing and **b** assuming the MM theory of cost of capital. Ignore taxation.

(Answers in Appendix E)

15.3 Ascertaining the cost of each type of finance

Determining the cost of each type of finance employed by a company is not easy, for two reasons:

■ As we are concerned with the appraisal of *future* investment cash flows, we have to estimate *future* costs of capital covering the investment period.

■ Although *explicit* rates of interest are associated with *new issues* of loan capital, other costs of capital will have to be *imputed* from stock market information; this is particularly so in the case of equity capital.

Cost of borrowed funds

New loans The cost of loan capital is basically the rate charged by the lender. On *new loans* this will be the explicitly agreed rate of interest (known as the 'coupon rate'). If a variable interest rate is charged, the expected average rate over the loan period will be more appropriate.

However, because loan interest can be deducted from profit for tax purposes, its effective cost is $I(1 - t)$, where I is the gross interest rate, and t the company's tax rate. For example, interest of 10% with a 50% tax rate, will reduce to $10 (1 - 0.50) = 5\%$.

In addition, there are usually administrative costs associated with an issue of loan stock or debentures and possibly also a discount allowed on issue. A £100 unit of loan stock might be issued at £99 to make it attractive, and issue costs of 1% incurred. The net proceeds of each £100 stock are therefore £98, and the cost of this capital changes to $(10 \div 98) (1 - 0.50) = 5.1\%$.

Imputed cost of loan capital

If you can buy a £100 nominal value 5% debenture on the stock market for £50, what is the effective gross rate of interest receivable by you? What does this tell you about the effect on market prices of loan stocks of a general change in interest rates?

The effective rate of interest is $(5 \div 50) \times 100 = 10\%$. When the general level of interest rates increases, market prices of existing fixed interest stocks fall; when rates decrease, fixed interest stock prices rise.

It follows that, if a company has 8% debentures in its present capital structure, and the current market price of each £100 debenture is £80, the market rate of interest is $(8 \div 80) \times 100 = 10\%$. A new issue of similar risk debentures would have to be offered at this rate; therefore this is the cost to include in the weighted average cost of capital.

Another way to illustrate that 10% is the imputed cost of debenture capital is to point to the company's right to purchase its own debentures on the market. At £80, they present an investment opportunity to the company of 10%, by reason of interest saved; therefore this opportunity cost is the effective cost of debenture capital.

A final point regarding cost of existing loan capital is that the market price of such capital is increased by accumulating interest. For example, a £100 10% debenture, interest payable half-yearly, might be quoted at £105 just before a half-yearly interest payment is due. Therefore, when calculating the cost of loan capital, the accumulated interest should be deducted from the market price to leave only the capital value of the stock. Thus the cost of our 10% debenture would be $(10(1 - t)) \div (105 - 5)$.

Imputed cost of redeemable loans   When a loan is scheduled to be repaid at a relatively early date, and interest rates have changed since the loan was first contracted, the current interest rate on the loan is ascertained by calculating the DCF yield rate that equates the present value of all future payments on the loan to its current market value. The resultant rate is known as the 'yield to redemption'.

An approximate short-cut arithmetic calculation of the yield to redemption is given by:

$$r = \frac{I(1 - t) + (1/n)\,(V_n - V_0)}{\tfrac{1}{2}(V_n + V_0)}$$

where

r = yield to redemption
t = the company's tax rate
n = years to final redemption date
V_n = loan value payable in n years
V_0 = market value of loan stock now

This might look fearsome at first glance, but it simply expresses the *annual* interest and capital appreciation as a percentage of the *average* value of the loan up to the repayment date.

For example, a £100 10% debenture, with a current market value of £80, repayable in five years' time, assuming a tax rate of 50%, has a yield rate of

$$\frac{10(1 - 0.50) + \frac{1}{5}(100 - 80)}{\frac{1}{2}(100 + 80)} = \frac{5 + 4}{90} = 10\%$$

EXERCISE 15.4

Check the last calculation by applying 10% DCF factors to the five-year interest and capital cash flows. Their present value should approximately equal £80 – the current market price.

Year	Interest less Tax	Loan repaid £	10% DCF factors £	Present value £
1	5		0.909	4.545
2	5		0.826	4.130
3	5		0.751	3.755
4	5		0.683	3.415
5	5	100	0.621	65.205
				£81.050

The small difference is due to the use of *simple* interest in the short-cut method, as against *compound* interest in the DCF calculations.

Cost of preference capital

Relatively few preference share issues have been made since 1965, because in that year loan interest became deductible as an expense for business tax purposes. Preference dividend is not chargeable as an expense.

However, where they do feature as part of the planned capital structure of a firm, their cost is the explicit rate payable expressed as a percentage of the *current market price* of the share. For example, the cost of an 8% £1 preference share, with a market price of 60 pence, is $(8 \div 60) \times 100 = 13\%$ (approx).

Cost of equity capital

The holders of the equity shares, normally the ordinary shares, in a company are those entitled to the profits after the fixed obligations to lenders and preference shareholders have been met. No fixed amount is payable but shareholders do expect to receive dividends. In addition, as most companies retain and reinvest a part of their profits, shareholders also expect the market value of their shares to grow. If their expectations are not satisfied – that is, if the total return from their investment is not equal to that obtainable on a share of similar risk – they will probably sell their shares, causing the market price to fall.

The return expected by ordinary shareholders will be higher than that on borrowed capital because of the higher equity risk but, because the *express* wishes of its many shareholders are impossible to discover, a company has to impute a rate from market information.

From a company's viewpoint *dividends* are all that shareholders are paid and a change in ownership of a share does not alter this. At any time, therefore, the price an investor is prepared to pay for a share must represent the present value of all future dividends. It follows that the rate of return expected by shareholders can be imputed from the relationship between dividends and share market price.

Cost of equity capital assuming no growth in earnings

If all shareholders' earnings are distributed, there will be no growth and the cost of equity capital is the rate of return that discounts all dividends paid to infinity to the present market value of the share. This can be represented by the following equation:

$$V_0 = \frac{D}{(1 + r)} + \frac{D}{(1 + r)^2} \cdots \frac{D_\infty}{(1 + r)^\infty}$$

where

D = dividend paid each year
V_0 = present market value of the share
r = shareholders' expected rate of return
∞ = infinity

which simplifies to

$$V_0 = \frac{D}{r}$$

therefore

$$r = \frac{D}{V_0}$$

If the current market price of an ordinary share is £2.36, and the company expects to pay a constant dividend of 26 pence per share, what is the company's cost of equity capital?

$$r = \frac{D}{V_0} = \frac{26 \times 100}{236} = 11\%$$

Cost of equity capital with growth

The assumption of a constant dividend is rather unrealistic because most companies retain profit for investment. Growth in dividends must therefore be provided for in the share valuation model as shown below:

$$V_0 = \frac{D_0(1 + g)}{(1 + r)} + \frac{D_0(1 + g)^2}{(1 + r)^2} \cdots \frac{D_0(1 + g)^\infty}{(1 + r)^\infty}$$

where

V_0 = the present market share value
D_0 = current dividend
g = expected growth rate
r = shareholders' expected rate of return

which simplifies to

$$V_0 = \frac{D_0(1 + g)}{(r - g)}$$

therefore

$$r = \frac{D_0(1 + g)}{V_0} + g$$

and

$$r = \frac{D_1}{V_0} + g$$

which recognisably satisfies the equity shareholder's requirement for dividend yield plus growth.

Note: $D_0(1 + g)$ is effectively D_1, i.e. the next dividend payable one year hence.

The current market price of the Fortune plc ordinary share is £1.87. The company has just paid a dividend of 9 pence per share, and expects future dividends to grow at a constant rate of 10% per annum. Calculate the company's cost of equity capital using the dividend growth valuation model.

$$r = \frac{D_0(1 + g)}{V_0} + g = \frac{9(1 + 0.10)}{187} + 0.10$$

$$= \frac{9.9}{187} + 0.10$$

$$= 0.053 + 0.10$$

$$= 15\% \text{ (approx.)}$$

The most difficult factor to forecast is the growth rate. Recent experience may be a guide to future growth if it is thought that it will continue into the future and, of course, the company's corporate plan should incorporate the company's growth forecast.

Another factor is the cost of issuing shares which includes not only the administrative costs but also any reduction in the current market price that is normally made to make the issue attractive. These costs will reduce the amount received per share and thus add to the required rate of return.

Cost of retained earnings

In Chapter 13 it was pointed out that retained earnings as a source of investment finance is preferable to making a fresh issue of shares because it avoids issue costs. It was also pointed out that re-invested profit would be expected to earn a rate of return not less than the shareholders' existing cost of capital. This is, therefore, the opportunity cost of retentions.

Cost of equity capital and the capital asset pricing model (CAPM)

When changes in the national or international economic or political outlook occur, share market indices, such as the FTSE 100 Index, also change according to whether the forecasts are optimistic or gloomy. Such indices reflect the general movement in share prices.

Obtain a recent copy of a financial newspaper which lists share prices daily (e.g. the *Financial Times*), if possible for a day following one on which some bright or pessimistic news was announced. Which way did prices move in general?

Calculate the percentage increase or decrease in the FTSE 100 Share Index. Now calculate the percentage increases or decreases in the prices of several shares chosen at random from different sectors of the market. Do these differ substantially from the change in the FTSE 100?

If you were to analyse the percentage changes in the prices of different shares compared with market index changes over a longer period, you would discover that some shares are more volatile than others.

The sensitivity of the price movements of a share compared with those of the market index reflects its *market risk*, and risk-averse investors will demand rates of return related to this risk.

In the section on diversification at the end of Chapter 6 (section 6.7), you saw how risk can be considerably reduced by combining investments into portfolios. But even if all the shares on the stock market were combined into one portfolio, risk would not be entirely eliminated. The unavoidable element is the *market risk* or 'systematic' risk which afflicts all stocks and shares on the market.

The diversifiable or 'unsystematic' risk relates to the *operating* characteristics of each individual share, and because it can be virtually eliminated by diversification, i.e. holding a portfolio of shares, it does not feature in the price investors are prepared to pay for the security (see Figure 15.1).

There is a direct link between the price of a share and the shareholders' required rate of return. The CAPM approach suggests that the latter is only related to market risk. If, therefore, we compare the annual returns of a share over a period, with those of the market portfolio, represented say by the FT 100, we should be able to ascertain whether the share is more or less risky than the market portfolio, and ascribe a higher or lower risk premium to it accordingly. Annual returns can be calculated by adding the dividend paid to the growth in the value of the share and relating the total to the market value of the share at the start of the year.

For example, a share purchased for £1 at the beginning of a year, which increases in value by the end of the year to £1.20, and which has paid a dividend of 10 pence during the year, has yielded an annual return of:

$$\frac{(£1.20 - 1.00) + 0.10}{£1.00} = 30\%$$

Given that a number of years' total returns for a share and for the market portfolio are calculated, they can be plotted on a graph to determine their relationship. Before this is done, however, the risk-free rate is deducted from the returns of the individual share and the market portfolio as it is included in both. Remember that it is only the *market-related risk* that we are trying to isolate.

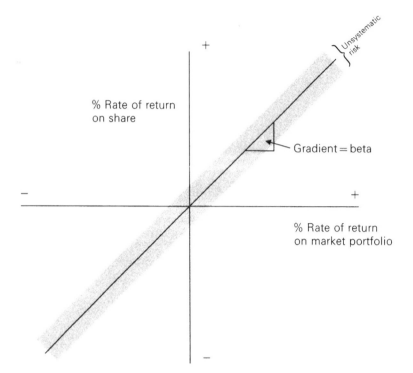

Figure 15.1 Excess returns of a share related to those on the market portfolio

Each coordinate on Figure 15.1 represents the return on the share (vertical axis), at the time when the market return was that read off the horizontal axis. The characteristic line drawn through the coordinates is the 'line of best fit', and its gradient measures the sensitivity of the returns on the share against those of the market. If the gradient is 1 (i.e. 45°), the share's returns vary proportionately with those of the market, it has the same risk quality as the market portfolio, and it has a coefficient, known as its beta, of 1.

If the gradient is steeper at, say 1.5, the share has greater risk than the market and its beta is also 1.5. As shown in Chapter 6 this implies that, if the return on the market portfolio changes, the return on the share will change more than proportionately.

Assuming we know the average return required on a portfolio consisting of all the shares on the market, and that the Treasury Bill rate is the risk-free rate, we can estimate the required rate of return on any share:

$$\begin{matrix} \text{Required rate} \\ \text{of return} \end{matrix} = \begin{matrix} \text{risk-free} \\ \text{rate (i)} \end{matrix} + \left(\begin{matrix} \text{return on market} \\ \text{portfolio} \end{matrix} - \begin{matrix} \text{risk-free} \\ \text{rate (i)} \end{matrix} \right) \begin{matrix} \text{beta of} \\ \text{the share} \end{matrix}$$

or

$$RS = i + (RM - i)B$$

In other words, the required return on a security (*RS*) comprises the risk-free rate (*i*) plus a premium for risk [(*RM* – *i*)*B*]. Note that the beta factor applies only to the risk premium of the market portfolio.

If the risk-free rate is 6%, the expected market rate 12%, and the beta of a share 0.9, calculate the return required on the share.

$$RS = i(RM - i)B$$
$$= 0.06 + (0.12 - 0.06)0.9 = 0.06 + 0.054 = 0.114 = 11.4\%$$

We now have an alternative to the dividend valuation model with which to estimate the cost of equity capital. As explained in Chapter 6, this is the capital asset pricing model (CAPM), and whilst it is based upon simplifying assumptions about the efficiency of capital markets, continuing research appears substantially to support its risk/return, market-based approach. Theoretically the dividend model and the CAPM, both being market-based, should give the same result; but they both suffer similar difficulties in forecasting. Future growth has to be forecast for the dividend model; whilst for the CAPM overall market conditions, betas and the risk-free rate have all got to be forecast for the period to which the cost of capital relates.

One advantage of the CAPM to companies who engage in different activities with different risks is that an appropriate rate of return *for each activity* can be approximated by applying the return of a company in a similar risk activity. You will recall that this method of dealing with risk was also discussed in Chapter 6 under 'the risk/return relationship'.

Weighting the costs of capital

In estimating a company's required rate of return on a continuing series of investments it is important to recognise four things:

- Past costs of capital are irrelevant; the costs must be those applicable to the *future investment* period.
- A *weighted average* of the costs of the different types of finance to be used must be calculated; for if the cost of the next tranche of capital obtained was applied, the required rate of return would change according to the type of capital used. This would lead to the acceptance of projects with lower returns when loan capital was obtained, and the rejection of projects not able to meet the cost of equity capital when that was obtained.
- The desired capital structure of a company cannot be constantly maintained. Profit generated by operations will be continuously available for investment, thus adding to equity capital; and loan capital is more likely to be obtained at infrequent intervals in large amounts. It is desirable for a company to use the *target* structure that it considers optimal in calculating its weighted average cost of capital, to stabilise investment decisions.
- However, in the case of a very large investment project which will significantly change the size and structure of a company's capital, the rate to apply to this project would be the *marginal* cost. This implies that the size of the new project will have an appreciable effect on the risk of existing activities, thereby increasing

their required rate of return. This increase must therefore be added to the cost of capital of the proposed project.

TO SUM UP

■ Efficient financial planning should not only ensure that investment funding is available when it is required, but also at the lowest overall cost. The result should be to maximise shareholder wealth.

■ This chapter has examined the traditional weighted average cost of capital (WACC), and compared it with the Modigliani and Miller model. Fear of corporate bankruptcy appears to be the main argument for the continuing use of the traditional model.

QUESTIONS 15.2

1 The capital structure of a company shown in its balance sheet is as follows:

	£
200,000 £1 ordinary shares	200,000
Retained profit	100,000
Shareholders' capital	300,000
10% debentures (repayable 2003)	150,000
	£450,000

The current market price of its ordinary share is £2.50, and a dividend of 10 pence has just been paid. A constant growth rate of 8% is expected during the next ten years. The debentures (nominal value £100) are quoted on the market at £90.

Assuming that the company believes that its present balance sheet capital structure is optimal, and will be maintained during the next ten years, calculate the company's weighted average cost of capital. Corporation tax can be taken as 50%.

2 The present capital structure of Newton Computers plc is as follows:

	£000
Called-up ordinary share capital (£1 shares)	800
Retained earnings	400
	1,200
10% loan	600
	£1,800

▶

The current market price of the ordinary share is £2.20, and a dividend of 10 pence per share has just been paid. Newton Computers considers that its present growth rate of 10% per annum will continue into the foreseeable future, that its gearing is optimal and will be maintained in future in proportion to the *current market values* of its share and loan capital. The loan stock has a market price of £88 per £100 stock unit, including half-yearly interest due immediately, and is repayable in five years at £100. Assume a corporation tax rate of 50%.

Required:

1 Calculate the weighted average cost of capital of the company (use the dividend valuation model for this purpose).

2 If the interest rate on Treasury Bills is 8%, the average rate of return on all market shares 11% and the beta of Newton Computers 1.2, calculate its cost of equity capital using the CAPM.

3 What is the purpose of the weighted average cost of capital?

4 Is a company's weighted average cost of capital necessarily applicable to each of its investment projects?

(Answers in Appendix E)

FURTHER READING

Arnold, G. (2002) *Corporate Financial Management*, Financial Times Pitman, chapters 16 and 18.

Lumby, S. and C. Jones (1999) *Investment Appraisal and Financial Decisions*, Chapman & Hall, chapters 16–19.

McLaney, E.J. (2000) *Business Finance: Theory and Practice*, Prentice Hall, chapters 10 and 11.

Pike, R. and B. Neale (2003) *Corporate Finance and Investment*, Prentice Hall, chapters 20 and 21.

Samuels, R., F. Wilkes and R. Brayshaw (1999) *Management of Company Finance*, Chapman & Hall, chapter 18.

IV Share Valuation and Dividend Policy

The investor and share valuation

- An investor with a building society savings account knows precisely the rate of interest receivable on his or her savings and can make direct comparisons with *current* returns on alternative 'safe' investments. He or she is not concerned about the underlying or future earnings of the building society.

- By comparison, an investor in ordinary shares has to forecast the *future* returns from his or her investment. He or she normally expects to receive a continuing, fairly stable but growing annual dividend and a progressive increase in the value of the shares, and should therefore subject proposed investments to the same principles of appraisal as those applied to businesses and dealt with in Chapter 3.

- Theoretically the *current* market value of the shares should represent the present value of future dividends, plus the expected proceeds of their sale some time in the future. But, as these cash flows are the product of company investment projects, it follows that share values represent the present value of future cash flows from these projects. We discuss theoretical and traditional share valuation in more detail later in this chapter.

- An investor's judgement about the future prospects of a company will inevitably take account of its past and present earnings record, evidenced partly by the profitability ratios discussed in Chapter 2. But he or she will particularly want to know how much of the company's profits relates to shareholders, and how much has been distributed as dividends.

- Dividends are the *annual* reward to shareholders, whilst retained and reinvested provide the prospect of future growth in earnings. The ratios used by investors to assess the performance of their investments are the subject of the first section of this chapter.

LEARNING OBJECTIVES

When you have completed this chapter you should be able to:

1 Evaluate the performance and share value of a company by using appropriate ratios.

2 Discuss theoretical share valuation.

3 Explain the meaning and relevance of 'efficient stock markets'.

4 Discuss the circumstances under which more traditional ways of valuing a company's shares may be adopted.

5 Explain and illustrate the various traditional methods of valuing the shares of a company, when a quoted market price may not be wholly appropriate.

16.1 How investors evaluate the performance of their shares

Shown below is the profit and loss account of Norfolk Agrimek plc, manufacturers of agriculture machinery and implements, which has 10,000,000 £1 ordinary shares in issue, at a current market price per share of £4.

Norfolk Agrimek plc Profit and loss account for the year to 19X3		£000s
Net trading profit		3,100
add Extraordinary profit on the sale of property		100
		3,200
less Corporation tax		1,000
Earnings applicable to shareholders		2,200
less Dividends		
Preference	100	
Ordinary	1,000	1,100
Earnings for the year carried forward		1,100

How can a shareholder use this information to appraise his investment? One way would be to compare this year's figures with those for last year, to determine whether there is any deterioration or improvement. Another approach would be to calculate the return on total capital employed illustrated in Chapter 2. However neither of these measurements is close enough to the requirements of the individual share-holder. Only *earnings* and *dividends* per share, *related to share market price, can do this.*

Earnings per share (EPS)

This is calculated by dividing total earnings after tax, before adding extraordinary items but deducting preference share dividends, by the total number of ordinary shares in issue.

EXERCISE 16.1

From the above information, calculate Norfolk Agrimek's EPS.

(Shareholders' earnings − extraordinary profit − preference dividend) ÷ number of shares in issue

$$= (2,200,000 - 100,000 - 100,000) \div 10,000,000 = 20 \text{ pence}$$

Given the number of shares does not change, this is an *absolute* measure of profit earned for ordinary shareholders, out of which their dividend is paid. A growing EPS will be expected if profits are withheld and reinvested in the company.

The number of shares in issue can change from year to year, however, and it is important to recognise this when comparing EPS this year with other years. Shares can increase in number when a 'rights' issue is made, which can dilute EPS. Another way in which earnings per share can be diluted is to make a 'bonus' issue of shares. Such an issue does not increase a company's total capital value; it merely increases the *number* of shares issued. For example, if Norfolk Agrimek had reserves of £20 million, it could *capitalise*, say, £10 million of this by issuing one new share for each share already held. The result would be that issued ordinary share capital increases to £20 million, and there are now 20 million shares in issue. Each shareholder has twice as many shares as he held before, but the theoretical value of each is half of what it was. Because shares have a lower market price they are more marketable.

If a bonus issue is made during a year, therefore, due recognition should be given to this when comparing with the previous year's EPS.

Price/earnings ratio

The opinions of investors as to whether past growth in EPS, together with other factors, will lead to more growth in the future, are reflected in the market price of the share. Investors will pay a higher price both for growth and for a share whose earnings are thought to be subject to a relatively low level of risk.

The price/earnings ratio (PE) is a widely accepted measure of the relative growth and risk rating of a share. It is calculated by dividing the share market price by the last reported EPS.

EXERCISE 16.2

Calculate Norfolk Agrimek's PE ratio.

$$\text{Market price} \div \text{EPS} = 400 \div 20 = 20$$

Note that the *last reported EPS* is used in the calculation, in harness with a market price which reflects expected *future growth*.

Generally, a high PE rating indicates a high-growth expectancy, and a low one, a company that is dragging its feet. This does not imply that low PE companies should be ignored as investments. For example, a company with a current low PE may be in the process of being reorganised under new management, and may be attractive as a speculative investment. Remember that the market price of a share is only as good as the information made available to the market. A company's manager may have more faith in the future of the company than the stock market.

Earnings yield

This is the reciprocal of the PE ratio, i.e. current EPS as a % of market price.

EXERCISE 16.3

Calculate Norfolk Agrimek's earnings yield.

$$\text{EPS} \div \text{market price} \times 100 = 20 \div 400 \times 100 = 5\%$$

A high market price will result in a low earnings yield, and be a signal of high growth potential; conversely, a high earnings yield indicates that investors are more uncertain about *future* growth and require a higher *current* yield to compensate for this.

This ratio has largely been superseded by the PE ratio in recent years, and is not published in the list of daily share prices.

Dividend yield

Dividends mean much more to small investors than earnings because they can be compared with yields on alternative investments. Investment yields are normally quoted *gross*, that is before deduction of any income tax payable. Therefore, as dividends are paid without deduction of tax (i.e. year 2003), the amount shown in company accounts as dividend paid, is the basis for the dividend yield calculation.

EXERCISE 16.4

Calculate **a** Norfolk Agrimek's dividend per ordinary share, and **b** the company's dividend yield.

a Dividend per ordinary share = £1000,000 ÷ 10,000,000 = 10 pence
b Dividend yield = (10 ÷ 400) × 100 = 2.5%

Why is it that investors will accept such a low return compared with the higher yields on other shares, and fixed-interest securities? It can only be that investors expect a compensating high growth rate in future dividends, and this is reflected in a high share price. When future growth is not expected to be so high, investors look for a compensating higher dividend yield.

Dividend cover

This measures the number of times that dividend paid is covered by earnings. It is an indicator of growth through retained earnings, and also of the company's ability to maintain the current dividend.

EXERCISE 16.5

Calculate Norfolk Agrimek's dividend cover. *Hint:* Use the earnings figure from the EPS calculation.

Earnings per share (EPS) ÷ dividend per share (DPS) = 20 ÷ 10 = 2

Earnings £1 of dividend paid by Norfolk is being matched by an equivalent reinvestment of £1.

Asset backing

EXERCISE 16.6

a Obtain a recent copy of the published annual accounts of a limited company, and from the balance sheet calculate the value of each ordinary share. This is done by dividing the share capital and reserves appropriate to ordinary shareholders by the number of ordinary shares in issue.
b Now compare this value with the quoted market price.

Theoretically the values should be the same, but in most cases will not be. This is because shares tend to be valued by the market on an expected dividend basis whereas balance sheet values depend on the accounting conventions applied in the valuation of assets and liabilities.

Although a share can be sold at its stock market value at any time, the balance sheet may indicate a considerably higher value (i.e. asset backing). In these circumstances, an investor might be advised to hold on to his shares as they could be undervalued. If this is so, and a potential purchaser appears on the horizon, the market price is likely to increase.

Whilst asset value is not so important as earnings and dividends when investment in shares is being considered, it is a factor that cannot be ignored, as assets may have an intrinsic value quite apart from their earning capacity.

1 The number of shares issued by Consolidated Plastics plc is 5,000,000. Its EPS is 30 pence. What is the profit applicable to ordinary shareholders?

2 If the PE ratio of Consolidated Plastics is 25, what is the market price of its shares?

3 What is the earnings yield of Consolidated Plastics?

4 The dividend yield of Consolidated Plastics is 2%.

   Calculate **a** dividend in pence per share, **b** dividend cover.

5 Do you consider Consolidated Plastics to be a high growth share? Explain.

(Answers in Appendix E)

16.2 Theoretical share valuation

Constant dividends and share valuation

In the introduction to this chapter it was implied that the current market price of a share represents the present value of expected future dividends on that share. In other words, it is the amount that an investor is prepared to pay now for the flow of future dividends. The *process* of transferring shares does not affect their market price. The company's share register merely records that a share now belongs to someone else, and the transfer simply diverts that dividend on that share to the new holder. The total dividend paid by the company remains unchanged.

You will recall from Chapter 3 that the amount someone will be prepared to pay now (i.e. the present value), for an amount receivable in one year's time is $A_1 \div (1 + r)$, where A_1 is the amount receivable, and r is the investor's required rate of return, incorporating both the costs of waiting and risk. Thus the present value of £100 receivable in one year's time at 10% is $100 \div 1.10 = £90.91$.

It can also be shown that the present value of a *perpetual* annual amount receivable (a perpetuity) is $A \div r$, where A is the perpetuity, and r the investor's required rate of return.

Assuming that a company pays a constant dividend (a perpetuity) of 30 pence per share, and the shareholders' required rate of return is 20%, what is the present value of the share?

$$V_0 = D \div r = £0.30 \div 0.20 = £1.50$$

where

V_0 = value now

D = perpetual dividend

r = shareholder's required rate of return

Investment of retained earnings and share valuation

Where a company uses retained profit for reinvestment, this should increase future dividends, and the total value of the company's shares should increase by the net present value of the investment project, *as soon as shareholders are aware that the project is to go ahead*.

For example, where a company pays a constant dividend of £10,000 the total value of its shares before acceptance of a project is:

$$D \div r = 10,000 \div 0.10 = £100,000$$

where r is 10% – the investor's required rate of return

Should £5,000 of the next dividend payable be invested in a project at the end of year 1 to yield £4,000 in each of years 2 and 3, and the dividend be increased accordingly in those two years, then the market value of the company after acceptance of the project will be:

$$V_0 = \frac{5,000}{(1.10)} + \frac{14,000}{(1.10)^2} + \frac{14,000}{(1.10)^3} + \frac{10,000}{(1.10)^4} \ldots \frac{10,000}{(1.10)^\infty}$$

$$= 4,545 + 11,570 + 10,518 + \frac{100,000}{(1.10)^3}$$

$$= £101,763$$

Note: ∞ = infinity

which shows an increase in total value of £101,763 – 100,000 = £1,763.

Note that dividend is reduced in year 1, increased in years 2 and 3, but resumes its normal pattern again from the end of year 4. Note also that the £100,000 discounted at the end of year 3 represents the present value at that time of the constant dividend of £10,000 from year 4 onwards.

EXERCISE 16.8

Now check that the investment project NPV agrees with the £1,763 increase in market value.

	Cash flow	PV factor @ 10%	Present value
Year 1	−5,000	0.90	−4,545
2	+4,000	0.826	+3,304
3	+4,000	0.751	+3,004
Net present value			+£1,763

Dividend growth and share valuation

Assuming that shareholders expect that a company's dividend will grow at a constant rate, then the present value of the future dividend stream can be found as follows:

$$V_0 = \frac{D_0(1+g)}{1+r} + \frac{D_0(1+g)^2}{(1+r)^2} + \frac{D_0(1+g)^3}{(1+r)^3} \dots \frac{D_0(1+g)^\infty}{(1+r)^\infty}$$

where

D_0 = the current dividend

g = the constant growth rate expected

r = the shareholders' expected rate of return

It can be shown that this simplifies to:

$$V_0 = \frac{D_0(1+g)}{r-g} \text{ or } \frac{D_1}{r-g}$$

where D_1 is the dividend payable in a year's time.

A company has just paid a dividend of 25 pence per share, which is expected to grow in future at a constant rate of 8%. Assuming a shareholders' discount rate of 13%, calculate the present value of the company's share.

$$V_0 = \frac{D_0(1+g)}{r-g} + \frac{0.25(1.08)}{0.13-0.08} = £5.40$$

16.3 Efficient stock markets

The concept that price is the present value of a future stream of dividends inherently assumes that investors have *full knowledge* of:

- all *investment opportunities* available to companies;
- *general economic trends*;
- the overall state of the *financial markets*;

and that they react immediately to this information by buying or selling shares because they believe them to be worth more or less than their current prices. If this is the case, the stock market can be said to be 'efficient' in that it reflects the intrinsic value of this information in the market prices of shares.

New information made public regarding prospective investments by a company *ought* to change the intrinsic value of its shares but because investors interpret the information differently the price will fluctuate randomly around the intrinsic value. Thus the price of a share is said to 'take a random walk' around its intrinsic value.

If we accept that the 'efficient market' and 'random walk' theories are broadly true, as research seems to bear out, then stock market analysts are in no better position than anyone else to predict share price movements. Despite this, analysts do exist in very large numbers, adopting either *technical* or *fundamental* analysis in assessing investments.

Technical analysis or *charting* examines long-, medium- and short-term trends of past share movements, assumes that the same patterns will repeat themselves and attempts to *predict* future share prices. However, the 'random walk' theory would appear to dismiss the validity of technical analysis.

Fundamental analysis is roughly in tune with the efficient market theory, for its adherents analyse all available information past and present, to calculate the 'intrinsic' value of a share, and advise investors accordingly.

QUESTIONS 16.2

1 Given a required rate of return of 10%, what is the maximum price you would pay for a share that is currently paying 30 pence dividend if: **a** dividend is expected to remain constant; **b** dividend is expected to grow at 5% per annum for ever?

2 What are the conditions associated with an efficient capital market?

(Answers in Appendix E)

16.4 Why value shares?

This may seem a strange question to ask following a statement that the Stock Exchange is an efficient market for shares! However, because there is usually a wide spread between share buying and selling prices, and because trading in certain shares may be limited, it cannot be guaranteed that the listed prices will always represent their true value.

You will recall that the efficient market theory is founded on *publicly known information*. However, this information may not be complete, in that:

- *company investment plans* will not all be public information;
- the value placed upon a *company's assets* by a potential buyer may be different from the value based upon share price;
- the majority of companies, mainly *private*, are not listed on the Stock Exchange;
- *holders of a large number of shares* in a company may be in a strong bargaining position to insist on a higher than listed price;
- a company seeking *fresh capital* may have to price a new issue of shares below market price to make them attractive.

Circumstances requiring the valuation of shares includes:

- proposed *amalgamation* of two or more businesses;
- purchase of shares in a company by *another company*;
- sales of shares in *unquoted, mainly private companies*;
- *valuation for tax purposes*;
- privatisation of a *nationalised company*;
- *flotation* of a fresh issues of shares.

16.5 Methods of share valuation

If a share is listed, its quoted price always provides a value reference point. In other cases, a company's articles of association may specify the basis to be used to value its shares.

Valuation bases used include:

- net asset values – **i** as a 'going concern' **ii** at break-up values;
- capitalised earnings – **i** using an implied rate of return, **ii** using an appropriate PE ratio;
- imputed dividend yield.

Each of these methods is discussed below, drawing on the following information relating to Compact Containers Ltd, a private limited company.

Compact Containers Ltd Balance sheet at 31 December 19X4	£000	£000
Fixed assets:		
Land and buildings (net)	600	
Plant and machinery (net)	500	1,100
Current assets:		
Cash	90	
Debtors	220	
Stocks	330	
	640	
less Current liabilities:		
Trade creditors	120	
Taxation	40	
	160	480
		£1,580
200,000 ordinary shares of £1 each		200
Retained earnings		980
		1,180
100,000 12% preference shares of £1 each		100
10% loan (repayable in 8 years)		300
		£1,580

Year	Profit applicable to ordinary shareholders £000	Dividends paid £000
19X4	248	80
19X3	200	60
19X2	180	60
19X1	160	50

Net asset basis

Bearing in mind that asset values in a balance sheet are usually stated at *historic cost*, and that even those values depend upon the accounting policies of the company, it will be necessary to adjust them to current values.

With increasing property values *land and buildings* could be undervalued; excepting perhaps for *leasehold* properties that may be subject to contingent liabilities for renewing dilapidations at the end of the terms of the leases.

Plant and machinery should be revalued at replacement cost *less* appropriate depreciation, and *investments* valued at current market prices.

Stock is valued at cost or realisable value, whichever is the lower, and a provision for bad debts made against debtors where this is thought necessary.

Assuming the net assets of Compact Containers Ltd are undervalued by £100,000, the value of its ordinary shares would be:

		£000
Net assets value per balance sheet		1,580
add Revaluation of assets		100
		1,680
	£000	
less Preference shareholders	100	
10% loan	300	400
Net asset value attributable to ordinary shareholders		£1,280
Number of shares		200
Value per share: £1,280/200		£6.40

Break-up or liquidation value would be considerably below the going-concern value, and would be the minimum price payable. In most cases it would be used only if the business is not worth continuing. Businesses are sometimes purchased with the sole objective of selling off all or part of their assets. This is referred to as *asset-stripping*, and the asset-stripper would fix his or her maximum price at a level that takes into account the potential sales and operating values of each of the separate assets.

Capitalised earnings – using an implied rate of return of PE ratio

This approach is the most logical to use if one agrees that an investment in the shares of a company is made in the expectation that the resources purchased will generate sufficient earnings to repay the price paid within a reasonable time and yield a satisfactory rate of return on capital invested.

It is the basis most appropriate to a prospective purchaser of a *controlling* interest in the company, as he will be able to influence operating policy and thus total profit.

The two basic factors in capitalising earnings are:

- expected level of earnings;
- required rate of return or PE ratio to apply to those earnings.

The appropriate level of earnings will be the ordinary shareholders' *future maintainable profit*; and if the profits of the most recent years are used as a guide for this purpose, adjustments will have to be made for non-continuing and extraordinary income and expenditure, and changes in accounting principles.

The *rate of return* to apply to future maintainable earnings will be that appropriate to the risks inherent in those earnings. The average *earnings yields* or PE ratios (discussed earlier in this chapter) of *quoted* companies with similar risks will be a guide here, subject to the chosen earnings yield being adjusted upwards, or the PE downwards, by, say 25% if it is a private company whose shares are being valued. This is because a private company may be little known to the investing public and therefore riskier as an investment.

If we assume that the most recent Compact Containers profit of £248,000 represents a reasonable figure of future maintainable annual earnings, and that an earnings yield of 20% is appropriate, the capitalised earnings value of its shares is: £248,000 ÷ 0.20 = £1,240,000.

If the PE ratio of the company whose earnings yield has been applied above is used instead, it will be the reciprocal of the earnings yield, i.e. 1 ÷ 0.20 = 5, and the value of the Compact shares is the same: £248,000 × 5 = £1,240,000. In each case the value per share is £1,240,000 ÷ 200,000 = £6.20.

Dividend yield valuation

Although a *small investor* in an unquoted company would look for good dividend cover to provide growth, she has little management influence over total earnings which may, in any case, fluctuate considerably. She will therefore tend to value her shares on the basis of dividends rather than earnings, and for this purpose will seek out the dividend yield on the shares of a *quoted* company of comparable size, risk and growth potential. It will be impossible to discover an exactly similar company so an average of the yields of two or three companies of similar size will be a reasonable proxy.

A low dividend yield normally implies high growth prospects and would be accompanied also by a relatively high dividend cover. A potential investor may, therefore, take a sceptical view of an unquoted company which is currently distributing high dividends (i.e. low dividend cover), even though it may have growth potential, and adjust the expected dividend yield upwards accordingly. She would make a further adjustment if the company was little known and therefore risky.

As dividend yields are quoted gross, the dividend paid by Compact Containers must be grossed up by a factor of 100/80, assuming a standard rate of tax of 20%. If an expected dividend yield of 8% is used, the value of Compact's shares using the latest dividend of £80,000 is:

$$(80,000 \times 100) \div (80 \times 0.08 \times 200,000) = £6.25$$

16.6 General considerations affecting share valuation

■ Before attempting to value shares, a close scrutiny of the company's memorandum and articles of association will reveal how such valuation may be influenced by *special capital, dividend and repayment priorities*, as well as any special rights reserved for the benefit of directors.

■ It should be confirmed that there is *adequate liquid capital* either existing or readily available to continue and develop the business effectively, and that there will be no early liability to repay capital.

■ *Adequate asset and earnings cover for capital and dividends* is of prime importance.

■ *Valuation* is what a willing buyer and seller agree it is, and whichever methods are used initially, the valuations emerging will merely serve as starting-points and as a basis for negotiations. The value eventually agreed will, at best, be a compromise of subjective judgement and strategic adjustments on both sides.

■ Because valuation is made for different purposes, *different methods or a combination of them* will probably be used. For example, the assets method may be adopted when the main interest is in securing and eventually disposing of certain assets. Where assets have high intrinsic value, for example property, this method will tend to dominate. The assets basis will also be appropriate when the bulk of the assets is of the liquid type, and therefore probably realistically valued already; for example those of investment trusts, banks and insurance companies.

■ On the other hand, the *capitalised earnings basis* is the logical approach to valuing 'going concern' assets, for without a continuing stream of future earnings, assets are only worth their break-up values.

■ Whatever method of valuation is used, *management expertise* within the target business must be taken into account. Clearly, the future earnings of, say, a currently highly successful financial institution may be highly dependent upon the continued loyalty of its present management team.

TO SUM UP

■ In this chapter you have seen not only how individual shareholders might assess the performance and value of their shares, but also how other interested parties could value a company, in circumstances when a quoted share price might not be available nor wholly appropriate.

■ Such an approach may be adopted in the case of a proposed business merger (see Chapter 18).

QUESTION 16.3

One of the directors of Alton Engineers Ltd, a private company engaged in the manufacture of small machine tools, wishes to sell some shares and has requested advice regarding the price that might be asked for them. You are given a copy of the last balance sheet and other financial information below:

Alton Engineers Ltd
Balance sheet at 31 December 20X3

	Cost £	Aggregate depreciation £	Net £
Fixed assets:			
Land and buildings	750	90	660
Plant and machinery	1,000	470	530
Furniture and fixtures	50	30	20
	1,800	590	1,210
Current assets			
Stock	350		
Debtors	280		
Short-term investments	50		
Cash	20		
	700		
less Current liabilities			
Trade creditors	200		
Net working capital			500
			£1,710
Shareholders' capital and reserves:			
Called-up share capital – ordinary shares 50p			400
Profit and loss account			1,010
			1,410
Creditors falling due after more than one year:			
13% term loan (repayable in five years)			300
			£1,710

Note:

Because of increased property values, land is thought to be worth £100,000 more than its balance sheet value. All the above figures are £000.

▶

▶

Operating results for the last three years (£000)			
	20X3	20X2	20X1
Turnover	4,000	3,500	2,800
Net profit after tax	256	210	154
Ordinary dividend paid	101	90	80

Information gleaned from the financial press regarding the recent performance of two companies in the same industry, and of approximately equal size, is as follows:

	P/E ratio	Gross dividend yield	Dividend cover
Zena Corporation	12	5%	3.0
Yani Engineers	10	6%	2.8

Assume that the current standard rate of income tax is 20%.

   Required: Advise the director regarding the valuation of the shares.

(Answers in Appendix E)

FURTHER READING

Arnold, G. (2002) *Corporate Financial Management*, Financial Times Pitman, chapters 14 and 17.

Lumby, S. and C. Jones (1999) *Investment Appraisal and Financial Decisions*, Chapman & Hall, chapters 15 and 21.

McLaney, E.J. (2000) *Business Finance: Theory and Practice*, Prentice Hall, chapter 9.

Pike, R. and B. Neale (2003) *Corporate Finance and Investment*, Prentice Hall, chapter 4.

Samuels, R., F. Wilkes and R. Brayshaw (1999) *Management of Company Finance*, Chapman & Hall, chapters 13 and 15.

17 Dividend policy and share valuation

INTRODUCTION

- Retained profit provides a significant proportion of new finance. This is not surprising for, apart from borrowing, the alternatives are:

  1 that existing shareholders dig more deeply into their own pockets by way of a rights issue;

  2 that the company makes a public issue of shares.

- Only when other sources are exhausted will the latter course be followed for this would dilute existing shareholders' control over the company.

- Regarding a rights issue, it would be illogical for a company requiring finance, and having profit readily available, to distribute it all as dividends and then ask for some of it back. However, companies *do* continue to pay dividends while making issues of shares, so how are their dividend, financing and investment policies reconciled? Is there an optimum dividend policy that maximises shareholder wealth? This question has exercised the minds of academics and financial managers in recent years, but without any completely satisfactory answer being produced.

- In this chapter we look at whether a company's dividend policy affects its share valuation.

LEARNING OBJECTIVES

When you have completed this chapter you should be able to:

1 Explain the residual theory of dividend policy.

2 Discuss and illustrate the Modigliani and Miller hypothesis that a company's dividend policy has no effect on the value of its shares.

3 Explain the costs associated with dividend policy.

4 Discuss the arguments supporting the relevance of dividend policy.

5 Enumerate the practical factors affecting dividend policy.

6 Explain the scrip and share repurchase alternatives to *cash* dividends.

17.1 Dividends as a residual profit decision

It would seem sensible for a company to continue to reinvest profit as long as projects can be found that yield returns higher than its cost of capital. In this way, the company can earn a higher return for shareholders than they can earn for themselves by reinvesting dividends. Such a policy can be optimal, however, only if the company maintains its target gearing ratio by adding an appropriate proportion of borrowed funds to the retained earnings. If not, the company's cost of capital would increase because of its disproportionate volume of higher-cost equity capital; this would be reflected in a reduced share price.

EXERCISE 17.1

Laser Engineering Ltd has the chance to invest in the five projects listed below:

Project	Capital outlay	DCF yield rate
A	70,000	18
B	100,000	17
C	130,000	16
D	50,000	15
E	100,000	14

The company's cost of capital is 16%, its optimal debt to net assets ratio is 30% and the current year's profit available to equity shareholders is £350,000.

Required:
a State which projects would be accepted, and what is the total finance required for those projects.
b Assuming that the company wishes to maintain its gearing ratio, how much of the required finance will be borrowed?
c How much of this year's profit can be distributed?

a *A, B* and *C*, with yields greater than or equal to the company's cost of capital; total finance required £300,000.
b Amount to be borrowed: 30% of £300,000 = £90,000.
c This year's profit: £350,000
   less amount to be reinvested – £300,000–90,000:   210,000

   Profit for distribution: 140,000

Laser Engineering shareholders obtain the best of both worlds. They can invest the £140,000 received as dividends to earn a higher rate of return than the company could earn for them; and the £210,000 retained by the company is reinvested to shareholders' advantage. Shareholders' wealth is optimised, and the dividend paid is simply the *residual profit after investment policy has been approved.*

If companies look upon dividends as what remains after investments are decided then the search for an optimum dividend policy is pointless. Shareholders wanting dividends can always make them for themselves by selling some of their shares.

Further support for the 'residual' theory of dividends, and the argument that a change in dividend policy does not affect share values, was advanced by Modigliani and Miller in 1961. They contended that in a perfect market the increase in total value of a company after it has accepted an investment project is the same, whether internal or external finance is used.

We can look again at the dividend valuation model discussed in Chapter 16, which showed that $V_0 = D \div r$, where V_0 is the present value of a share; D is an assumed constant dividend; and r the shareholders' required rate of return.

Thus if D is £2,000 then $V_0 = £2,000 \div 0.10 = £20,000$, where $r = 10\%$.

EXERCISE 17.2

Given the above data, if a dividend is *currently* due, but not yet paid, what would the present value of the company be?

$V_0 = £2,000 + (2,000 \div 0.10) = £22,000$ – which simply shows the value to include the current, unpaid dividend.

EXERCISE 17.3

If the dividend currently due was invested in a project yielding £300 per annum in perpetuity, what would be the net present value of the project if the shareholders' required rate of return is 10%?

	£
Value of £300 in perpetuity at 10% = £300 ÷ 0.10 =	3,000
less Capital invested	2,000
Net present value	**£1,000**

The value of the company should therefore increase by £1,000.

EXERCISE 17.4

Assuming that the £300 additional earnings from the internally financed project is used to increase the annual dividend, show the revised present value of the company.

$V_0 = £2,300 \div 0.10 = £23,000$ – i.e. an increase of £1,000 over the previous value, this being the net present value of the new project. The dividend forgone is, of course, still included in the total value.

Now assume that the current dividend is paid to shareholders, and the new project is financed by an issue of shares, on which 10% is still the required rate of return. What is the present value of the company, and how much of that value relates to the shares held before the new issue?

$V_0 = £2,300 \div 0.10 = £23,000$ – of which a capitalised expected annual dividend of $£200 \div 0.10 = £2,000$ relates to the new shares; leaving £21,000 appropriate to the original shares – the same as before. Alternatively:

952 new shares	@ 2.10 =	2,000
1000 old shares	@ 2.10 =	21,000
		£23,000

One deficiency in the Modigliani and Miller hypothesis, however, is that they ignore costs associated with an issue of shares, which can be quite considerable.

QUESTIONS 17.1

1 'The residual theory of dividends assumes that a stable dividend policy is followed, with the residue of profit being reinvested within the company.' True or false? Explain.

2 'Retained earnings and external finance are interchangeable for investment purposes' (Modigliani and Miller). Did they mean by this:
  a that they are both sources of cash;
  b that existing shareholders' wealth is unchanged whatever the choice of finance; or
  c that the cash required would come from the same source – shareholders?

(Answers in Appendix E)

17.2 Costs associated with dividend policy

Capital flotation costs are a deterrent to substituting external finance for retained earnings but there are other costs affected by the dividend decision.

If shareholders are left to make their own dividends by selling some shares, this involves brokerage and other selling costs which, on a small number of shares, can be extremely uneconomic. In addition, if they have to be sold during a period of low share prices, capital losses may be suffered.

From the investors' viewpoint, profitably invested retained earnings should increase share values, enabling shareholders to create their own dividends. Selling shares creates a liability to capital gains tax, currently 20%, 23% or 40%, but subject to a fairly generous exemption limit. By comparison, dividends in the hands of shareholders attract higher rates of income tax (up to 40% at 2003 rates). Thus higher-rate taxpayers may prefer comparatively low dividend payouts to minimise their tax burden.

Financial institutions confuse the taxation picture even more, through their major holdings in the shares of quoted companies. They are able to set off dividends received against dividends paid for tax purposes but some may be liable to capital gains tax if they sell shares to make dividends.

The effect of taxation on dividend decisions is difficult to analyse. It may be argued that companies attract investors who can match their personal taxation regimes to company dividend policy, and that those who do not want to join a particular 'taxation club' will invest elsewhere. If this is true, however, a change in a company's dividend policy would probably not find favour with its shareholder clientele, and would consequently affect share values, which seems to support the argument that dividend policy matters.

QUESTION 17.2

List, in two columns, the costs and taxes incurred by shareholders in financing investment by **a** retained earnings, and **b** external finance.

(Answer in Appendix E)

17.3 Other arguments supporting the relevance of dividend policy

---

EXERCISE 17.6

As a potential investor, how would you react to the following questions?

1 Would you prefer cash dividends now, against the promise of future, perhaps uncertain, dividends?

2 Would you prefer a stable, growing dividend to one that fluctuates in sympathy with company investment needs?

3 If a company, in whose shares you invest, increases or decreases its dividend, would this change your personal investment policy?

In answer to question **1** you probably opted for cash now rather than cash you may never see. The future is uncertain and most people take much convincing that it is in their interests to postpone income. Although the equity shareholder by definition is the risk-bearer, he is also entitled to a reasonable resolution of dividend prospects to compensate for the additional risk he carries. An investor will almost certainly pay a higher price for earlier rather than later dividends.

In question **2**, by definition, a fluctuating dividend is more risky than a stable dividend. Investors will pay more for stability, especially if it is linked with steady growth. Research has shown that, in general, dividends follow a pattern of stability with growth. Maintenance of the previous year's dividend is the first consideration, with growth added when directors feel that a higher plateau of profitability has been consolidated.

As regards question **3**, you would no doubt be very happy about an increase, and might even be prompted to buy more shares – thus helping to push the market price up. Conversely a decreased dividend would cause you to review your investment, perhaps even to sell your shares to take advantage of better investment opportunities elsewhere. Investors tend to believe that dividend changes provide information regarding a company's future prospects, and they react accordingly. For example, in 1980 ICI cut its dividend for the first time in years, and this harmed the market price of its shares considerably. The directors were reacting to the continuing recession, expecting that future earnings would not be sufficient to support a continuation of the previous dividend payout.

Dividend policy does therefore appear to be relevant to share valuation, but as stated in the introduction to this chapter, it is left to the individual company to reconcile this policy with uncertainty, costs, taxation and other factors to be discussed in the next section.

17.4 Practical factors affecting dividend policy

Whatever dividend policy is thought to be best for a company in theory, certain practical factors influence the decision.

Availability of profit   The Companies Act 1985 provides that dividends can only be paid out of accumulated *realised* profit *less realised* losses, whether these are capital or revenue. Previous or current years' losses must be made good before a distribution can be made. If an asset is sold, any *realised* profit arising can be distributed; but any profit arising from a revaluation of an asset cannot be distributed – unless and until the asset is sold.

The additional cost of replacing productive assets at inflated prices should be provided for in determining profit available for distribution.

Availability of cash   Profit may be earned during a year and yet it may not be possible to pay a dividend because of lack of cash. This can arise for various reasons.

It may already have been expended or be needed to replace fixed and working assets, perhaps at inflated prices. Large customers may not yet have paid their accounts or cash may be needed to repay a loan.

Government restrictions   Dividends may be restricted by government prices and incomes policies.

Other restrictions   The company's articles of association may limit the payment of dividends or a lender may insert a condition into a loan agreement to restrict the level of dividends.

Similar firms' policies   A company's dividend policy cannot be so outrageously different from policies followed by similar companies in the same industry, otherwise the market price of its shares could fall.

17.5 Alternatives to cash dividends

In recent years companies have introduced more flexibility into their dividend policy by either:

- issuing shares in place of cash dividends (i.e. a 'scrip' dividend); or
- repurchasing their shares.

Scrip dividends

Companies may give their shareholders the option to receive shares rather than cash. This has the effect of maintaining company liquidity, and enabling the company to increase earnings by investing the retained cash. Shareholders may have to pay income tax on the value of shares received.

Thus, a shareholder can increase his investment in a company, without the expense associated with a public issue or a purchase on the stock market, but at the same time retains the option to convert his shares into cash at a future date.

Repurchasing shares

Since 1981 companies have been allowed to purchase their own shares subject to certain restrictions, and the prior authorisation of their shareholders. This is normally done by utilising distributable profits, and the shares must be cancelled after purchase.

Repurchase of shares may be carried out for any of the following reasons:

- to repay *surplus* cash to shareholders;
- to increase gearing by reducing equity capital;
- to increase EPS by reducing the number of shares related to an unchanging level of profit, and hopefully, therefore, the value of each remaining share;
- to purchase the shares of a large shareholder.

The liquidity of the stock market is improved by the cash distribution, if the latter is reinvested advantageously.

TO SUM UP

■ In this chapter we have examined the arguments for and against the relevance of dividends to share valuation.

■ Most companies and their shareholders do, however, settle for a planned and publicised policy of stable and growing dividends, any change to which might be interpreted by investors as information signalling a more volatile or reducing future income. This would tend to lower the value of the company.

QUESTIONS 17.3

1 A company has just made a profit after tax of £350,000. Its investment schedule shows that £300,000 could be invested in projects yielding more than the company's cost of capital. Assuming that the company has a target gearing ratio of 33⅓%, how much dividend could be paid this year?

2 Which of the following support the argument that dividend policy is relevant to the optimisation of shareholder wealth?
   a the certainty of dividends now is preferred to dividends later;
   b directors have the power to change dividends;
   c dividends provide information regarding the expected future fortunes of the company;
   d shareholders prefer stable, growing dividends;
   e dividends are only payable to registered shareholders;
   f dividends should be reconciled with the taxation position of shareholders;
   g shareholders would prefer that profit be distributed as dividends.

3 Given the following information, what dividend can be paid by each company?

	Alpha £	Beta £	Gamma £
Profit/(loss) brought forward from the previous year	(1,000)	2,000	(3,000)
Trading profit/(loss) for the current year	5,000	4,000	2,000
Loss suffered on sale of property	–	(1,000)	–
Revaluation of property	–	–	10,000

4 What is the effect on company liquidity of a a scrip dividend, and b share repurchase?

(Answers in Appendix E)

FURTHER READING

Arnold, G. (2002) *Corporate Financial Management*, Financial Times Pitman, chapter 19.

Lumby, S. and C. Jones (1999), *Investment Appraisal and Financial Decisions*, Chapman & Hall, chapter 22.

McLaney, E.J. (2002) *Business Finance: Theory and Practice*, Prentice Hall, chapter 12.

Pike, R. and B. Neale (2003) *Corporate Finance and Investment*, Prentice Hall, chapter 19.

Samuels, R., F. Wilkes and R. Brayshaw (1999) *Management of Company Finance*, Chapman & Hall, chapter 17.

V External Expansion

Business mergers

■ Most businesses achieve growth organically. They expand existing activities, or diversify into new ones. This is almost always so as regards small and medium-sized enterprises. But mature, larger companies, may reach a stage when further expansion may be more economically and advantageously achieved by amalgamating with another company.

■ This chapter draws upon previous material regarding the evaluation of company performance, and valuation of their shares (Chapter 16). Also on the alternative types of securities as well as cash that may be included in the terms of the offer to merge (Chapters 12 and 13).

When you have completed this chapter you should be able to:

1 Identify and discuss the reasons for, and benefits of merging.

2 Describe and demonstrate how merging companies may be valued.

3 Using given data, show how the financial terms of an offer to merge may be evaluated, both by the offeror and offeree companies' shareholders.

4 Discuss the factors determining the consideration comprising an offer to merge.

5 Recall the regulations governing mergers.

6 Describe the defensive action that may be taken against a proposed merger.

18.1 Why merge?

Mergers are almost inevitable as firms:

■ quicken growth by *acquiring existing companies* rather than expanding internally, especially as shares can be issued instead of cash;

- combine to *ward off competitors*;
- *absorb other firms* that are underutilising their assets;
- combine to *secure their survival* in industries that are declining;
- take over suppliers to safeguard their *sources of materials*;
- increasingly have to *compete on a global scale*.

Multinational companies, in particular, have radically changed the economic complexion of the world, and are the objects of much international economic and political controversy.

Some amalgamations will subsequently yield net economic benefits. For example, the merger of two business units engaged in the same stage of production or service, e.g. breweries (referred to as *horizontal* integration), would give the opportunity to reduce joint costs of their production, marketing and distribution facilities by retaining the most efficient units and discontinuing the least efficient. Again, when business units engaged in complementary stages of a production or service process combine, e.g. breweries with hotels and pubs (known as *vertical* integration), production and marketing benefits could follow.

Research has revealed, however, that not all amalgamations are economically beneficial. This could be so of mergers of firms engaged in production or services that have no apparent business link, e.g. shipping with properties. Such combinations are referred to as *conglomerates*, and the forces motivating their growth appear to be mainly those of *risk diversification* (see Chapter 6, section 6.7) and, in some cases, the power ambitions or desire for security of their leading shareholder/directors.

In recent years many conglomerates have found it beneficial to *demerge*, i.e. sell those parts of their businesses that were not related to their mainstream activities, to their managers (management buyouts), or to outsiders. This has provided finance with which to develop and expand their remaining activities.

Alternatively, demerger may involve the splitting of the activities of a large company (possibly a conglomerate), into separate corporate entities, with their own management teams. Shareholders in the original company are given a proportionate number of shares in each of the newly-created companies. The 1990s' demerges of the Hanson Group, ICI, and British Gas are significant examples of this strategy. In each case, it was considered that more value could be unlocked by demerger, though in the case of British Gas demerger was encouraged by regulatory pressure.

A particular phenomenon of the 1980s in the USA was in the use of so-called 'junk bonds', sponsored mainly by finance house Drexel Burnham Lambert. These carried high rates of interest and therefore high risk. Cash raised by issuing them caused an 'explosion' of take-over activity, as predators stalked businesses that were not using their resources efficiently. To the extent that this made sleepy companies wake up, it was economically beneficial. But 'junk bonds' were also used for unsound hostile megabids and management buyouts.

From your earlier reading you learned that highly geared companies are vulnerable in a recession, and issuers of these high interest bonds began to fail in the late 1980s as they were unable to meet their interest commitments. Holders of 'junk bonds' also suffered as their market prices fell, and it can be presumed that such high-risk securities will not feature very often in future takeover bids.

18.2 Assessing the benefits of merging

Pike Electronics plc have expanded rapidly and hold a fairly strong position in a highly competitive industry. Further internal growth is contemplated, but as part of their corporate strategy they plan to merge with, or acquire the assets of, another company. Given that the advantages of amalgamations can be summarised under the headings of management, supplies, research and development, production, marketing, and finance, what characteristics would Pike be looking for in a possible candidate for merging?

It is possible that Pike Electronics might be looking for an opportunity to widen its product range, with other operating advantages of lesser importance, but putting the widest interpretation on the question, Pike Electronics' requirements could encompass any or all of the following:

Management Securing the management talent of another company to strengthen its own team. Indeed, management may be the prime asset in some targeted companies, e.g. a financial institution.

Supplies Safeguarding sources of materials or components, e.g. buying a company that manufacturers a particularly strategic silicon chip.

Increased requirements of materials common to the merged companies can reduce costs through the negotiation of quantity discounts. Likewise, a policy of standardising on a reduced range of materials will reduce costs.

Research and Development Expertise in similar or different fields would complement Pike's own research effort.

Production Merging similar operations could yield economies of scale; acquisition of advanced production technology that would otherwise take years to develop within Pike Electronics; standardising production by adopting the most profitable of each company's products.

Marketing Acquiring a new range of products to complement those of Pike Electronics; gaining access to new markets and distribution networks, both at home and overseas; rationalising advertising costs; diversifying into other activities to counter the effects of a decline in its traditional business.

Finance Acquisition of unused cash resources, or other assets to sell and convert into cash (known as 'asset-stripping'); combining with a company that has better asset backing, i.e. net asset value per ordinary share.

Accumulated tax losses in the acquired company could be offset against future profits in this company generated by the merger. Earnings per share (EPS) might be increased (see section 18.4), and merging with a company with high gearing would reduce the overall cost of capital of the acquiring company.

The merging of the assets of two companies should logically result in their *joint* value being greater than the sum of their previous separate values. This benefit is commonly referred to as *synergy*, or the '2 + 2 = 5 effect', and it can come about only if the total operational net cash flow after the merger is enhanced for any of the above reasons. As already stated, one of the reasons for conglomerate mergers not living up to expectations is because the marriage of unrelated activities will not necessarily lead to synergy. Merger benefits usually flow out of the rationalisation of like functions or the strengthening of existing operational advantages, and these benefits are worth paying for.

If the acquiring company cannot offer the shareholders of a target company more than the current market value of their shares, a merger would appear not to be worthwhile. On the other hand, a merger should always be for the mutual benefit of both sets of shareholders.

18.3 Valuation of merging companies

The merger of two companies is normally effected by the exchange of shares in one company for those in another. It follows that the share valuations should be acceptable to both parties.

We have already covered the principles of share valuation, but it will be worth your while to reread Chapter 16 before proceeding with this chapter.

The three basic methods discussed in that chapter were net assets value; price earnings (PE) ratio times expected earnings per share (EPS); and dividend yield. The last two methods are most appropriate to the valuation of a private limited company; and the first when the intention is to purchase only part of the assets of another company, or where the assets to be acquired are predominantly liquid, and therefore realistically valued in the current balance sheet.

Another approach to valuation is for the potential acquirer to treat the prospective acquisition as the appraisal of an investment, which of course it is. The intention is to pay cash, shares, loan stock or a mixture of these, in exchange for assets which will generate a future cash flow. The price to pay is the present value of that forecast cash flow, discounted at an appropriate risk-related rate of return.

The difficulty of this approach is the estimation of future cash flows. Net cash flows of 'going concern' companies will continue indefinitely given that assets are replaced. However, when it is considered that the present value of £1 in ten years' time at 15% is only £0.25, and much less at higher rates of interest, then an appraisal covering, say, ten years will probably be satisfactory. In any case, forecasting net operating cash flows for a longer period might be an impracticable proposition. In the case of a merger, the important point is to include the value of the benefits of merging.

Pike Electronics plc estimate that the net profit after tax of Newton Computers plc, for the foreseeable future, will be £400,000 per annum (including synergy), with depreciation of fixed assets averaging £100,000 per annum. Asset replacement during the next ten years will cost £80,000, £100,000, £120,000 and £150,000, in years 1, 3, 6 and 8 respectively.

If Pike Electronics look for an investment rate of return of 15%, what is the maximum price they should pay for Newton Computers? *Hint:* treat the net cash flow after year 10 as a perpetuity, and discount it at its capital value at the end of year 10.

All figures to the nearest £000					
Year	Net profit after tax £	Add back depreciation £	Assets replacement £	Net cash flow £	DCF factor @ 15% £	Present value £
1	400	100	(80)	420	0.870	365
2	400	100	–	500	0.756	378
3	400	100	(100)	400	0.657	263
4	400	100	–	500	0.572	286
5	400	100	–	500	0.497	249
6	400	100	(120)	380	0.432	164
7	400	100	–	500	0.376	188
8	400	100	(150)	350	0.327	114
9	400	100	–	500	0.284	142
10	400	100	–	500	0.247	124
10				3,333*	0.247	823
Maximum offer price for Newton Computers						£3,096

*Capitalised value of a perpetuity of £500 @ 15% = £500 ÷ 0.15 = £3,333.

The above value would then be considered along with those produced by other methods, and an initial offer made to the shareholders of Newton Computers. This should be pitched so as to leave room for subsequent adjustment upwards, but must be credible otherwise further negotiations could be soured.

As stated in the final section of Chapter 16, valuation is what a willing buyer and seller agree it is; whichever methods are used initially, the valuations emerging will merely serve as starting-points and as a basis for negotiations. The value eventually agreed will at best be a compromise of subjective judgement and strategic adjustment on both sides.

18.4 Financial evaluation of an offer to buy shares

What financial consequences will both sets of shareholders concerned in a proposed merger expect in assessing the offer? Assume that both companies are quoted. *Hint*: shareholders will expect to be better off after the merger than before.

Shareholders will look for:

- an increase in the *value of their shares*;
- an increase in *earnings per share*;
- the maintenance of, or an increase in, *dividends*.

The Pike and Newton data given below refers to the year just ended.

	Pike	Newton
Net profit after tax	£576,000	£337,500
Number of ordinary shares in issue (£1)	2,400,000	1,500,000
EPS	24p	22.5p
Market price of share	£3.60	£2.70
PE ratio	15	12
Dividend	8p	9p
Total market value	£8.64 million	£4.05 million

a If an offer for the shares of Newton was made by Pike on the basis of the above share valuations, how many Pike shares would be issued in exchange for Newton shares?

b Calculate the post-merger EPS of Pike based upon the total of both companies' existing earnings, and the increased number of shares in Pike.

a The *exchange ratio* based upon share value is 2.70 ÷ 3.60 = 0.75; that is, three shares in Pike will be exchanged for every four in Newton. This will mean the issue of (1,500,000 ÷ 4) × 3 = 1,125,000 shares in Pike.

b

total post-merger earnings ÷ post-merger number of shares
(576,000 + 337,500) ÷ (2,400,000 + 1,125,000)
EPS (post-merger) = 25.91 pence

Note how the EPS of Pike has increased from 24 to 25.91 pence. Recalling that the Newton shareholders have only three shares in Pike for every four previously held in Newton, the effective EPS per old share of Newton has fallen to (25.91 ÷ 4) × 3 =

19.43 pence, a deterioration of approximately 3 pence per share. This has resulted because of the superior *quality* of Pike's earnings, denoted by its PE ratio. Quality implies better growth prospects and lower risk related to earnings. Whenever the PE ratio of one of the companies in a merger is higher than that of the other, the resultant EPS favours the former company and discriminates against the other.

Clearly, if Newton shareholders were to make their decision solely on the basis of post-merger EPS, the Pike offer would be rejected. However, if they believed that the subsequent market value of their shares would increase, the offer might begin to look more attractive.

EXERCISE 18.5

If the total post-merger earnings of Pike are valued by the stock market on a PE ratio of 15:

a What would be the value of each Pike share after the merger?

b Using the value calculated in **a** compare the effective value of a share held by a Newton shareholder before and after the merger.

a EPS × PE ratio = 25.91 × 15 = £3.89 (approx.).

b The effective post-merger value of a Newton share is (3.89 × 3) ÷ 4 = £2.92. This compares with the pre-merger value of £2.70, an increase of 0.22. However, the increase is speculative, and depends heavily on the assumption that the Pike PE ratio will remain at 15 – despite the lower ratio of Newton. It is highly probable that Newton shareholders would look for more cash 'on the table', and therefore a higher offer than £2.70 per share.

EXERCISE 18.6

If the terms of the offer were five Pike shares for every six in Newton:

a What value would Pike be putting on each Newton share?

b What PE ratio is being attributed to each Newton share?

c What would be the post-merger EPS if synergy is forecast to increase Newton profit to £424,000?

d If a post-merger Pike PE ratio of 14 is adopted by the market, what would be the value of a Pike share?

a Value placed on Newton share = (3.60 × 5) ÷ 6 = £3.00.

b Revised PE of Newton = 300 ÷ 22.50 = 13 (approx.).

c Post-merger

$$\text{EPS} = (576{,}000 + 424{,}000) \div (2{,}400{,}000 + 1{,}250{,}000)$$
$$= 1{,}000{,}000 \div 3{,}650{,}000 = 27.4 \text{ pence}$$

d Value of Pike share = 27.4 × 14 = £3.84.

The offer now looks much more realistic. Newton shareholders are receiving a premium of 30 pence on the current market price, and if synergistic expectations are realistic the effective post-merger value will grow to £3.84 × (5 ÷ 6) = £3.20. With a post-merger EPS of 27.4 pence their previous dividend could be held, with expectations of further growth.

Pike shareholders should also approve, with the promise of a 24 pence accretion on their share value, together with growing dividends.

But what if the post-merger earnings per share were to be diluted? You will recall that this could happen if a higher PE ratio was placed on the earnings of the *offeree* company, than on those of the *offeror*. Would the offeror shareholders approve such a deterioration in their earnings?

The answer is that, if either synergy or growth result in an *early* increase in earnings, at a rate higher than could have been expected without the merger, the merger may be acceptable to the offeror shareholders.

The success of merger valuation negotiations depends very heavily on the predictions of synergy and growth, with this being reflected in an initial offer realistically priced above the current market value of the offeree's shares. How much above will be influenced greatly by the degree to which the market price has anticipated the offer.

QUESTIONS 18.1

1 The market price of a takeover bidder's shares is £4.80. If 5 shares in the bidder company are to be exchanged for every 8 in the biddee company, what is the value put on the biddee's shares? What is the exchange ratio?

2 'If a biddee's PE ratio is higher than the bidder's, the EPS of the bidder after the merger will increase.' True or false? Explain.

(Answers in Appendix E)

18.5 Merger, acquisition, takeover, or strategic alliance?

Merger

Although the word 'merger' has been used so far as a generic term describing the fusion of assets of two or more businesses, it is normally reserved for schemes of arrangement where:

- both sets of shareholders *agree to the merger*;
- the *separate businesses continue* after amalgamation;
- previous shareholders remain *members of the enlarged unit* and retain some control over it;
- the amalgamating businesses are of *comparable size*.

A merger is most often effected by issue of shares in one company in exchange for those in another, the issuing company becoming the holding company, with the other company retaining separate legal identity.

Another approach is for a *new* holding company to be formed to issue shares in exchange for those in the merging companies, which retain their separate legal identities. Although the creation of a new holding company will cause additional expense, overriding reasons for its formation might include the following:

- the holding company can concentrate upon *overall policy making*, leaving operational companies to their separate specialised activities;
- should an operational company go into liquidation, its *creditors' claims* cannot be transferred to the assets of other group companies, unless this has been agreed;
- the shareholders of a purchased company may prefer to *retain some control over a new holding company* rather than be 'absorbed' by a competitor; this only applies of course, where the consideration for the merger is comprised of shares – not cash.

Acquisition

An acquisition is where an acquired company's members give up membership of their company, the consideration for the purchase of their shares or assets being cash, loan stock, convertible loan stock or a mixture of these. The acquired company can either be wound up or continue, but its membership is liquidated. Acquisitions usually apply to small companies that are unable to raise further capital or need cash to pay an inheritance tax liability or are too small to compete.

Takeover

A takeover occurs where one company has already purchased a substantial interest in the shares of another on the stock market and makes an offer for the remainder of the shares. The offer may be wholly in shares of the bidder company but often comprises a package of shares, cash and loan stock. The biddee company is usually smaller than the bidder, but not necessarily. Bids are not always welcomed by the target company shareholders and are frequently bitterly contested.

Reverse takeover

A company wishing to takeover another smaller company may deem it advantageous to encourage the latter to make a 'reverse bid' for the larger company's shares. The result is that the enlarged capital of the smaller company, now the holding company, will mostly be controlled by the larger company and previous shareholders of the smaller company will be minority shareholders though still retaining their same interest in asset value.

A reverse takeover may be resorted to:

- when the larger company is unquoted, and the smaller quoted, and it is desired to *maintain the stock exchange quotation*;
- when it is intended that the smaller company will act as the *future administrative unit*, and the larger company the operating unit;
- when the larger company is highly geared, and the smaller company all equity financed, a reverse takeover will obviate the need to obtain the consent of the *large company's preference shareholders, and/or debenture holders*;
- when the smaller company has the *better profit record*.

Strategic alliance

Where the opportunities for organic growth are limited, and full-blooded merger is not desirable, external growth by way of a strategic alliance is a possible option.

A strategic alliance is a cooperative agreement between two (or more) companies, usually competing in the same industry, to pool resources to develop a new product or process, and/or to gain access to new markets. It may involve the voluntary transfer of technology, expertise, and/or markets to the project, and may be established by setting up a joint venture company, or simply an agreement to collaborate. Firms from the same or different countries may form such alliances.

Such an agreement may be the only way of gaining access to restrictive overseas markets, and/or offsetting the high costs of developing new products or processes; as happened in the motor manufacturing industry during the 1980s. Other examples include the collaborative agreement between British Aerospace and other European aerospace companies to produce the Airbus; and the agreement between the BBC and BSkyB to collaborate in the introduction of digital television.

The possible disadvantages of such an arrangement are that there may be *involuntary* transfers of technical know-how and markets to alliance partners but of course this can work to the mutual advantage of all partners.

18.6 The offer terms – cash or securities?

A typical offer to purchase the shares or assets of another company might read as follows: '£1 in cash for each share held in the offeree company, plus two shares in the offeror company for every three in the offeree company.' If the market price of the offeror's shares is £2.50 at the time of the offer, the value being placed on each of the offeree's shares is £1 + ((2 × £2.50) ÷ 3) = £2.67. This offer would then be evaluated by both sets of shareholders, as discussed in the previous section.

But what factors determine the consideration comprising the offer? Why shares? Why not cash? It would be impossible to construct one financing model to cover all permutations of circumstances, but the major influences on the cash or securities decision are discussed below.

Cash will be the whole or part of the package when:

- the offeror has available, or can readily acquire, the necessary *funds*;
- existing shareholders wish to retain their *control over the offeror company*; issuing shares would result in shared ownership in future;
- *gearing in the purchasing company is already high*, thus inhibiting a loan stock or preference share issue;
- there is *insufficient security* to cover an issue of loan stock.

The main drawback to paying in cash instead of securities is that the offeree company's shareholders might be liable to tax on the capital gains arising from the sale proceeds.

Ordinary shares might be used as the whole or part of the consideration for the following reasons:

- when the offeror is *short of cash*;
- when it is thought desirable to issue *equity shares* to the present managers of the offeree company as an incentive to continuing effort in the merged companies;
- they may be more attractive to shareholders in the offeree company who are currently paying *high rates of tax*;
- when offeree shareholders *prefer not to pay capital gains tax* on a cash offer;
- when gearing is *already high* in the offeror company.

Preference shares could be part of the offer package:

- because generally they have *no voting rights*, and this would ensure that control would be maintained in the hands of existing equity shareholders;
- because the *borrowing base* of the merged companies would be broadened;
- when the bulk of the offeree's shares are in the hands of *institutions* such as charitable trusts, who are not liable to tax, and would therefore welcome a high fixed dividend.

Loan stock (including debentures)   The main arguments for issuing loan stock are:

- it enables the offeror shareholders to *retain control* of their company;
- it reduces the amount of *cash* that otherwise might have to be paid;
- the *cost of servicing* it is reduced considerably because interest is chargeable against profit for tax purposes.

This last argument is particularly important when the merger might result in the initial dilution of the EPS of the offeror company. Because fewer new shares will be issued, and the *net* cost of loan interest is relatively low, EPS should gain.

Arguments against issuing loan stock are:

- Extending the borrowing powers specified in the articles of association of the offeror company would be an expensive procedure.
- The *future borrowing base* of the company will be narrowed.

■ It could worsen an already *highly geared capital structure* in the issuing company.

■ It creates a *contractual commitment to pay interest*, whereas dividend can be deferred if profits are insufficient in any year.

Convertible loan stock – more flexible than pure loan stock because it gives recipients the future option of either retaining a fixed return security or converting it to equity shares. In addition, the income from loan stock may be higher than the dividend income previously received, with the prospect of future growth, if and when the stock is converted into shares.

From the offeror's viewpoint the initial cost could be quite low, partly because the interest rate can be pitched lower than that on straight loans and partly because it is deductible from profit for tax purposes. This would help to prevent dilution of EPS up to the conversion date, during which time expected benefits of the merger accrue. Thereafter enhanced profit ought to cover the dividend requirements of the additional equity shares.

QUESTIONS 18.2

The consideration comprised in a merger offer could include cash, ordinary shares, preference shares, loan stock and convertible loan stock. Which of these would be issued to match each of the following statements?

a It has no voting rights, therefore control remains in the hands of equity shareholders.

b When the gearing of the offeror is already high.

c It would attract capital gains tax in the hands of the recipients.

d It has the early benefits of loan stock and, possibly, the future benefits of ordinary shares.

(Answers in Appendix E)

18.7 The regulation of mergers

Influenced largely by the need to protect the public interest, and those of shareholders, and arising from unfortunate irregularities connected with past mergers, proposals are now regulated by:

■ the *City Code on Mergers and Takeovers*
■ the Competition Act 1998, and the Enterprise Act 2002
■ the Companies Acts
■ European Union regulations.

The City Code on Mergers and Takeovers

This was first published in 1968 (and last updated 2000) by a City working party set up by the Governor of the Bank of England to regularise merger procedure and practices on a voluntary basis, rather than to submit to regulation by legislation.

It is administered by the City Panel on Takeovers and Mergers, a small but efficient full-time body headed by a director-general. They ensure that public companies follow the letter of the code and *private* companies the spirit of the code.

The code contains general principles, with a supporting set of rules governing standards to be observed in merger negotiations. It is the responsibility of the panel to interpret and administer the code. A particularly important requirement of the code is that companies (acting alone or in concert) who hold at least 30% of the voting shares of another company, are obliged to make an offer for the remaining shares at the highest price paid for those shares during the preceding twelve months.

The code is intended to frustrate efforts to start false markets in the shares of merger parties, to protect minorities, to regulate the power of directors in negotiations, to ensure that adequate information is available to all parties involved in negotiations. It lacks the force of law but a reprimand from the panel, or suspension of its Stock Exchange quotation, would not be taken lightly by an erring party to a merger.

Corporation and Enterprise Acts

A proposed merger can be referred to the Competition Commission by the Secretary of State for Trade and Industry and the Director-General of Fair Trading to investigate and report on the possible existence of a monopoly situation. A monopoly might exist if at least one-quarter of the market is supplied by one person or group, if this is deemed to *operate against the public interest*. The commission has the unenviable task of having to weigh the technical advantages of the merger against the likely constraints on free competition, and the necessity to promote consumer interests.

The commission's brief is to recommend to the Secretary of State for Trade and Industry what action to take. Few references are made to the Commission and of those, only a small number are successful in preventing a merger.

Companies Acts

Persons holding more than 5% of the shares of a company must inform it of the fact, and be entered on a special register. This provides information of potential bidders for shares.

Further, the Companies Act 1985 prescribes criminal sanctions against any person(s) connected with a company during the previous six months, who discloses or uses unpublished, price-sensitive information in connection with transactions in the securities of a company on a recognised stock exchange. This is intended to frustrate those who would seek profit by what is known as 'insider dealing'. The Companies Act also prescribes that any company acquiring over 90% of the shares of another company may acquire the remaining shares compulsorily.

EU regulations

European Commission regulations forbid mergers which might lead to domination, and therefore exploitation, of the European Single Market.

18.8 Defensive action against a merger

Once a bid is made, action to evade it is strictly limited and expensive, but the following actions have been taken in the past to ward off takeover bids:

- make a counter-bid for the bidder;
- reference to the Office of Fair Trading or to the Department of Trade and Industry;
- seek a more acceptable merger partner (a 'white knight');
- an increase in dividend by the offeree company – though it is doubtful whether the panel would condone such action;
- revalue the company's assets;
- issue realistic profit forecasts for each of the merging companies;
- make a bonus issue of shares to existing shareholders;
- encourage a management buyout;
- sell assets to thwart the bidder (the 'crown jewels' strategy).

TO SUM UP

- From a microeconomic viewpoint, an offer to merge may be considered as a particular form of investment, and appraised as such. Both sets of shareholders involved will expect an increase in their future wealth as a result in merger.

- From a macroeconomic point of view however, the regulatory authorities are concerned that mergers referred to them will not conflict with the public interest.

- In this chapter, we have drawn upon previously discussed valuation and analytical material to see how both sets of shareholders may assess a proposal to merge.

Delor Cosmetics plc manufacture and sell a complete range of cosmetics, including a spray-on perfume. The ingredients for this product are manufactured by Delor then shipped to Airpak Ltd for aerosol packaging.

The spray-on range is to be extended and much investigation has gone into the alternatives of either extending the existing plant of Delor or merging with an existing aerosol specialist company. Airpak has been selected to fill this role, not only because of its expertise and the relationship that already exists between the two companies but also because it markets a wide range of spray-on products to other industries. A merger would thus provide an element of diversification for Delor.

The summarised balance sheets for the year just ended, together with other relevant information, are shown below:

Balance sheets		
	Delor	Airpak
Net assets	5,250,000	1,700,000
Financed by:		
Ordinary shares (£1 each)	1,000,000	450,000
Reserves	4,250,000	1,250,000
	5,250,000	1,700,000
Profit after tax	£375,000	£115,740

Delor has made an offer to the shareholders of Airpak which puts a PE ratio of 14 on Airpak shares. The stock market currently rates Delor on a PE of 16. Current dividend payments by Delor and Airpak are covered 3 times and 2 times respectively.

Assume that synergy would boost before tax profit by 10% immediately after the merger. Corporation tax assumed to be 50%.

Required:
1 Calculate:
   a The existing earnings per share (EPS) for each company.
   b The existing dividend per share (DPS) for each company.
   c The current market price of the Delor share, and the value ascribed to the Airpak share by the Delor offer.
   d The share exchange ratio, and the number of Delor shares that would have to be issued to Airpak shareholders if the offer was accepted.
   e A comparison of the effective EPS of both companies before and after the merger.
   f The expected value of a Delor share after the merger assuming that the previous PE of 16 is held.
   g A comparison of the effective value of an Airpak share before and after the merger, assuming the conditions in **f** above.
   h The effective dividend per old Airpak share if Delor retained its dividend cover at 3 times.

▶

▶

2 Do you think that Airpak and Delor shareholders would approve the offer?

3 Assume the value per Airpak share calculated in **1c** above. Suppose that Delor made an alternative offer of 2 of their shares for every 5 in Airpak, plus 11% convertible loan stock for the balance of the offer price.

    a   Compare the net income (i.e. after a 30% rate of income tax) of Airpak's shareholders before and after the merger. Assume that Delor retains its 3 times dividend cover.

    b   Would this comparison influence your decision in question 2 above?

(Answers in Appendix E)

FURTHER READING

Arnold, G. (2002) *Corporate Financial Management*, Financial Times Pitman, chapter 20.

McLaney, E.J. (2000) *Business Finance: Theory and Practice*, Prentice Hall, chapter 14.

Pike, R. and B. Neale (2003) *Corporate Finance and Investment*, Prentice Hall, chapter 22.

Samuels, R., F. Wilkes and R. Brayshaw (1999) *Management of Company Finance*, Chapman & Hall, chapter 24.

Working Capital Management

Financing working capital

- Invested capital includes fixed and current assets. It is the latter *less* suppliers' and other short-term credit, which is referred to as *net current assets* or *working capital*.

- The terms *fixed* and *current* assets are used to differentiate between those resources that will not completely revert to cash within a year and those that will, respectively.

- The planning and control of current assets warrant the same skill and care as is lavished on fixed assets, the twin objectives of current asset management being:

  1 to *minimise* the time between the initial input of materials and other resources into the operating process, and the eventual payment by customers for goods or services supplied; this is known as the *cash operating cycle*, and success in this aim will reduce investment in stocks, debtors and liquid assets to a minimum;

  2 to finance those assets as efficiently as possible; with the overall objective of optimising the return on total capital employed.

When you have completed this chapter you should be able to:

1 Explain the risk/return trade-off of investment in working capital.

2 Estimate the working capital requirement of a proposed project.

3 Explain and calculate appropriate ratios, and the cash operating cycle used to monitor ongoing investment in working capital.

4 Describe how working capital is financed to attain a balance of risks with costs.

19.1 Working capital investment – a risk/return trade-off

Most people with bank current accounts maintain cash balances sufficient to meet their daily needs and for emergencies. Any money held in excess of these needs is wasted, as it could be better invested elsewhere to earn higher interest.

Anyone who finances needs by running an ever-increasing overdraft which is not backed by easily realisable assets runs the risk of bankruptcy. Somewhere between these extremes, a balance between risk and return must be struck; this applies not only to individuals but also to businesses.

For example, *too high* an investment in stock reduces the risk of running out of stock, but also reduces profit because the wasted resources could be better invested elsewhere. Conversely, *too low* an investment in stock increases the risk of running out of stock and therefore of losing orders, even though it releases resources for alternative investment.

19.2 How much working capital?

The total working capital of a business is a composite result of the management policies adopted in respect of each of its elements. Clearly, in most cases, it will not be a static requirement. Seasonal changes in demand and supply, and the introduction of new, and cessation of existing products, will cause it to fluctuate.

Periodic cash flow forecasts are probably the best indicators of ongoing working capital needs, as illustrated in Chapters 8 and 20.

However, a 'snapshot' calculation can be made by taking the following factors into account:

- planned *production volumes*
- *forecast costs* per unit of output
- the *length of the production cycle* (or 'lead time')
- planned *stock levels*
- credit terms *allowed to customers*
- credit terms *received from suppliers*.

EXERCISE 19.1

A company will shortly be producing a new product. Calculate the maximum additional working capital required using the following information:

Annual output: 12,000 units – to be evenly produced throughout the year.

Production cost and selling price per unit:

▶

▶

	£
Raw material	30
Labour	10
Overheads	10
Total cost	50
Profit	20
Selling price	70

(a) One month's stock of raw materials is held at all times.

(b) Each unit takes one month to produce, on average; all material being input at the commencement of the process.

(c) Work-in-progress is half complete on average

(d) 1½ month's finished units are held in stock.

(e) Customers are allowed 2 months' credit.

(f) Suppliers of raw materials and overheads allow 1½ months' credit.

(g) Production wages are paid ¼ month in arrears.

(h) Assume each month has four weeks, and that there are twelve months in a year.

Hint: Items (a)–(e) will require additional working capital, but be partly financed by (f) and (g).

The additional working capital required would be:

		£	£
Raw materials	1 mth 1,000 × £30		30,000
Work-in-progress:			
Material	1 mth 1,000 × £30	30,000	
Labour	½ mth 500 × £10	5,000	
Overheads	½ mth 500 × £10	5,000	
			40,000
Finished units	1½ mth 1,000 × £50		75,000
Debtors	2 mth 2,000 × £50		100,000
less:			245,000
Creditors – Materials	1½ mth 1,500 × £30	45,000	
– Wages	¼ mth 250 × £10	2,500	
– Overheads	1½ mth 1,500 × £10	15,000	
			62,500
Net additional working capital required			182,500

Notes:

1 Work-in-progress:
   – Fully complete as to material – introduced at commencement of production.
   – Labour and overhead half-complete, shown as equivalent to 500 units.

2 Debtors – funds required to finance debtors over the credit period, are at production cost only.

19.3 Controlling working capital – ratio analysis

The data given below relates to Apex and Base, two similar-sized companies in the same line of business. Before completing the following assignment which involves the calculation of ratios, it might be helpful for you to refer back to Chapter 2 on ratio analysis, and in particular the section entitled 'Can the business pay its way?'

Now calculate the following ratios relating to the accounts of Apex and Base:

a Current ratio;
b Acid test ratio;
c Number of days' sales outstanding;
d Number of days' stock held;
e Number of days' creditors outstanding;
f Cash as a percentage of current assets;
g Sales to capital employed.

Balance sheets of Apex and Base			£000	
		Apex		Base
Sources of funds:				
Share capital – ordinary £1		500		500
Retained profit		1,100		500
		1,600		1,000
Uses of funds				
Fixed assets (net)		800		800
Current assets:				
Stock	400		200	
Debtors	400		200	
Cash	200		50	
	1,000		450	
Current liabilities				
Trade creditors	150		200	
Taxation	50		50	
	200		250	
		800		200
Net assets:		1,600		1,000
Sales	1,500		1,500	
Profit after tax	105		105	
Profit % of net assets	6½		10½	

	Apex	Base
a Current ratio	5:1	1.8:1
b Acid test	3:1	1:1
c Debtors – days outstanding	97	49
d Stock – days outstanding	97	49
e Creditors – days outstanding	36	49
f Cash as a % of current assets	20%	11%
g Sales to capital employed	0.9:1	1.5:1

EXERCISE 19.3

1 What is the overall reason for the difference in profit % between Apex and Base?

2 What are the factors contributing to this difference?

3 In which company would you invest? Why?

1 A lower capital employed by Base has earned the same profit as Apex, resulting in a higher return per £100 capital invested by Base.

2 Apex has at least double the investment in each of the current assets, and also a lower amount owing to creditors.

3 Given the higher return on capital invested, I would prefer Base's shares to those of Apex. The comparative statistics show Base to be better financially managed than Apex, the latter company carrying too high a level of current assets to support its turnover.

The Apex Company is a classic case of *overcapitalisation* (or *undertrading*), with resultant lower profit return. Conversely, too *aggressive* a working capital policy, with current assets 'cut to the bone', might result in lost orders, either because minimal stocks cannot cope with the volume of orders or because customers are deterred by tight credit policies.

19.4 Controlling working capital – cash operating cycle

The *cash operating cycle* is the interval of time between purchasing production materials and payment for finished output by customers, taking account of credit allowed by suppliers.

It therefore measures the total time that funds are invested in working capital.

A comparison of the total time, and the turnover times of each of its components, with predetermined targets, will indicate where remedial action is called for.

Given below is a schedule of the values of stocks, debtors and creditors of Apex Engineering Ltd at the end of a year. Alongside are the annual totals of the profit and loss accounts to which they relate.

	£000		£000
Stock – Materials	30	Purchases	360
Debtors	140	Sales	840
Stock – WIP	40	Cost of Sales	600
Stock – Finished	75	Cost of Sales	600
Trade Creditors	62	Purchases	360

Required:

Calculate the number of days that each of the stocks and debtors, *less* creditors, at the end of the year, represent as a proportion of the annual figures shown on the right. What is the cash operating cycle in days?

Cash operating cycle		
		Days
Stock – Material	30/360 × 365	30
Debtors	140/840 × 365	61
Stock – WIP	40/600 × 365	24
Stock – Finished	75/600 × 365	46
		161
less: Creditors	62/360 × 365	63
		98

19.5 Financing working capital

Investment plans of a business need finance to cover:

- a *permanent* and growing layer of fixed and net current assets;
- *fluctuating* current asset requirements arising mainly from seasonal and customer demand factors.

Permanent investment is usually financed by long- and medium-term capital, and as you have already seen, a business must decide upon an acceptable ratio of debt to equity capital; the debt proportion being financed by a judicious mixture of long- and medium-term instruments, with the object of minimising the cost of capital at an acceptable risk.

Company treasury managers can reduce some of this risk by arrangements with banks or the London International Financial Futures and Options Exchange (LIFFE), which protect against future adverse changes in interest rates.

But there still remains the problem of how to finance fluctuating net current assets.

Figure 19.1 shows alternative net working capital financing strategies, ranging from the most (*D*) to the least (*A*) risk. It is assumed:

- that fixed assets are largely financed by *long- or medium-term capital*;
- that the *servicing* of borrowed capital in the form of interest and capital repayments is met out of current net earnings, or alternatively, in the case of capital payment, by a renegotiated loan;
- that taxation and dividends are paid out of *current earnings*.

Strategy A uses *long-term finance* only, fully covering the risk of running out of cash due to fluctuating cashflows (the wavy line). The safety built into the permanence of this arrangement, however, has its costs. These are:

- *higher cost* of long- against short-term capital;
- risk of being *locked in* by a high interest rate, if interest rates fall;
- the need to pay *interest* in the troughs between fluctuations when the capital is not required – lessened to some extent by short-term investment interest on the surplus.

Strategy B leaves some fluctuating needs to be covered by *short-term finance*. It is more risky, therefore, than *A* because liquidity problems could arise if repayment of the short-term capital was due at a time when alternative financing might be difficult to arrange. In addition, short-term interest rates are more volatile than long-term, which makes cash flows less certain.

Strategy C covers all cyclical fluctuations by *cheaper* short-term borrowing, at the same time providing *flexibility* to repay the finance when it is not required. This is

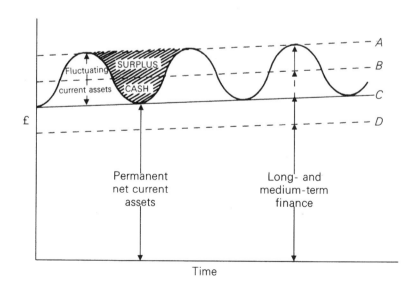

Figure 19.1
Financing working capital – balancing risk with cost

Note: permanent net current assets are after deducting normal trade credit, accruals and other continuing current liabilities

a lower cost arrangement than either *A* or *B*, but with a higher level of the risks specified in *B*.

Strategy D permits short-term financing of a layer of permanent net current assets – an extremely risky policy, especially if the assets financed are not easily realisable. This policy presents the greatest risk of insolvency.

Strategies B or *C* appear to strike a balance between the extremes of *A* and *D*. The choice will ultimately be influenced by the perceived risk of running out of cash.

TO SUM UP

■ In this chapter we have examined the *overall* control and financing of working capital. In Chapters 20–22 we take a closer look at the control of liquidity, stock and debtors.

QUESTIONS 19.1

1 Assume that, two years later, Base, the company cited in Exercise 19.2, shows the following position:

Source of funds:		£000
Share capital – ordinary £1		500
Retained profit		1,100
		£1,600
Uses of funds:		
Fixed assets (net)		1,600
Current assets:		
Stock	400	
Debtors	400	
Cash	–	
	800	
Current liabilities:		
Trade creditors	300	
Taxation	100	
Overdraft	400	
	800	–
		£1,600
Sales		£3,000
Profit after tax		180
Profit % of net assets		11¼%

▶

Required:

Using the above information, **a** calculate the same ratios as those produced in Exercise 19.2, **b** comment on the company's financial position.

2 At the end of last year the *cash operating cycle* of Briggs Engineering plc was 145 days, comprising the current assets and liabilities shown below:

	Turnover period days	Turnover factor
Raw material stock	80	Purchases
Finished goods stock	45	Cost of sales
Debtors	60	Sales
	185	
less Creditors	40	Purchases
	145	

The 'turnover period' is calculated by relating each working capital item to its 'turnover factor', and multiplying by 365. For example:

$$(\text{Stock of raw materials} \div \text{purchases}) \times 365 = 80 \text{ days}$$

Stock of raw materials at the beginning of last year was £20,000, purchases during the year were £130,031, and the gross profit for the year £78,469.

Required:

1 Calculate the value of net current assets at the end of the year.

2 Given that Briggs' target 'turnover periods' for the year were 65, 35, 50 and 50 days respectively, for each of the working capital items, what should the investment in net current assets have been?

(Answers in Appendix E)

FURTHER READING

Arnold, G. (2002) *Corporate Financial Management*, Financial Times Pitman, chapter 13.

McLaney, E.J. (2000) *Business Finance: Theory and Practice*, Prentice Hall, chapter 13.

Pike, R. and B. Neale (2003) *Corporate Finance and Investment*, Prentice Hall, chapter 14.

Samuels, R., F. Wilkes and R. Brayshaw (1999) *Management of Company Finance*, Chapman & Hall, chapter 19.

20 Controlling liquidity

INTRODUCTION

■ The importance of *cash flow* was emphasised in your earlier study of investment appraisal, its availability to pay dividends, and in Chapter 19 in the calculation of the cash operating cycle. Liquidity is clearly the vital lubricant of an ongoing business.

■ We therefore need to plan our future cash requirements, with the aim of balancing adequacy with the cost of holding cash.

LEARNING OBJECTIVES

When you have completed this chapter you should be able to:

1 Define liquid assets and explain the need for liquidity.

2 Describe how cash flow may be speeded up, and managed more efficiently.

3 Compile a cash forecast from given data, and explain the importance of routine cash forecasting.

4 Describe how cash inventory models based upon the availability of a range of short-term investments, can be used to minimise the cost of managing cash.

20.1 What are liquid assets?

Liquid assets include cash in hand and in bank current accounts and assets easily and quickly convertible into cash. The latter covers bank and finance house deposits, and marketable securities of all kinds. Marketable securities usually have short maturity dates but equity shares, quoted on a Stock Exchange and therefore easily realisable, may be included in a portfolio of liquid assets.

20.2 Why do we need liquidity?

Why do any of us need an easily accessible reserve of cash?

First, we need it to pay for goods and services received and ordered. Even if your electricity supplier allows time to pay, you must eventually hand over cash for electricity consumed. Such payments are part of our normal day-by-day *transactions*.

Second, it is wise to maintain an emergency cash float in case something unexpected happens. Such a *precautionary* balance may be required for expenditure on wedding presents, or to pay an unexpected car repair bill.

Businesses also need liquidity to meet normal *transactions* expenditure on wages, materials, expenses and taxes; and as a *precaution* to deal with uncertainty of their cash flows. Any cash held in excess of *transaction* and *precautionary* requirements is wasteful unless it is held to meet some planned expenditure, such as impending plant replacement or taxation.

20.3 Efficient cash management – a prerequisite

Efficient cash management is a prerequisite for determining and maintaining optimum cash levels in business. Cash forecasting is of no avail if cash management systems are inefficient. Assuming that its control of debtors is efficient (see Chapter 22), and that customers pay their accounts within the time allowed, a business must ensure that customers' payments are speedily transmitted into its bank account.

Although this process appears straightforward, there are several ways in which it can be quickened:

- Ensure that cash/cheques are *banked daily*; the cost in interest lost because firms make only a weekly journey to the bank is surprisingly high.
- *Centralised banking.* Countrywide depots, shops and branches should be instructed to bank daily receipts for the *direct credit* of head office current account – ensuring that all cash is pooled and more efficiently deployed to benefit the whole business. Banks now offer a wide-ranging cash management service to companies with a large number of subsidiaries or branches. By computer transfers of cash between companies and across frontiers in different currencies, they enable the most efficient use to be made of short-term surplus funds within the group.
- Arrange the *direct debit* customers in respect of regular payments due; Automobile Association subscriptions and utility payments are dealt with this way, and hire purchase instalments are largely directly debited.
- Arrange with the bank for *express clearance* of large-value cheques through the Clearing House Automated Payment System (CHAPS); a fee is charged for this service but earlier access to cash should yield a benefit much greater than the fee.

- *Collect* large payments from customers *personally* to cut down postal delays; security companies or sales representatives may be useful here.
- The growing use of *electronic funds transfer* systems, allowing customers to pay their debts into suppliers' bank accounts by direct computer transfer, e.g. Banker's Automated Clearing Service (BACS).

Other ways to improve cash management include:

- arranging *insurance cover* for cash in transit, and other balances held;
- reducing the number of, and amounts held, in cash *floats*;
- ensuring a good relationship is maintained with the *bank*;
- monitoring *internal check systems* on cash frequently;
- covering the risk of foreign currency fluctuations by *forward dealing*;
- preparing *detailed short-term cash forecasts* covering different time horizons;
- ensuring that *excess cash* is held in short-term investments to help earn its keep.

QUESTION 20.1

Crane Auto Engineers plc maintained a centralised London bank deposit account, into which branches credited their net cash receipts at the end of each four-weekly period. The net cash flow for the Norwich branch was £100,000 per four-weekly period.

The recently appointed Norwich accountant realised that the delay in banking was losing the company interest, and he produced figures to illustrate the loss.

Assuming that the net receipts per four-weekly period are received in equal instalments at the end of each week, show how much additional interest could be earned by crediting the London account each week instead of every four weeks. The deposit interest rate is 13% per annum.

(Answer in Appendix E)

20.4 What volume of liquid funds should be held?

If businesses knew future cash flows *with certainty*, cash forecasts would indicate precisely how much was needed at all times. In these circumstances strategy *C* in Figure 19.1, p. 271, would suit, with short-term funding arranged well in advance to cover known periods of cash shortage. Conversely, known cash surpluses could be invested to mature precisely when funds are required. With certainty, liquidity funding could be managed most efficiently and economically.

Uncertainty is the normal business condition, however, and strategies *A* or *B* in Figure 19.1 may be more appropriate – providing permanent cash buffers to cover exceptional cash shortages. Holding cash has its opportunity cost, of course, and management must decide between covering the risk of running out of cash and reducing profitability. Policy will depend on the stage of business development, forecasts of future growth and short- and long-term cash forecasts.

In the early stages, a growing business will tend to rely heavily on short-term borrowed capital because other sources of funds will be unavailable. The danger is that, if the business cycle turns down or government credit restrictions are introduced, the business can be most vulnerable. Worse, it could be heading for insolvency if overdrafts are restricted or are called in by the bank. This is a possibility, even if the current trading position of a business is very healthy.

As a business grows and improves its credit standing, it should be able to negotiate temporary borrowing to close a liquidity gap, but this will depend partly on what security it can offer for loans or overdrafts, and on general financial market conditions. If borrowing conditions become critical, and an issue of shares is not feasible, more drastic action may be needed if a business is to survive. The following options are available:

- *rephase the repayment of existing debt capital* to increase current liquidity;
- *time-related* actions such as delaying payment to suppliers, speeding up collection of debts and delaying capital expenditure;
- *volume-related* actions, including cutting down on overtime, shift-work and part-time working, also temporary lay-offs;
- *scale-related* actions, including reduced operating budgets, restrictions on capital expenditure, research and development, and marketing, reduction of inventory levels, reduced dividends;
- *divestment* of non-core activity, subsidiary companies and loss-making divisions and projects, selling undeveloped land and other surplus assets.

QUESTIONS 20.2

1 Decisions about volume of liquid funds to hold are based on assessment of the return/risk trade-off. What does this mean?

2 Which of the following actions, taken to improve liquidity, are related to **a** time, **b** volume, **c** scale, **d** divestment of activity?
 i Sale of surplus office block;
 ii Reduction of overtime;
 iii Delayed capital expenditure;
 iv Reduction of inventory levels.

(Answers in Appendix E)

20.5 Cash forecasting

In Chapter 8 we discussed short-term cash forecasting in the context of determining initial financing requirements. It is vital, however, that cash forecasting is a continuing exercise with forecasts covering different time horizons. Weekly forecasts for three months ahead; monthly forecasts for the coming twelve or twenty-four months; longer forecasts for up to five or ten years.

Cash forecasts help by pointing up any expected periods of cash shortage for which provision can be planned well in advance; or periods of cash surplus providing short-term investment funds.

The four most important features of preparing cash forecasts are:

- Account for *all* cash receipts and payments, including those of a capital nature; taxes; dividends, grants received; VAT; as well as all the normal operating cash flows.
- The expected *timing* of receipts and payments should be reflected in the forecast, attention being paid to credit terms received from, and allowed to, suppliers and customers respectively. Note particularly the exact timing of large payments for assets or repayment of capital.
- The forecasts should be *updated* as frequently as uncertainty and change dictate; the use of PCs and laptops and financial software make this feasible for the smallest of businesses.
- *Deviations* in forecasts will inevitably occur but, by producing a range of forecasts based on varying assumptions, they can be estimated. Alternatively, the *sensitivity* of forecasts to change can be examined by simulating the effect on net cash flows, of changes in single variables, or combinations of variables. These are areas in which the computer and financial models are increasingly applied.

QUESTION 20.3

The estimated sales of Eco Cleaning Equipment plc for the next ten months, October to July, are as shown below:

	£000		£000
October	120	March	200
November	160	April	240
December	280	May	320
January	160	June	360
February	160	July	320

Experience has shown that 75% of a month's sales are paid for in the month following, 20% two months following, and 5% three months following. Manufacturing materials are approximately 30% of sales value and are purchased and paid for one month before the month of sale. Wages and salaries represent approximately 40% of sales value, and are paid in the month of sale. Expenses representing 10% of sales value are paid one month later than the month of sale.

▶

▶

Capital expenditure costing £90,000 is due for payment in March; a dividend of £40,000 is payable in April; and £80,000 corporation tax is due to payment in August next. A government grant of £30,000 in respect of the equipment purchased is receivable in June. The balance of cash at the end of December is £30,000.

Required:

a Construct a cash forecast covering the months January to June.

b By using a computer financial model, the accountant forecasts that:

i for the months January–March there is minimal risk of the cash balance falling below £20,000;

ii the distribution of possible net cash balances for May reveals a 30% probability of a cash deficit of £60,000. What action might the accountant take as a result of this information?

(Answers in Appendix E)

20.6 The range of short-term investments available

It is important to make maximum use of liquid assets with as little as possible being held as cash at any time, the remainder being placed in short-term investments. The investments most used for this purpose are:

- *Overnight loans* to banks and discount houses.
- *Clearing bank deposit accounts*; seven days' notice of withdrawal required, but easily realisable in an emergency.
- *Finance, discount house and merchant bank deposits*; have a higher interest rate than clearing banks, but longer notice of withdrawal is required.
- *Foreign and other bank deposit accounts*; higher interest, but possibly greater risk.
- *Treasury Bills*; maximum 3 months maturity; £50,000 minimum investment.
- *Bills of exchange*; maturing in 3–6 months' time.
- *Certificates of deposit* issued by banks and commercial and industrial companies; evidencing loans for fixed amounts, fixed periods and fixed rates of interest.
- *Certificates of tax deposits* issued by the Inland Revenue.
- *Local authority deposits and loans* for periods ranging from weekly to two-yearly.
- *Government bonds with short maturities*; no Capital Gains tax if held for more than one year.
- Deposits in the *Eurocurrency markets* (see Chapter 10).

These various homes offer a choice of maturities and returns to tailor a portfolio that will satisfy the six characteristics of short-term investment. These are: easy realisability, short maturities, low default risk, low arrangement expense, fair rate of return, and tax efficiency.

20.7 Keeping the cash balance to a minimum

What do you think are the main objectives of managing short-term investments?

- To maximise the *return on the investment.*
- To arrange for the *maturities and cash requirements* to coincide.
- To maintain an *easily accessible bank deposit balance or overdraft facility*, as a hedge against the uncertainty of cash flows.

Mathematical models have been used successfully to optimise transfers into and out of short-term investments. These models recognise that there are costs associated with *holding* cash (i.e. interest forgone), and cost of *withdrawing* cash from investments (i.e. administration and brokerage).

An inventory model assumes a cash deposit into short-term securities at the start of a period, followed by smooth, predictable withdrawals to meet transaction requirements. The objective is to find the optimal level of cash withdrawal which minimises the total costs of holding and withdrawing cash.

Using the following symbols and assuming the conditions outlined in the Baumol model above, construct two separate models to show:

a the total cost of holding cash;
b the total cost of withdrawals.

T = total amount deposited at the commencement of a period
C = optimal cash withdrawal
i = interest rate on short-term securities
b = fixed costs of each withdrawal.

The total cost of holding cash is $i(C \div 2)$. The total cost of withdrawals is $b(T \div C)$. As C grows larger, total withdrawal cost reduces, but holding cost increases. The optimal level of C will therefore be when withdrawal and holding costs are equal, i.e. when

$$i(C \div 2) = b(T \div C)$$
$$\text{and } iC^2 = 2bT$$
$$\text{and } C^2 = (2bT) \div i$$
$$\text{therefore } C = \sqrt{((2bT) \div i)}$$

A company deposits its sales receipts of £50,000 into short-term investments at the beginning of a period. The investment interest is 8% and the fixed cost of withdrawing cash is £20 per withdrawal. Payments are predictable and even throughout the period. What is the optimal level of cash withdrawal?

$$C = \sqrt{((2bT) \div i)} = \sqrt{((2 \times 20 \times 50{,}0000) \div 0.08)}$$
$$= \sqrt{(2{,}000{,}000 \div 0.08)} = £5{,}000$$

Although this model captures the essential elements of the problem, it is rather unrealistic in its assumptions regarding cash flows of the average company, which are frequently not predictable or smooth. Other, more sophisticated models have been developed to overcome the problems of cash flow uncertainty, which calculate the minimum and maximum cash balances within which a company can operate most economically, e.g. the Miller–Orr model.

TO SUM UP

- This chapter has focused on the importance of liquidity in business. As with all beneficial resources, it is held at a cost, which can be minimised by efficient planning and management.

- However, it is also clear that control of liquidity will rest to a large extent upon the efficient management of the other components of working capital.

- We look at the control of stocks and debtors in Chapters 21 and 22.

QUESTIONS 20.4

1 There are many ways of speeding the process of transmitting the cash received from customers into supplier's bank accounts.
  a Describe four such methods.
  b What is the benefit of speeding up the process?

2 In what three essential respects does a cash forecast differ from a profit and loss account?

3 a What are the costs of holding cash?
  b If the maturities of short-term investments do not coincide with the need for cash, what costs will be incurred?

(Answers in Appendix E)

FURTHER READING

Arnold, G. (2002) *Corporate Financial Management*, Financial Times Pitman, chapter 13.

McLaney, E.J. (2000) *Business Finance: Theory and Practice*, Prentice Hall, chapter 13.

Pike, R. and B. Neale (2003) *Corporate Finance and Investment*, Prentice Hall, chapter 15.

Samuels, R., F. Wilkes and R. Brayshaw (1999) *Management of Company Finance*, Chapman & Hall, chapter 20.

Controlling stocks

■ Successful management of working capital reflects the degree of control exercised over each of its components – stocks, debtors, and liquid assets. This does not mean that the separate elements of working capital are independent of one another. A change in policy in one will probably effect the value of another. For example, a critical liquidity problem might be solved temporarily by reducing stock levels to release cash, but stock shortages can result in lost sales and therefore a reduction in liquidity. Again, if customers can be persuaded to order in large quantities in return for quantity discounts, this would probably reduce finished goods stocks but increase debtors and possibly bad debts. Thus stock policy may affect, and be affected by, debtors and liquidity.

■ Controlled investment in stock plays a critical role in achievement of business objectives. Too high a stock level relative to a given volume of sales will reduce return on investment; too low a level, whilst reducing investment, may also reduce sales and therefore profit proportionately more. This is another example of the need to consider the trade-off between return and risk when making business decisions.

■ Stock control problems will largely be related to whether a business manufactures or distributes products, the complexities of the production process, and the range and variety of products supplied. In manufacturing, the production cycle usually necessitates the holding of raw materials, work-in-progress, and finished goods stocks. Whereas in distribution, wholesale warehouses and retail outlets hold only stocks of finished goods.

Problems in stock control may be alerted by applying the stock turnover ratios discussed and illustrated in Chapters 2 and 19.

When you have completed this chapter you should be able to:

1 Describe the factors influencing stock levels.

2 Discuss how stock levels may be optimised.

3 Explain the 'Pareto curve' influence on the management of stocks.

4 Calculate economic order quantity (EOQ) levels.

5 Discuss the need to determine re-order levels and safety stocks.

21.1 What factors influence stock levels?

EXERCISE 21.1

From each of the following hints, see if you can deduce a factor that influences the level of *finished goods* stocks in different industries.

1 Number of customers.

2 Foodstuffs.

3 Fashion, style and technology.

4 Harvests, fireworks, Christmas crackers.

5 Keen competition.

6 Nationwide distribution.

7 Quantity discounts.

8 Unique specifications.

9 Lost customers.

1 Anticipated *demand* from customers.

2 The rate of *deterioration* (shelf-life) of the product.

3 The pace of *obsolescence*, changes in style and technological development will constrain stockholding.

4 *Seasonal* nature of the product. For example, harvested foods may be wholly processed immediately after being gathered, thus boosting stock level at that time; Christmas crackers, fireworks and sledges peak in different seasons, but will probably be made for stock throughout the year, to reap the economies of even production levels.

5 *Uncertainty* of demand will call for higher stocks.

6 The need to *decentralise* stockholding into a network of national distribution depots may increase total stock.

7 *Transfer stocks* to customers by persuading them to purchase in larger quantities.

8 Whether goods are *made to order* or for stock.

9 *Lost profit contribution* has to be balanced against the cost of holding higher stocks.

The nature of, and demand for, the product largely influences *finished goods* stock levels. Likewise, *raw material* stocks will be affected by the nature of the product, with perishability a prime determinant of how much material can be economically held.

Uncertainty of product demand may also affect holdings of raw materials and components but the major factor here will be rate of usage in production and the time taken to replace stocks from suppliers.

Work-in-progress stocks depend on production processing time. Partly finished confectionery stock will be low, therefore, whilst that in a factory producing computers will be high. It should be noted that increased output does not necessarily increase raw material and work-in-progress stocks, if the additional output is completed in overtime or additional shifts worked.

21.2 Optimum stock levels

In manufacturing, the ideal situation is to carry no stocks of raw materials and finished goods, and a bare minimum of work-in-progress, but this can only be achieved if:

- raw materials are available from suppliers *immediately they are required*; and finished products are delivered to customers immediately after they are completed (the 'just-in-time' or JIT approach);
- raw material and component purchase prices are no different whether one *buys for stock or for continuous delivery*;
- sales are *stable* and can be *forecast accurately*;
- *production is efficiently organised* and always proceeds on schedule;
- *production facilities are flexible* and easily adapted to changes in customer demand;
- optimum use is made of *computer aided manufacturing* (CAM) techniques;
- *total quality management* (TQM) techniques are applied in production.

Although several of these conditions might be encountered in industry, it is doubtful whether all can be found together in a single manufacturer. Risks opportunities and the circumstances discussed in the previous section may dictate that 'buffer' stocks be maintained by the majority of firms.

From the *production manager's* viewpoint, uncertainties of raw material supply must be provided for. In addition, fluctuating or seasonal finished product demand will provide encouragement to:

■ ensure there are *adequate levels of raw materials and components* to take the strain of a sudden increase in product demand; and

■ *produce for stock* to realise lower costs per unit resulting from longer production runs.

The *sales manager* will be concerned primarily that adequate levels of finished goods are available to meet the customers' demands. Hold-ups in production and fluctuating demand can be insured against by holding larger finished goods stocks.

On the other hand, the *financial manager* has to reconcile the vested interest in flexibility and safety of managerial colleagues with the financial constraint of minimising total capital invested in stocks. To achieve this compromise, s/he will aim to:

■ reduce to a minimum the *total cost of* holding and acquiring stocks;

■ decide the *stock reorder level* for each item held, to ensure that demand can be met;

■ add a *safety stock* to each item that is subject to uncertain demand or supply.

21.3 Minimising the stock control effort

It is well recognised in various value areas, comprising a number of items, that a comparatively low proportion of the items represents a high proportion of total value. Conversely a high proportion of items represent a relatively low proportion of the total value (the *Pareto curve*). This is so in the case of debtors and stocks in most firms. The pattern might be:

Turnover	Over £50	£10–£50	Under £10
% of total annual value	65	25	10
Number of items	10	20	70

In the case of stock, the word 'value' refers not so much to value of individual items as to value in usage – which relates more to turnover. For example, a £10 stock item 'turned over' 50 times in a year represents £500 usage value, whereas a £50 item turned over 4 times has a £200 usage value.

Note particularly that the above table shows that 90% of the value represents only 30% of the items.

Close control of the high value items, perhaps by using the kind of mathematical approach discussed on pp. 287–8, will pay off handsomely; whereas the much larger effort needed to control the majority of items in stock will pay relatively poor rewards and can probably be dealt with by using less costly rule-of-thumb methods.

21.4 How much to order?

We stated earlier that one of the financial manager's prime aims is to reduce to a minimum the *total* cost of holding and acquiring stocks. Assuming that demand for an item is known, this minimum can be directly related to the frequency and size of orders.

If Percy Bend, a plumber, uses 10,000 of a certain pipe fitting fairly evenly throughout the year, and places only one order per year with his supplier, what would be his maximum and average stock levels?

Given that Percy just runs out of stock when the order is delivered, his maximum stock will be 10,000, and his average stock $10,000 \div 2 = 5,000$. That is, half the time his stock will be greater than 5,000, and during the other half of the year less than 5,000.

Obviously the costs of *holding* such a large stock would be high, and would include storage-related costs such as rates, heating, maintenance; insurance of both buildings and stocks; interest on the capital invested in stock; and deterioration and obsolescence.

Against that, *ordering* costs such as clerical salaries, costs of receiving and handling deliveries, would be relatively low – restricted in Percy's case to one order and one delivery. If two orders are placed, ordering costs will increase, but holding costs will diminish considerably as the average stock will drop to $5,000 \div 2 = 2,500$.

We see that ordering cost grows as more orders are placed but stock holding costs diminish, until a point is reached at which ordering and holding costs are equal and their total is at a minimum. This point will indicate the most *economic order quantity* (EOQ), and can be represented by the following model:

$$\left(\frac{Q}{2} \times H\right) + \left(\frac{A}{Q} \times C\right)$$

where

Q = quantity ordered
H = holding cost per unit
C = cost of placing an order
A = annual usage

1 Assuming that Percy Bend's annual holding cost per fitting is 8 pence, and the cost of placing an order £4, draw up a schedule showing the total cost of holding and ordering the fitting if the number of orders placed are 1, 2, 4, 5, 8, 10, 25, 50. What is the EOQ?

2 Now check the answer in Exercise 1 by applying the EOQ model.

(Answers in Appendix E)

The EOQ model is widely applied in industry but may need modification when the following limitations and circumstances apply:

- where it is possible to *substitute materials*, switch to production of another item easily or defer sales without loss, lower stock levels are possible;
- where *seasonal or climatic conditions* impose a peak inventory requirement on firms;
- *quantity discounts* are not catered for in the simplest formula. Where the savings from such discount exceed the extra cost of stockholding, a revised order quantity should be calculated to take this into account;
- *anticipated price movements and changes in fashion or technology* influence the building up or running down of stocks, to the extent that demand cannot be easily estimated or is volatile;
- in order to accommodate a supplier and obtain the keenest prices, it might be more advantageous to accept a *delivery schedule imposed by the supplier*. This applies particularly to long-term fixed-price contracts;
- where there are *temporary restrictions on storage capacity*;
- in manufacturing, where the cost of placing an order (*C*) on an outside supplier is replaced by the cost of *instigating and setting-up a production run*.

21.5 When to order?

Percy Bend's demand for the fitting is approximately 200 per week, with orders being placed every five weeks. If the supplier takes five weeks to deliver an order, then patently Percy will have to place a further order immediately upon receiving each delivery, i.e. when the stock level is 1,000, otherwise he will run out of stock.

However, supposing the supplier can meet each order in two weeks, at what stock level should Percy place each order to avoid running out of stock? The answer is delivery time × average usage per week, i.e. 2 × 200 = 400 fittings, as depicted in Figure 21.1.

When delivery times and demand are uncertain, safety stocks may have to be carried to avoid production disruption and possible loss of customer orders. The

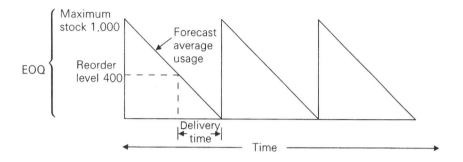

Figure 21.1
Reorder level when demand and delivery times are known

optimal safety stock will be that at which the total of the cost of holding safety stock and the profit from lost customers is minimised. If too much safety stock is carried, to the extent that no customers are lost, the cost of stockholding could well exceed the total of holding lower stocks and losing a few orders.

The most obvious way to provide safety stock is to set a re-order level higher than indicated by average demand and the supplier's normal delivery time; that is, to order sooner than average usage requires. How much higher will be related to the probability of demand being higher than normal, and the cost of lost customers at different levels of safety stock. Mathematical models can be used to calculate safety stock but, owing to the subjective nature of some of the variables involved, particularly the value of lost custom, managerial judgement based on experience must play a large part in its determination.

TO SUM UP

■ In this chapter we have seen how the risk of running out of stock has to be balanced against the cost of holding stock, in order to minimise the investment in this resource. The 'just-in-Time' (JIT) approach has been successfully introduced by many manufacturers in recent years.

■ Mathematical models can be applied to achieve this objective, but management experience and 'rule of thumb' methods may be just as effective in some circumstances.

QUESTIONS 21.2

1 The holding and 'out-of-stock' costs associated with safety stocks of 50, 100, 150 and 200 units are respectively £20, £40, £60, £90; and £80, £50, £20, £10.
  a What is the optimal level of safety stock?
  b If this level of safety stock related to Percy Bend's pipe fitting, what would be the re-order level?

▶

▶

2 Which of the following will **a** restrict or **b** increase stockholding? Explain.
   i   A doubling of sales.
   ii   A product subject to rapid deterioration.
   iii Uncertainty of demand
   iv   Offer of quantity discounts to customers.
   v   High volume of 'made to order' products.

3 New Plastics plc supply a container that is in regular and steady demand. Total annual sales are 80,000, and the annual cost of holding a container in stock is one penny. The cost of placing an order on the supplier is £3. Calculate:
   a The economic order quantity (use the EOQ model).
   b The total cost of holding and ordering stock.
   c Whether a quantity discount of 0.1 penny per container makes worthwhile placing orders in 15,000 batches.

(Answers in Appendix E)

FURTHER READING

Arnold, G. (2002) *Corporate Financial Management,* Financial Times Pitman, chapter 13.

McLaney, E.J. (2000) *Business Finance: Theory and Practice,* Prentice Hall, chapter 13.

Pike, R. and B. Neale (2003) *Corporate Finance and Investment,* Prentice Hall, chapter 15.

Samuels, R., F. Wilkes and R. Brayshaw (1999) *Management of Company Finance,* Chapman & Hall, chapter 23.

Controlling debtors **22**

INTRODUCTION

■ Investment in debtors must be worthwhile. In the simplest case, a business that is considering a change of policy from cash on delivery to granting credit would do so only if it estimates that additional profit earned on increased sales will yield a return greater than the opportunity cost of capital. Further changes in policy on credit must always meet the same criterion of profitability.

■ The consequential effects on stock levels and cash flow of changing credit policy must also be taken into account. For example, an extension of credit terms to encourage sales will increase debtors but may also push up stock levels required to support this higher level of sales. Cash flow will also be affected by delayed payment by debtors.

■ Investment in debtors can be released by factoring or invoice discounting but this can be fairly expensive unless, in the case of factoring, it is outweighed by considerable improvement in debt collection by the factor.

LEARNING OBJECTIVES

When you have completed this chapter you should be able to:

1 Specify and explain each of the factors governing the investment in debtors.

2 Discuss the methods employed to assess the credit status of potential customers.

3 Discuss the elements normally covered by credit terms.

4 Calculate from given data the benefits and costs of changing credit terms.

5 Specify and explain the major elements of a procedure for efficient management of debtors.

22.1 What factors govern investment in debtors?

QUESTION 22.1

The sales director of a company argued that if a change in credit policy increased *total* sales, then such a change was desirable. Do you agree?

(Answers in Appendix E)

Pike Electronics plc had experienced a rapid growth in sales thanks to dynamic marketing and production policies in this expanding and highly competitive area of the economy. The level of debtors had risen along with sales as the company offered normal credit terms to its customers both at home and overseas. As the investment in accounts receivable was now alarmingly high, and bad debts were rising, the managing director called for a review by the finance director of the company policies and practices concerning debtors.

EXERCISE 22.1

Using the above information, plus your own knowledge and experience, specify briefly the aspects upon which the level of debtors depends and upon which the Pike review will report.

Although practice will vary from industry to industry, certain factors are common to all businesses:

- The volume of *credit* sales will be a prime determinant, this in turn depending upon the general state of the economy, but particularly upon that of the industry concerned. Seasonality of sales and the incidence of customers' orders may also cause debtors to fluctuate.
- The *credit policies* followed, including:
  - i   the efficacy of investigating into potential customers' credit standing;
  - ii the establishment of realistic *credit terms* covering maximum value, credit period and cash discounts. Credit terms in most industries are customary, but competition tends to induce firms to modify these when it is considerable desirable;
  - iii the level of customer *riskiness* accepted by the firm; extending credit to risky customers will increase sales and debtors, but will also increase bad debts, investment cost and administrative expense;
  - iv any special terms offered to *export* customers.

■ The *paying practices* of credit customers do not always accord with agreed terms. Some flexibility may have to be allowed, particularly in respect of large and valued customers. However, the statutory requirement for large public companies to disclose their payment policies in their annual accounts has applied pressure to late payers; as has the proposal to impose statutory interest for late payment.

■ The effectiveness of *debt collection* organisation and procedures. Control costs should not exceed the value of debts prevented from going bad.

QUESTION 22.2

Upon which of the following circumstances will the level of investment in debtors in a business primarily depend?

a The type of item bought by the customer.
b The level of customer riskiness.
c Special terms offered to export customers.
d The distance of the customer from supplies.
e The paying practices of customers.
f The effectiveness of debt collection.
g The total number of employees.
h The efficacy of credit status investigation.
i Realistic credit terms.
j Dividend paid to shareholders.
k The volume of credit sales.

(Answers in Appendix E)

22.2 Assessing the credit status of customers

As a result of the Pike Electronics' debtors' review, a qualified credit controller was appointed to head the accounts receivable section. One of the first tasks was to examine the various methods used by the company to obtain information upon which to base credit decisions:

■ *Credit agency ratings* published by Dun & Bradstreet, for example, on most businesses. The company had a regular subscription arrangement with this agency. Information used to compile these ratings tends to be limited to that already obtainable from published accounts.

■ *Financial statements* obtained directly from potential customers, whether published or not, revealing liquidity, gearing, trading and other relevant information.

■ *Sales representatives and company officers* are used for direct enquiry purposes.

- *Trade associations*, e.g. the Building Trades' and Motor Traders' Associations, who have organised credit reference departments, provide information regarding 'blacklisted' businesses who have defaulted on their debts.
- *Bankers' references*, usually made through the company's bank on the potential customer's bank. This is not a very penetrating investigation, normally being limited to an acknowledgement that an account is kept and has been maintained satisfactorily.
- *Trade references* provided by the potential customer. Recommendations from existing trading connections of the customer are obviously more satisfactorily than bank references, although they could be chosen by the customer to paint the most favourable picture.

Because of the danger of losing sales through delayed credit enquiries, Pike Electronics tended to rely almost wholly upon agency credit ratings and sales representatives' reports in assessment of potential customers. Unfortunately this 'broad brush' approach had proved less than rigorous, leading to increased bad debts. Moderate agency ratings were sometimes not reinforced by calling for special agency reports, and, in the case of potentially large customers, no special action was taken.

The credit controller therefore recommended the following additional guidelines:

- *non-existent or poor agency ratings* should always be followed up by trade and bank references in the case of potentially low value customers;
- as regards large order customers, a *special agency report*, and usually a direct personal approach for further financial information where this was not already available.

QUESTION 22.3

'Credit agency ratings can be relied upon wholly to decide the credit status of a potential customer'. True or false? Explain.

(Answer in Appendix E)

22.3 Establishing credit terms

Credit terms cover the maximum value allowed to each customer, the maximum time allowed for payment and frequently the offer of cash discounts for early payment of debts. Normally, if a customer is granted credit, s/he is subject to the suppliers' *standard* time and cash discount conditions but maybe restricted as regards credit value. The plastic credit card system (e.g. Mastercard) is a good example of this. Payment conditions, and interest on outstanding balances, are standard terms but the maximum credit value allowed varies with the customer's credit rating.

Maximum credit allowance   A business may use *disciminant analysis* to rate the credit standing of its customers. This statistical technique weights the various factors covered by credit investigation such as liquidity, profitability, gearing, debt payment record, and ascribes a credit value (a rating) to each customer. The higher the rating, the more credit will be allowed; whereas lower-rated customers may be requested to pay in advance or on delivery of goods.

The credit allowance may be further restricted so that the firm does not over-rely upon the payment practices of a few large customers. The supplier may calculate this amount as a conservative proportion of a customer's net asset value or of its own estimated *total* debtors.

Credit period   The *minimum* credit period will be that customary in the particular industry but, as customers' cash flow conditions vary (e.g. they may be seasonal), some flexibility will have to be introduced in allowing time to pay. Typical terms are payment within 30 days of date of invoice (i.e. net 30 days), and payment by the end of the month following the date of invoice.

In long-term contract industries such as construction, work-in-progress payments are the norm. These are made at contractually specified stages of job completion, which are usually certified by an independent surveyor or other technical expert.

Cash discount   This might be offered to shorten the average payment period and thus reduce investment in debtors. For example, if the terms of payment are currently net 30 days, and all customers pay their accounts on time, the value of debtors outstanding should be equivalent to 30 days' sales. If terms are changed to 2½% discount for payment within 10 days of invoice date otherwise net 30 days (i.e. 2½/10, N/30), and all debtors take advantage of the discount, investment in debtors will amount to 10 days' sales.

The value of cash discount to debtors is considerable. Using the data in the previous paragraph for example, on sales of £100 per month the effective rate of return on £100 paid 20 days earlier would be:

$$\left(\frac{2\frac{1}{2}}{97\frac{1}{2}} \times \frac{365}{20} \times \right) \times 100 = 46.8\% \text{ p.a.}$$

Note that only £97.50 is received promptly after deduction of 2½% cash discount, but that this repeats itself approximately 18 times (365 ÷ 20) each year.

From the supplier's viewpoint the discount is an additional cost, but may be worth incurring if sales are increased or alternatively not lost to competitors (see section 22.4).

1 What are the determinants of **a** the maximum credit value allowed to a customer, **b** the credit period?

2 What is the effective % annual cost to a customer who does not take advantage of a 2% cash discount for payment within 7 days, net 30 days?

(Answers in Appendix E)

22.4 Changing credit terms

Caution should be exercised in changing credit policy for not only must *customers'* reactions be anticipated but also those of competitors. The overall principle is that the benefits should always be worth more than the costs.

Extending credit terms to increase sales

The total annual sales of Unique Ltd are currently £2.4 million. The selling price of its product is £8 and its variable cost £6. The company is considering extending its average credit period to customers from one to two months, and estimates that this change will increase sales to £3 million.

Existing customers are expected to take full advantage of the new terms, and the firm has sufficient existing capacity to increase production to the anticipated new level. The company's marginal cost of capital is 25%.

If Unique Ltd's new policy succeeds, how much additional profit will be realised by the company?

Increase in sales £3 – 2.4 million = £600,000

$$\% \text{ Contribution per product } \frac{£8 - 6}{8} \times 100 = 25\%$$

Increased contribution 25% × £600,000 = £150,000

Against this benefit of £150,000 has to be set the opportunity investment cost of the higher level of debtors, resulting from the delay in payment of an additional month.

In this respect, however, there is a difference between the increased investment in *existing customers'* debts, and those of *new customers*. The *sales* value of existing debtors, i.e. *including profit*, is deferred for payment by one further month, whereas additional investment in new debtors comprises *variable cost* of sales only.

a Calculate total debtors on existing sales under Unique Ltd's old credit policy of one month.

b Calculate the value of debtors relating to *existing* customers under the new policy.

c Show the increase in debtors relating to existing customers.

d Calculate the value of investment in debtors relating to *new* sales (***Reminder:*** variable cost only).

a Present level of debtors: £2.4 million ÷ 12 = £200,00

b New level of debtors – existing customers: £2.4 million ÷ 6 = £400,000

c Additional investment – existing customers: (**b** – **a**) = £200,00

d Variable cost of debtors relating to new sales: (£600,00 × 0.75) ÷ 6 = £75,000

a Given Unique Ltd's 25% cost of capital, what is the cost of carrying additional debtors?

b Should the new policy be implemented?

a Total additional investment in debtors: £200,000 + 75,000 = £275,000. Opportunity cost of additional investment: 25% of £275,000 = £68,750.

b As the increased contribution from new sales, £150,000, is greater than the opportunity cost of carrying additional debtors, £68,750, the policy should be implemented.

Impact of bad debts and other costs

If customers are allowed to delay payment of their debts, some will default. Further, the longer the credit period allowed the higher the incidence of bad debts as credit is allowed to lower-quality (high-risk) customers. Costs of vetting new customers and collecting debts will probably increase.

Assume that Unique Ltd's existing bad debts are 0.5% of sales, but this will increase to 10% in respect of the additional sales. The additional annual cost of vetting new customers and collecting debts will be £12,000. Should the new credit policy be implemented in the light of these extra costs?

	£
Increased contribution from new sales (see previous activity)	150,000
less Additional cost of bad debts 10% of £600,000 = 60,000	
Additional administration costs = 12,000	
Additional debtors opportunity cost	
(see previous activity) = 68,750	140,750
Net increased profit	£9,250

The marginal increase in profit is now so small that the risks of introducing the new policy will have to be carefully assessed. Sensitivity analysis may help here. An additional point to note is that if productive capacity is not currently available to cope with additional demand, the costs of providing it will obviously nullify the proposal.

Offering or changing cash discount

Introducing or changing cash discount may embrace all the costs and benefits discussed above, as well as adding the cost of discount. Offering discount may attract additional sales and, therefore, increase debtors, if demand for the product is highly sensitive to price changes (i.e. is elastic). At the same time, earlier payment of debts will reduce investment in accounts receivable.

Pike Electronics' new credit controller had recommended that the company's credit terms should be changed to 2% discount to customers who pay within 10 days of date of invoice, otherwise net 30 days, considering that this policy would result in:

- the company's annual sales increasing from £3 million to £3.1 million, and that existing capacity could cope with this increase;
- bad debts decreasing from 2% to 1% of all sales;
- the average collection period reducing from its present 50 days to 20 days;
- 80% of all customers taking advantage of the cash discount;
- administrative costs reducing by £2000 per annum.

EXERCISE 22.6

Produce the calculations submitted by Pike Electronics' new credit controller to justify his proposals, assuming that the company's cost of capital is 15%, and its contribution to sales ratio is 20%

	£
Costs:	
Cash discount 0.02 x 0.80 × £3.1 million	= 49,600
Benefits:	
Reduction in bad debts – existing 2% × £3 million = 60,000	
– new 1% × £3.1 million = 31,000	= 29,000
Additional contribution 20% of £100,000	= 20,000
Reduction in administrative costs	= 2,000
Reduction in opportunity cost of debtors:	
Existing level of debtors 50/365 × £3 million = 410,959	
New level of debtors 20/365 × £3.1 million = 169,863	
Costs:	
15% of = 241,096	= 36,164
	87,164
Net benefit of offering discounts	37,564

It is possible of course that alternative changes in credit policy maybe more advantageous than those considered above. For example, a 3% cash discount would increase costs even more, but produce considerably higher sales and low bad debt, investment and administrative costs. In examining such alternatives the *optimal* point is that at which the *marginal benefits* are just equal to the *marginal costs*.

QUESTIONS 22.5

1 If a company extends its credit period total debtors can be expected to be higher. Why will the new level of existing customers' debts be valued on a basis different from that applied to new customers?

2 What determines the rate of opportunity cost applied to investment in debtors consequent upon a change in credit policy?

3 Why should the rate of bad debts increase when the credit period is extended?

4 As regards each of the following, state which may **a** increase or **b** decrease if cash discounts are offered for prompt payment of debts?
   a Total debtors.
   b Debt collection costs.
   c Sales.
   d Investment opportunity cost.
   e Contribution from sales.
   f Average debt collection period.

(Answers in Appendix E)

Debt collection

The cost of each additional day's sales remaining unpaid can be high. For example, with a turnover of £3.5 million, approximately £10,000 of capital would be tied up in debtors for each day's sales outstanding. If the average collection period for debtors is, say, five days more than planned, then £50,000 is over-invested in debtors, and, at an opportunity cost of 20%, this reduces profit by £10,000 per annum. Additional bad debts and administrative costs arising from the excess debtors would further diminish profit.

The need to inject adequate resources into the collection of debts is therefore equally as important as optimising credit terms.

This point was not lost on Mary, managing director of Pike Electronics plc, and she asked her new credit controller to outline a procedure that would deal with the company's debt collection most effectively at lower cost.

The following were the major points he submitted to Mary:

- *Invoices and monthly statements of account* should be forwarded to customers promptly.
- Prompt and courteous attention should be given to all customer's *complaints* whether concerned with the goods supplied or with invoices, and allowances made by sending credit notes when justified.
- *A progression of applications* for payment should be made, first by statement, then by either telephone or post. A telephone request is more personal, and can very often obtain better results than standard letters requesting payment. Progressively insistent letters should follow until the only course is to place the debt with agents or solicitors for collection.
- *Action through reputable debt collection agencies*, which act on commission, is normally effective in dealing with all but the hard cases, with follow-up solicitors' letters as final requests for payment.
- *Action through the courts* would be resorted to only after solicitors' direct action had failed. Court action should be deferred for as long as possible, for it is expensive and often yields less than a direct compromise arrangement with the debtor.
- *In dealing with individual debts*:
  a if a debtor appears able to pay, *rigorous collection procedures* are in order;
  b if the account is *small* it will probably be less costly to proceed no further than a collection agency;
  c if the debtor is a valued customer but is in temporary financial difficulties, *a compromise deferment of payment* may be in order;
  d *revise or withdraw credit facilities* in the case of particularly bad payers: cash on delivery terms might be in order here;
  e concentrate the collection effort on the small number of *large-value debts*.
- *Arrange credit insurance* for above-normal credit risks, i.e. for exceptionally large amounts of extended credit periods. This relates particularly to export sales, when the government's Export Credits Guarantee Department (ECGD) or an independent insurer should be approached.
- *Produce regularly updated statistics* of debtors, including:

a monthly analyses into types of customers, amounts outstanding, ages of debts and progress made in the collection of older debts;

b graphs showing monthly trend figures of debtors against a moving annual sales figure;

c the days' sales outstanding ratio.

The Pike Electronics' credit controller also produced an analysis of estimated staff and other costs required to support the proposed procedure most effectively. In his opinion, any increase in this level of cost would not be justified by the consequent savings in bad debts and investment in debtors; conversely, less expenditure would result in *marginally* higher bad debts and increased debtors.

TO SUM UP

■ Efficient debtor control releases resources for alternative profitable investment, and thus adds to the wealth of the owners of a business.

■ In this chapter we have discussed how this can be achieved by analysing the costs and benefits of proposed changes in credit terms, as well as ensuring that an efficient system of debtors' control is established.

QUESTIONS 22.6

1 The annual sales of Unique Ltd are £2 million. Its current cost of debt collection is £30,000 per annum, with bad debts of 1% of sales, and the average debt collection period 45 days.

   Would it be worth increasing its debt collection expenditure by £15,000 if bad debts fell to 0.5% of sales, and the average debt collection period to 35 days? The company's marginal cost of capital is 20%.

2 Approximately a third of a company's sales relates to two categories of customers, X and Y, whose credit is limited in value. The current bad debt experience on each of them is 1% and 2% of sales respectively, but it is estimated that these credit restrictions are losing sales valued at £200,000 and £100,000, respectively.

   If the company were to grant these customers unlimited credit and thus to recapture the lost sales, the bad debts are likely to increase to 5% and 10%, respectively on the increased turnover, and the average collection period on the new sales would be two months. Assuming a contribution to sales ratio of 10%, and an opportunity investment rate of 12%, calculate whether the company should extend these credit terms.

(Answer in Appendix E)

FURTHER READING

Arnold, G. (2002) *Corporate Financial Management*, Financial Times Pitman, chapter 12.

McLaney, E.J. (2000) *Business Finance: Theory and Practice*, Prentice Hall, chapter 13.

Pike, R. and B. Neale (2003) *Corporate Finance and Investment*, Prentice Hall, chapter 15.

Samuels, R., F. Wilkes and R. Brayshaw (1999) *Management of Company Finance*, Chapman & Hall, chapter 22.

International Trade and Investment

Managing international trade and investment

INTRODUCTION

■ Exporting to, and investing in, overseas countries can be rewarding but also risky. Differences in political philosophies, economic policies, cultures, currencies, and sheer distance between the home and overseas countries all contribute to this risk.

■ Traders and investors must be aware of these difficulties, and, as far as possible, protect against loss.

LEARNING OBJECTIVES

When you have completed this chapter you should be able to:

1 Specify and discuss the aspects to which a prospective overseas trader or investor should direct his or her attention.

2 List and discuss the ways in which an exporter may receive payment from his or her overseas customers.

3 Explain how an exporter may insure against the risk of non-payment.

4 Discuss how an exporter may finance his or her shipments.

5 Explain why exchange rates fluctuate and what actions can be taken to protect against the risk of currency loss.

6 Specify and discuss the actions that can be taken by an overseas investor to protect against political and exchange rate risks.

23.1 Trading overseas

A business planning to trade or invest overseas must take account of the following aspects:

■ The *prospective market* for its goods and services, including demand, local customs and taste, and whether it is a free enterprise or centrally controlled economic system. The DTI Overseas Trade Services, Regional Offices and local Business Links, foreign embassies, and most clearing banks, can help with relevant information.

- *Location* of the manufacturing/servicing facilities, including the possibility of setting-up a subsidiary company to operate in the overseas country. The decision to invest overseas will largely be based on comparative economic advantage. A well-developed infrastructure, availability and cost of suitable labour, materials sourcing, and the offer of grants and tax breaks by the overseas government will loom large in this decision.

- *Alternative methods of entry* into prospective overseas markets, e.g. licensing/franchising, manufacture and/or marketing to overseas companies; or by setting-up joint ventures with overseas firms.

- *Selling methods* to be adopted; which might involve setting up a direct selling organisation in the country concerned; appointment of local overseas agents; selling through UK resident buying houses, confirming houses or exporting merchants, who would all control selling independently of the manufacturer.

- *Exchange control and other regulations* in overseas countries that might restrict the types of goods allowed to be imported, control their specification, impose duties upon them and restrict payment for them.

- How goods/services are to be *shipped* – whether through the firm's own export department or an outside forwarding agent; packing requirements; transportation; documentation; terms of the contract. Goods are generally invoiced at prices to include all costs up to the time they are put on board a ship or aircraft ('free on board' – FOB), or include the further costs of carriage, insurance and freight (CIF) to the dockside/airport in the buyer's country.

- How and when *payment* is to be received for the goods/services supplied.

23.2 Receiving payment for exports

The method of payment agreed between exporter and buyer will depend upon the degree of trust existing between the parties, the terms being offered by competitors, and the financial status of both parties. The favoured methods of payment are 'open account'; payment in advance of shipment; bills of exchange; and documentary letters of credit.

Open account　If the exporter is satisfied as to the integrity of the buyer, and there is little risk of exchange control regulations restricting the transfer of funds from the overseas country, business could be conducted in exactly the same way as with home customers. Payment is then made by the overseas buyer within a recognised credit period – say, monthly – in one of five different ways:

- *Buyer's cheque* – rather slow because of the length of time taken to clear the cheque.

■ *Banker's draft* – a cheque drawn by the buyer's overseas bank upon a UK bank, in sterling or foreign currency; the exporter receives payment immediately the draft is received.

■ *Mail payment order* – the buyer's overseas bank instructs a UK bank by airmail to pay the exporter.

■ *Telegraphic transfer* – of money by cable, telephone or telex, from the buyer's to the exporter's bank; this is the most expensive method.

■ *Electronic funds transfer* between the buyer's and exporter's banks, by a secure international telecommunications network known as SWIFT. This method is the fastest and is rapidly replacing mail and telegraphic transfers.

Payment in advance   Uncertainties attending overseas trade have led to the development of other means to ensure exporters receive payment for goods. The ideal arrangement is to receive cash in advance of shipment, but this is unusual, save when deposits or progress payments are agreed on lengthy building, civil or heavy engineering contracts.

Bills of exchange   The traditional, and most used, instrument for receiving payment is the bill of exchange, drawn by the exporter and handed to his bank together with the shipping documents, which might include invoices, bills of lading (shippers' receipts), insurance certificates and certificates of origin. At this stage the bank may be prepared to make an advance of, say, 80% of the bill, in anticipation of ultimate collection from the overseas customer.

The bank forwards the documents to its overseas branch or agent, and they are released to the overseas buyer when the latter either *pays* the bill of exchange if it is drawn 'at sight', or *accepts* it by signing it across its face. 'Acceptance' implies that the buyer agrees to pay the bill in full when it is presented to him on the date specified in the bill. The exporter may then discount (sell) it to his bank or a discount house, and thus obtain payment immediately. A guarantee issued by the Export Credits Guarantee Department (ECGD) (see section 23.3) may support such finance.

Documentary letters of credit   If a foreign customer is well known, a bill of exchange sent for 'collection' overseas will probably be used. However, if the exporter and overseas buyer are not known to each other, both their positions can be secured by the buyer's bank giving an undertaking through a UK bank, that payment will be made for the goods supplied, provided that the supplier complies with the terms of a letter of credit drawn in his favour.

To obtain payment, the exporter presents a bill of exchange and other export documents to the named paying bank, which either pays immediately, or accepts the bill, according to the terms of the credit. The bill can then be sold to a bank or discount house. The UK paying bank will eventually be reimbursed by the buyer's bank which, in turn, will look to the buyer for payment. For a small additional fee, the UK bank will *confirm* that it will pay the exporter, even if the foreign bank fails, which adds another conditional guarantee of payment for the exporter.

Thus the exporter is assured of receiving payment, and the buyer is secure in the knowledge that payment will not be made on his behalf until title to the goods has been passed to him.

Letters of credit may either be *irrevocable*, that is non-cancellable without the agreement of the buyer and seller, or *revocable*, in which case the credit can be cancelled by the buyer at any time *before* presentation of documents, without notice to the supplier. Revocable letters of credit are not used much because they add to the uncertainty.

QUESTION 23.1

When an exporter is unsure of a foreign customer's ability to pay for goods supplied, the credit of the latter's bank may be substituted for that of the customer. Under what method of payment for exports is this arrangement made?

(Answer in Appendix E)

23.3 Insurance against the risk of non-payment

The commercial and political risks of non-payment associated with exporting consumer goods, raw materials, etc. on credit terms of up to six months can be insured with private sector companies such as NCM Credit Insurance and Trade Indemnity plc; and with some banks – Barclays, for example, extend cover to small exporters.

Short-term insurance for sales of *high-value* capital goods and projects, and contracts for longer delivery periods, are primarily covered by the ECGD, a government department responsible to the Secretary of State for Trade and Industry. Set up in 1919 to provide an export credit service, and thus to encourage exporters, it is charged to break even on its activities. The ECGD also provides *guarantees* to banks which advance money to exporters (see following section).

Insurance for exporters available from the ECGD is covered by various policies:

- *Specific Guarantee policies*, covering commercial and political risks on *high-value* capital goods, and major constructional work projects and services, where payment is normally expected from the buyer shortly after delivery.

  Maximum loss covered is 90%, but the cover can be effected either from the date of contract or shipment.
- *Supplement Specific Guarantee policies*, covering contracts with longer credit periods.
- *Overseas investment insurance* offers UK investors protection against political risks in respect of new investment overseas. The scheme aims both to contribute to the development of the economies of the developing countries and to encourage UK overseas investment.
- *Bonds* are issued to overseas buyers by banks and insurance companies, backed by the ECGD, guaranteeing that the UK exporter will carry out the terms of the contract.

23.4 Finance for exports

Whether supplying goods for export or to the home market, a firm will need finance to cover each of the stages of manufacturing, stockholding and customer credit. In order to encourage exports, the government has urged banks and other lenders to favour exporters even in times of credit restrictions.

However, the uncertainties of exporting cause suppliers of finance to be cautious to the extent that they normally look for some form of insurance against non-payment by overseas buyers. Such insurance is provided by the ECGD and private sector companies whose facilities were described in section 23.3. This insurance backing can help to make finance available in several ways:

Bank overdrafts

These are the cheapest form of *pre-shipment* finance but will be looked upon more favourably if the exporter is covered by export insurance policies in his trading.

Discounting or borrowing against bills of exchange

As described in section 23.2, an exporter can be paid for his good by selling (discounting) a bill of exchange accepted by his buyer – or a UK acceptance house in the case of documentary credits – to his bank. Alternatively, a bank loan may be arranged on the security of such a bill.

Bank finance guaranteed by the ECGD

This embraces two types of bank loans: those to exporters (supplier credits), and those to overseas buyers (buyer credits):

Supplier credits for between two to five years on contracts valued from £25,000, can be arranged under an ECGD supplier credit financing facility, which gives up to 100% cover to the bank. These guarantees are given where an exporter is insured under either a 'specific' or a 'supplemental' specific guarantee policy. The UK bank advances up to 85% of the contract value to the exporter against a bill of exchange drawn on the buyer and supported by shipping documents.

Buyer credits are available to overseas purchasers of high-value UK capital goods and services. Contracts must be in access of £5 million and for periods of between two and five years. Banks will lend up to 85% of the contract value, to the buyer, which is the extent of the cover provided by the ECGD guarantee. The remaining 15% should be paid by the buyer to the exporter before the start of the credit period.

Under such credits the exporter can expect to receive cash from the buyer upon shipment of goods, although pre-shipment finance in the form of progress payments by the buyer can be arranged in respect of long-term construction contracts.

Project financing is a special kind of buyer credit used to finance a major construction project, e.g. a bridge, where the lenders place primary reliance on the subsequent revenues of the project for repayment.

Foreign currency loans

These are a method whereby an exporter can protect himself against adverse fluctuations in rates of exchange. The exporter borrows the invoiced amount of foreign currency and sells it for sterling at the current (spot) rate. When he receives payment from the overseas customer the foreign currency is repaid to the bank.

Export factoring

This type of financing is already familiar to you in connection with home trade. Subsidiaries of the clearing banks are active in this field and provide a debtors' ledger service and 70%–80% advances on outstanding debts.

Leasing

Another familiar form of home financing, this facility is extended to buyers in some overseas countries through specialist companies or subsidiaries of clearing banks. The lease can be written either in the UK or in the overseas country and, if in the latter, the tax advantages will vary from country to country.

Export finance houses

Loose associations of finance houses provide instalment credit for international trade. The exporter is paid immediately upon deposit of shipping documents with the finance house, the buyer agreeing to pay the finance house by instalments. Progressively higher rates of interest are charged to the buyer, in relation to the credit period. The buyer also pays a service fee to the finance house.

Countertrade is another term for barter, where payment for goods sold is settled by receiving goods instead of cash.

Forfaiting is a method of arranging medium-term instalment export finance. The buyer makes an initial payment (say, 15%), and the remainder is secured by promissory notes or drafts, which may be guaranteed by an overseas bank. The exporter obtains payment by discounting the notes or drafts with a bank, which in turn receives payment by periodic presentation of the notes to the buyer.

1 What facility other than export insurance is provided by the ECGD?
2 What is the essential difference between supplier and buyer credits arranged under ECGD guarantees?

(Answers in Appendix E)

23.5 Managing foreign currency – why exchange rates fluctuate

An exchange rate is the price of one currency expressed in terms of another and, like any other commodity, supply of or demand for a currency will cause the exchange rate to fluctuate. For example, if the dollar rate against the pound changes from $2 to $2.01, the demand for the pound has strengthened.

The fluctuations arise from many causes, including:

- *interest rate differentials* between countries – perhaps caused by government action to increase or decrease demand for its currency;
- a *change of confidence* by outsiders in the economic or political future of a country;
- a *favourable balance of payments* will tend to attract money into a country and vice versa;
- an *indigenous source of wealth* (e.g. North Sea Oil) will react favourably on a country's rates of exchange, even though the balance of trade may be against that country;
- *comparative rates of inflation and relative purchasing power of currencies*, influenced by government through its internal monetary policies;
- *exchange control regulations* to govern the purposes for which foreign currency can be purchased.

Export pricing in foreign currency

Fifty per cent of exports from the UK are paid for in cash or on credit terms of up to 60 days; but even in these cases, and certainly when transactions involve longer credit periods, there is exposure to exchange risks.

Any transaction under which a company is committed to receiving or paying foreign currency at some future date exposes the company to exchange risks. For example, if you invoiced your overseas customer $10,000 payable six months' hence, and the current (spot) rate for the pound against the dollar changed from $2 = £1 to $4 = £1 during that time, the sterling value of the invoice would have deteriorated from £5,000 to £2,500. It will be obvious to you that, whatever the method of payment, the currency to be used to settle the transaction has to be agreed.

If the overseas customer will agree, invoicing in the *exporter's* currency will favour the exporter and leave the risk of exchange loss with the customer. However, the buyer is often able to dictate that invoices are denominated in his home currency, which leaves the risk with the supplier – unless the terms of payment prescribe a fixed rate of exchange, thus pegging payment of currency to the exporter's currency at the date of shipment. Pricing in a foreign currency may be resorted to for other reasons:

- as an insurance against a *weakening home currency*;
- to match imports in the *same foreign currency*, thus offsetting any possible losses;
- where the selling company is a *subsidiary* of a foreign company – to ensure that the invoiced currency is that of the parent company;
- a *third currency* may be adopted by both parties to the contract when neither of their currencies is mutually acceptable. In this case both parties face a foreign exchange risk problem.

When an exporter knows that he will be paid in foreign currency at some future time he may act in one of the following ways:

- Convert the foreign currency into his *home currency* at the (spot) rate prevailing when the currency is received, i.e. accept the risk of currency loss, but create the possibility of currency gain.
- Borrow *an equivalent amount of foreign currency now*, and convert it into sterling, as explained in section 23.4. This eliminates the exchange risk, unless the buyer defaults on his payment, leaving the exporter exposed to the risk of having to buy foreign currency to repay his loan. The exporter will, of course, gain or lose, on the interest differential between the rate paid on the currency borrowed, and that earned on sterling invested.
- Have the proceeds paid into a *foreign currency account* specially maintained to set off receipts and payments in that currency – thus setting off losses against gains, i.e. 'matching'.
- Persuade his customer to *pay in advance* (a 'lead' payment) or to delay (a 'lagged' payment), according to the forecast of future exchange rates.
- Contract with a bank or a currency dealer to sell the foreign currency at a *predetermined rate* when it is received. The *forward* currency dealing is dealt with in more detail in the following two sections.
- Buy an *option* to sell the currency at an agreed rate (the exercise price) at a future date. If, by that date, the foreign currency weakens, the option would be exercised because more sterling would be received than at the spot rate. However, if the foreign currency strengthens, the option would not be exercised because conversion would yield less sterling than at the spot rate.

    The cost of the option is the commission paid to the writer of the option.

    Note that a currency option gives a *right* to buy or sell but not an obligation, whereas a forward currency contract (see below) imposes an *obligation* to buy or sell. The exporter would, of course, choose the cheapest but least risky option.

Under what circumstances will an exporter be exposed to exchange rate losses?

(Answers in Appendix E)

Forward foreign exchange contracts ('hedging')

A forward foreign exchange contract is between a UK importer or exporter and his bank (or other currency dealer), whereby each party agrees to deliver, at a specified future time, a certain amount in one currency, in exchange for a certain amount in another currency at an agreed rate of exchange.

By entering into a forward foreign exchange contract a UK importer or exporter can:

- fix at the time of the contract a price for the purchase or sale of a fixed amount of foreign currency at a *specified future date*;
- eliminate his or her *exchange risk* to future foreign exchange rate fluctuations;
- calculate the *exact sterling value* on an international commercial contract although payment is to be made in the future in a foreign currency.

Normally no cash is exchanged at the time the contract is taken out – unless the bank requires a cash deposit as security against a customer not meeting his contractual obligation on maturity of the contract.

Contracts are either 'fixed forward' (specified date) or 'option forward' (between two dates at a customer's specification).

Interpreting forward rates

Spot is the rate of exchange at which foreign currency is bought or sold now, for delivery now, whilst the *forward* rate is a rate quoted now for the purchase or sale of a stated amount of foreign currency at a specified time in the future, no matter how the spot rate might change in the intervening period. Spot, and one- and three-month forward rates, are published at the end of each day, but rates for these and longer periods are obtainable from banks and currency dealers in most currencies throughout each business day.

Forward rates are based on the spot rates *minus* a premium (pm) or *plus* a discount (dis). They are not forecasts by banks of what spot rates will be at some future date. Premium and discount are based chiefly on the differences in interbank interest rates obtainable on the currencies involved.

For example, the closing *spot* rates for the pound against the dollar might be quoted as \$1.5025–\$1.5035, the first rate being the dealer's *selling* rate, i.e. he will give a *low* number of dollars for pounds; and the second rate is his *buying* rate, i.e. he will expect a relatively *high* number of dollars in exchange for pounds.

In an adjacent column of the published rates, the 'one-month' figures may show 0.21¢–0.16¢ pm which, interpreted, means that *forward* US$ are at a premium (pm) over sterling, i.e. are dearer, and that the premiums quoted should be *deducted* from the complementary spot rates to give the *one-month forward selling and buying rates.*

EXERCISE 23.1

1 If an exporter is due to receive $10,000 from a customer in one month's time, and the rates of exchange are as quoted above, how much sterling will s/he receive if s/he has entered into a fixed forward contract for one month to sell dollars?

2 How much would s/he have received at the spot rate prevailing when the contract was first drawn?

1   Bank spot buying rate 1.5035

    less premium   0.0016

               1.5019 = *one-month forward buying rate*

   Amount received one month hence = 10,000 ÷ 1.5019 = 6,658

2   Amount receivable at current spot rate = 10,000 ÷ 1.5035 = £6,651

Note from this example that a premium shows that the currency is stronger than sterling in the forward market; thus UK exporters would receive more sterling than at the spot rate at the future date, and importers would have to pay more sterling.

A discount shows that the currency is weaker than sterling in the forward market; thus UK exporters would receive less sterling than at the current spot rate at the future date, and importers have to pay less sterling.

Thus when the forward rate is at a premium, a forward contract not only protects the exporter's expected profit, it also yields him or her an extra margin over the present spot rate. When the forward rate is at a discount, however, the expected profit is reduced, but it is protected against any further deterioration of the rate – the decreased margin being the exporter's cost for this insurance.

For importers, who are buying rather than selling foreign currencies, the implications of a premium and a discount are reversed.

With the benefit of hindsight, i.e. when future spot prices are known, forward contracts, which eliminate the possibility of gain from speculation, are not always the most profitable course of action, but they do provide a means of ensuring an exchange rate in advance in markets where fluctuations can be sudden, large and unpredictable. Exchange losses can be expensive to a company – no matter what their cause.

The closing figures for the pound against the dollar forward (three months) show:
$1.5510–$1,5520; 0.30¢–0.25¢ dis.

a What is the dealer's spot selling rate?

b What is the dealer's three-month forward selling rate?

c If an importer in the UK is due to pay his overseas supplier $40,000 in three
months' time, how much sterling would s/he require to pay the supplier on a
three-month forward exchange contract?

(Answers in Appendix E)

Eurocurrency

In 1991, the Maastricht Treaty laid plans for a Single European Currency to be introduced on 1 January 1999, subject to successful participant countries meeting specified
'convergence criteria' regarding inflation, interest rates, government debt and recent
currency performance in the then existing Exchange Rate Mechanism (ERM). The
planned common currency has since been named the 'Euro', and replaced all the separate currencies of member countries on 1 January 2002, excepting Britain, Denmark
and Sweden, who opted out of joining the Single Currency when the Maastricht Treaty
was agreed. Future membership of the Single Currency will require the approval of the
parliament of each country, subject to a national referendum in each.

Clearly, a single European currency should eliminate multi-currency uncertainty, currency transaction costs and the cost of 'hedging' against currency risk.
Currency stability, with the possibility of lower interest rate, should be of considerable benefit to forward business planning, with a consequential increase in trade
both within and outside Europe.

The main perceived disadvantage of a single currency is the loss of each country's sovereignty over its *monetary policy* and, to some extent, its *fiscal policy*.
Monetary policy would be managed by the European Central Bank (ECB), and
public expenditure and borrowing controlled, by the terms of the Maastricht
Treaty, through the Commission in Brussels.

23.6 Managing overseas assets and finance

Proposed overseas investments are evaluated by applying normal investment
appraisal techniques. Investment and operating cash flows, risk, and the appropriate discounting rate have accordingly to be forecast.

Where there is an established overseas subsidiary, finance for additional investment may be available locally in the form of retained earnings, depreciation provisions, and local borrowing. The *basic* cost of capital will then be a weighted average
of the parent company's opportunity cost, and the local borrowing rate. Where a

new subsidiary is to be set up to be wholly financed by fresh capital from the parent company, the *basic* cost of capital will be that of the parent company.

Overseas investment will inevitably require the application of a discounting rate which reflects not only the basic cost of capital, which you will recall incorporates both normal business and financial risks, but also a premium to cover the additional risks of the overseas operation. These are largely:

- *political risks*, caused by the imposition of exchange control regulations impeding repatriation of funds, additional taxes, or complete expropriation of overseas assets;
- *foreign exchange risks*, caused by exchange rate fluctuations.

The financial manager of a company with overseas assets must therefore be alive to problems and current trends in the international monetary markets, and manage her/his company's financial affairs accordingly.

S/he should mobilise the multinational companies' cash in countries with the strongest currencies, noting particularly that, although a high interest rate may attract money to a particular country, it may also hide a weak currency. If cash is held in a weak currency, the company may in future have to pay more locally for foreign currency.

If a devaluation of the company's home currency is forecast, the financial manager should:

- *advance payment to overseas creditors/lenders*; s/he will thus pay less foreign currency now, than at a future date when the exchange rate is low;
- when repayment of an overseas loan is imminent, *purchase foreign currency forward* to reduce the cost in sterling.

Where there may be a deterioration in the value of a foreign currency, in regard to operations in that country the financial manager should:

- *bring forward* payments of liabilities, dividends and management fees to the home country, whilst the cost of local foreign currency is relatively low; for example, if the dollar is currently worth £0.50 but is expected to fall to £0.25 in the near future, then an *early* remittance of dollars to the home country would yield more pounds than a delayed remittance; alternatively, the risk could be covered by 'hedging' operations;
- use any spare local cash to *stockpile imported material*, and bring forward contracts for the import of fixed assets by the overseas company, whilst the local currency is currently still strong;
- look for *local substitutes* to replace the future purchase of materials that are currently imported; future imports will cost more than at present;
- borrow locally, press local debtors for early payment, or defer local creditors to the latest possible date, to provide the *liquidity* to implement the three previous recommendations;
- *liquidate all foreign currency obligations* at the earliest date, to reduce the cost in local currency;

■ *reduce the net exposure to foreign currency fluctuations* by matching like currency inflows and outflows.

TO SUM UP

■ The basic principles of investment and trading are the same, whether at home or overseas. However, a business looking to expand abroad should research the additional political, cultural, financial and currency risks it faces, and take appropriate, timely, protective action.

■ These areas of risk, and the action that can be taken to reduce them, have been outlined in this chapter.

QUESTIONS 23.5

1 Under what arrangement is payment received for exports similar to receiving payments in the home market?

2 Of the sources of export finance available, which have their complement in the home market?

3 'Forward' exchange contracts are the only means whereby exporters can protect themselves against exposure to exchange rate losses.' 'True or false? Why?

4 Are each of the following statements true or false? State why.
  a 'If the US dollar is expected to weaken against the pound, a British subsidiary company in the USA should be instructed to defer payment of liabilities and management fees to the home company.'
  b 'The overseas company is due to repay a loan denominated in Deutschmarks at any time during the next six months. If the current rate of exchange is 2 Deutschmarks = 1 dollar, but this is expected to diminish progressively to 2.5 Deutschmarks = 1 dollar over the next six months, the company should repay the loan sooner rather than later.'

(Answers in Appendix E)

FURTHER READING

Lumby, S. and R. Jones (1999) *Investment Appraisal and Financial Decisions*, chapman & Hall, chapters 23–25.

McLaney, E.J. (2000) *Business Finance: Theory and Practice*, Prentice Hall, chapter 15.

Pike, R. and B. Neale (2003) *Corporate Finance and Investment*, Prentice Hall, chapters 8 and 17.

Samuels, R., F. Wilkes and R. Brayshaw (1999) *Management of Company Finance*, Chapman & Hall, chapters 21 and 26.

Compound sum of £1 (CVIF)

Period	1%	2%	3%	4%	5%	6%	7%
1	1.010	1.020	1.030	1.040	1.050	1.060	1.070
2	1.020	1.040	1.061	1.082	1.102	1.124	1.145
3	1.030	1.061	1.093	1.125	1.158	1.191	1.225
4	1.041	1.082	1.126	1.170	1.216	1.262	1.311
5	1.051	1.104	1.159	1.217	1.276	1.338	1.403
6	1.062	1.126	1.194	1.265	1.340	1.419	1.501
7	1.072	1.149	1.230	1.316	1.407	1.504	1.606
8	1.083	1.172	1.267	1.369	1.477	1.594	1.718
9	1.094	1.195	1.305	1.423	1.551	1.689	1.838
10	1.105	1.219	1.344	1.480	1.629	1.791	1.967
11	1.116	1.243	1.384	1.539	1.710	1.898	2.105
12	1.127	1.268	1.426	1.601	1.796	2.012	2.252
13	1.138	1.294	1.469	1.665	1.886	2.133	2.410
14	1.149	1.319	1.513	1.732	1.980	2.261	2.579
15	1.161	1.346	1.558	1.801	2.079	2.397	2.759
16	1.173	1.373	1.605	1.873	2.183	2.540	2.952
17	1.184	1.400	1.653	1.948	2.292	2.693	3.159
18	1.196	1.428	1.702	2.026	2.407	2.854	3.380
19	1.208	1.457	1.754	2.107	2.527	3.026	3.617
20	1.220	1.486	1.806	2.191	2.653	3.207	3.870
25	1.282	1.641	2.094	2.666	3.386	4.292	5.427
30	1.348	1.811	2.427	3.243	4.322	5.743	7.612

Period	8%	9%	10%	12%	14%	15%	16%
1	1.080	1.090	1.100	1.120	1.140	1.150	1.160
2	1.166	1.186	1.210	1.254	1.300	1.322	1.346
3	1.260	1.295	1.331	1.405	1.482	1.521	1.561
4	1.360	1.412	1.464	1.574	1.689	1.749	1.811
5	1.469	1.539	1.611	1.762	1.925	2.011	2.100
6	1.587	1.677	1.772	1.974	2.195	2.313	2.436
7	1.714	1.828	1.949	2.211	2.502	2.660	2.826
8	1.851	1.993	2.144	2.476	2.853	3.059	3.278
9	1.999	2.172	2.358	2.773	3.252	3.518	3.803
10	2.159	2.367	2.594	3.106	3.707	4.046	4.411
11	2.332	2.580	2.853	3.479	4.226	4.652	5.117
12	2.518	2.813	3.138	3.896	4.818	5.350	5.926
13	2.720	3.066	3.452	4.363	5.492	6.153	6.886
14	2.937	3.342	3.797	4.887	6.261	7.076	7.988
15	3.172	3.642	4.177	5.474	7.138	8.137	9.266
16	3.426	3.970	4.595	6.130	8.137	9.358	10.748
17	3.700	4.328	5.054	6.866	9.276	10.761	12.468
18	3.996	4.717	5.560	7.690	10.575	12.375	14.463
19	4.316	5.142	6.116	8.613	12.056	14.232	16.777
20	4.661	5.604	6.728	9.646	13.743	16.367	19.461
25	6.848	8.623	10.835	17.000	26.462	32.919	40.874
30	10.063	13.268	17.449	29.960	50.950	66.212	85.850

Period	18%	20%	24%	28%	32%	36%
1	1.180	1.200	1.240	1.280	1.320	1.360
2	1.392	1.440	1.538	1.638	1.742	1.850
3	1.643	1.728	1.907	2.067	2.300	2.515
4	1.939	2.074	2.364	2.684	3.036	3.421
5	2.288	2.488	2.932	3.436	4.007	4.653
6	2.700	2.986	3.635	4.398	5.290	6.328
7	3.185	3.583	4.508	5.629	6.983	8.605
8	3.759	4.300	5.590	7.206	9.217	11.703
9	4.435	5.160	6.931	9.223	12.166	15.917
10	5.234	6.192	8.594	11.806	16.060	21.647
11	6.176	7.430	10.657	15.112	21.199	29.439
12	7.288	8.916	13.215	19.343	27.983	40.037
13	8.599	10.699	16.386	24.759	36.937	54.451
14	10.147	12.839	20.319	31.961	48.757	74.053
15	11.974	15.407	25.196	40.565	64.359	100.712
16	14.129	18.488	31.243	51.923	84.954	136.970
17	16.672	22.186	38.741	66.461	112.140	186.280
18	19.673	26.623	48.039	85.071	148.020	253.340
19	23.214	31.948	59.568	108.890	195.390	344.540
20	27.393	38.338	73.864	139.380	257.920	468.570
25	62.669	95.396	216.542	478.900	1033.600	2180.100
30	143.371	237.376	634.820	1645.500	4142.100	10143.000

B

Present value of £1 (PVIF)

n Year	5%	6%	7%	8%	9%	10%	11%	12%	13%
0	1.000	1.000	1.000	1.000	1.000	1.000	1.000	1.000	1.000
1	0.952	0.943	0.935	0.926	0.917	0.909	0.901	0.893	0.885
2	0.907	0.890	0.873	0.857	0.842	0.826	0.812	0.797	0.783
3	0.864	0.840	0.816	0.794	0.772	0.751	0.731	0.712	0.693
4	0.823	0.792	0.763	0.735	0.708	0.683	0.659	0.636	0.613
5	0.784	0.747	0.713	0.681	0.650	0.621	0.593	0.567	0.543
6	0.746	0.705	0.666	0.630	0.596	0.564	0.535	0.507	0.480
7	0.711	0.665	0.623	0.583	0.547	0.513	0.482	0.452	0.425
8	0.677	0.627	0.582	0.540	0.502	0.467	0.434	0.404	0.376
9	0.645	0.592	0.544	0.500	0.460	0.424	0.391	0.361	0.333
10	0.614	0.558	0.508	0.463	0.422	0.386	0.352	0.322	0.295
11	0.585	0.527	0.475	0.429	0.388	0.350	0.317	0.287	0.261
12	0.557	0.497	0.444	0.397	0.356	0.319	0.286	0.257	0.231
13	0.530	0.469	0.415	0.368	0.326	0.290	0.258	0.229	0.204
14	0.505	0.442	0.388	0.340	0.299	0.263	0.232	0.205	0.181
15	0.481	0.417	0.362	0.315	0.275	0.239	0.209	0.183	0.160
16	0.458	0.394	0.339	0.292	0.252	0.218	0.188	0.163	0.141
17	0.436	0.371	0.317	0.270	0.231	0.198	0.170	0.146	0.125
18	0.416	0.350	0.296	0.250	0.212	0.180	0.153	0.130	0.111
19	0.396	0.331	0.277	0.232	0.194	0.164	0.138	0.116	0.098
20	0.377	0.312	0.258	0.215	0.178	0.149	0.124	0.104	0.087
25	0.295	0.233	0.184	0.146	0.116	0.092	0.074	0.059	0.047
30	0.231	0.174	0.131	0.099	0.075	0.057	0.044	0.033	0.026
35	0.181	0.130	0.094	0.068	0.049	0.036	0.026	0.019	0.014
40	0.142	0.097	0.067	0.046	0.032	0.022	0.015	0.011	0.008
45	0.111	0.073	0.048	0.031	0.021	0.014	0.009	0.006	0.004
50	0.087	0.054	0.034	0.021	0.013	0.009	0.005	0.003	0.002

Note: The above present value factors are based on year-end interest calculations.

n Year	14%	15%	16%	17%	18%	19%	20%	21%	22%	23%
0	1.000	1.000	1.000	1.000	1.000	1.000	1.000	1.000	1.000	1.000
1	0.877	0.870	0.862	0.855	0.847	0.840	0.833	0.826	0.820	0.813
2	0.769	0.756	0.743	0.731	0.718	0.706	0.694	0.683	0.672	0.661
3	0.675	0.658	0.641	0.624	0.609	0.593	0.579	0.564	0.551	0.537
4	0.592	0.572	0.552	0.534	0.516	0.499	0.482	0.467	0.451	0.437
5	0.519	0.497	0.476	0.456	0.437	0.419	0.402	0.386	0.370	0.355
6	0.456	0.432	0.410	0.390	0.370	0.352	0.335	0.319	0.303	0.289
7	0.400	0.376	0.354	0.333	0.314	0.296	0.279	0.263	0.249	0.235
8	0.351	0.327	0.305	0.285	0.266	0.249	0.233	0.218	0.204	0.191
9	0.308	0.284	0.263	0.243	0.225	0.290	0.194	0.180	0.167	0.155
10	0.270	0.247	0.227	0.208	0.191	0.176	0.162	0.149	0.137	0.126
11	0.237	0.215	0.195	0.178	0.162	0.148	0.135	0.123	0.112	0.103
12	0.208	0.187	0.168	0.152	0.137	0.124	0.112	0.102	0.092	0.083
13	0.182	0.163	0.145	0.130	0.116	0.104	0.093	0.084	0.075	0.068
14	0.160	0.141	0.125	0.111	0.099	0.088	0.078	0.069	0.062	0.055
15	0.140	0.123	0.108	0.095	0.084	0.074	0.065	0.057	0.051	0.045
16	0.123	0.107	0.093	0.081	0.071	0.062	0.054	0.047	0.042	0.036
17	0.108	0.093	0.080	0.069	0.060	0.052	0.045	0.039	0.034	0.030
18	0.095	0.081	0.069	0.059	0.051	0.044	0.038	0.032	0.028	0.024
19	0.083	0.070	0.060	0.051	0.043	0.037	0.031	0.027	0.023	0.020
20	0.073	0.061	0.051	0.043	0.037	0.031	0.026	0.022	0.019	0.016
25	0.038	0.030	0.025	0.020	0.016	0.013	0.011	0.009	0.007	0.006
30	0.020	0.015	0.012	0.009	0.007	0.005	0.004	0.003	0.003	0.002
35	0.010	0.008	0.006	0.004	0.003	0.002	0.002	0.001	0.001	0.001
40	0.005	0.004	0.003	0.002	0.001	0.001	0.001	0.000	0.000	0.000
45	0.003	0.002	0.001	0.001	0.001	0.000	0.000	0.000	0.000	0.000
50	0.001	0.001	0.001	0.000	0.000	0.000	0.000	0.000	0.000	0.000

n Year	24%	25%	26%	27%	28%	29%	30%	35%	40%
0	1.000	1.000	1.000	1.000	1.000	1.000	1.000	1.000	1.000
1	0.807	0.800	0.794	0.787	0.781	0.775	0.769	0.741	0.714
2	0.650	0.640	0.630	0.620	0.610	0.601	0.592	0.549	0.510
3	0.524	0.512	0.500	0.488	0.477	0.466	0.455	0.406	0.364
4	0.423	0.410	0.397	0.384	0.373	0.361	0.350	0.301	0.260
5	0.341	0.328	0.315	0.303	0.291	0.280	0.269	0.223	0.186
6	0.275	0.262	0.250	0.238	0.227	0.217	0.207	0.165	0.133
7	0.222	0.210	0.198	0.188	0.178	0.168	0.159	0.122	0.095
8	0.179	0.168	0.157	0.148	0.139	0.130	0.123	0.091	0.068
9	0.144	0.134	0.125	0.116	0.108	0.101	0.094	0.067	0.048
10	0.116	0.107	0.009	0.092	0.085	0.078	0.073	0.050	0.035
11	0.094	0.086	0.079	0.072	0.066	0.061	0.056	0.037	0.025
12	0.076	0.069	0.062	0.057	0.052	0.047	0.043	0.027	0.018
13	0.061	0.055	0.050	0.045	0.040	0.037	0.033	0.020	0.013
14	0.049	0.044	0.039	0.035	0.032	0.028	0.025	0.015	0.009
15	0.040	0.035	0.031	0.028	0.025	0.022	0.020	0.011	0.006
16	0.032	0.028	0.025	0.022	0.019	0.017	0.015	0.008	0.005
17	0.026	0.023	0.020	0.017	0.015	0.013	0.012	0.006	0.003
18	0.021	0.018	0.016	0.014	0.012	0.010	0.009	0.005	0.002
19	0.017	0.014	0.012	0.011	0.009	0.008	0.007	0.003	0.002
20	0.014	0.012	0.010	0.008	0.007	0.006	0.005	0.002	0.001
25	0.005	0.004	0.003	0.003	0.002	0.002	0.001	0.001	0.000
30	0.002	0.001	0.001	0.001	0.001	0.000	0.000	0.000	0.000
35	0.001	0.000	0.000	0.000	0.000	0.000	0.000	0.000	0.000
40	0.000	0.000	0.000	0.000	0.000	0.000	0.000	0.000	0.000
45	0.000	0.000	0.000	0.000	0.000	0.000	0.000	0.000	0.000
50	0.000	0.000	0.000	0.000	0.000	0.000	0.000	0.000	0.000

Present value of an annuity of £1 (PVIF$_a$)

n Year	5%	6%	7%	8%	9%	10%	11%	12%	13%
1	0.952	0.943	0.935	0.926	0.917	0.909	0.901	0.893	0.885
2	1.859	1.833	1.808	1.783	1.759	1.736	1.713	1.690	1.668
3	2.723	2.673	2.624	2.577	2.531	2.487	2.444	2.402	2.361
4	3.546	3.465	3.387	3.312	3.240	3.170	3.102	3.037	2.974
5	4.329	4.212	4.100	3.993	3.890	3.791	3.696	3.605	3.517
6	5.076	4.917	4.767	4.623	4.486	4.355	4.231	4.111	3.998
7	5.786	5.582	5.389	5.206	5.033	4.868	4.712	4.564	4.423
8	6.463	6.210	5.971	5.747	5.535	5.335	5.146	4.968	4.799
9	7.108	6.802	6.515	6.247	5.995	5.759	5.537	5.328	5.132
10	7.722	7.360	7.024	6.710	6.418	6.145	5.889	5.650	5.426
11	8.306	7.887	7.499	7.139	6.805	6.495	6.207	5.938	5.687
12	8.863	8.384	7.943	7.536	7.161	6.814	6.492	6.194	5.918
13	9.394	8.853	8.358	7.904	7.487	7.103	6.750	6.424	6.122
14	9.899	9.295	8.745	8.244	7.786	7.367	6.982	6.628	6.302
15	10.380	9.712	9.108	8.559	8.061	7.606	7.191	6.811	6.462
16	10.838	10.106	9.447	8.851	8.313	7.824	7.379	6.974	6.604
17	11.274	10.477	9.763	9.122	8.544	8.022	7.549	7.120	6.729
18	11.690	10.828	10.059	9.372	8.756	8.201	7.702	7.250	6.840
19	12.085	11.158	10.336	9.604	8.950	8.365	7.839	7.366	6.938
20	12.462	11.470	10.594	9.818	9.129	8.514	7.963	7.469	7.025
25	14.094	12.783	11.654	10.675	9.823	9.077	8.422	7.843	7.330
30	15.372	13.765	12.409	11.258	10.274	9.427	8.694	8.055	7.496
35	16.374	14.498	12.948	11.655	10.567	9.644	8.855	8.176	7.586
40	17.159	15.046	13.332	11.925	10.757	9.779	8.951	8.244	7.634
45	17.774	15.456	13.606	12.108	10.811	9.863	9.008	8.283	7.661
50	18.256	15.762	13.801	12.234	10.962	9.915	9.042	8.305	7.675

Note: The above present value factors are based on year-end interest calculations.

n Year	14%	15%	16%	17%	18%	19%	20%	21%	22%	23%
1	0.877	0.870	0.862	0.855	0.847	0.840	0.833	0.826	0.820	0.813
2	1.647	1.626	1.605	1.585	1.566	1.546	1.528	1.510	1.492	1.474
3	2.322	2.283	2.246	2.210	2.174	2.140	2.106	2.074	2.042	2.011
4	2.914	2.855	2.798	2.743	2.690	2.639	2.589	2.540	2.494	2.448
5	3.433	3.352	3.274	3.199	3.127	3.058	2.991	2.926	2.864	2.804
6	3.889	3.784	3.685	3.589	3.498	3.410	3.326	3.245	3.167	3.092
7	4.288	4.160	4.039	3.992	3.812	3.706	3.605	3.508	3.416	3.327
8	4.639	4.487	4.344	4.207	4.078	3.954	3.837	3.726	3.619	3.518
9	4.946	4.772	4.607	4.451	4.303	4.163	4.031	3.905	3.786	3.673
10	5.216	5.019	4.833	4.659	4.494	4.339	4.192	4.054	3.923	3.799
11	5.453	5.234	5.029	4.836	4.656	4.486	4.327	4.177	4.035	3.902
12	5.660	5.421	5.197	4.988	4.793	4.610	4.439	4.278	4.127	3.985
13	5.842	5.583	5.342	5.118	4.910	4.715	4.533	4.362	4.203	4.053
14	6.002	5.724	5.468	5.229	5.008	4.802	4.611	4.432	4.265	4.108
15	6.142	5.847	5.575	5.324	5.092	4.876	4.675	4.490	4.315	4.153
16	6.265	5.954	5.669	5.405	5.162	4.938	4.730	4.536	4.357	4.190
17	6.373	6.047	5.749	5.475	5.222	4.990	4.775	4.576	4.391	4.219
18	6.467	6.128	5.818	5.534	5.273	5.033	4.812	4.608	4.419	4.243
19	6.550	6.198	5.877	5.584	5.316	5.070	4.844	4.635	4.442	4.263
20	6.623	6.259	5.929	5.628	5.353	5.101	4.870	4.657	4.460	4.279
25	6.873	6.464	6.097	5.766	5.467	5.195	4.948	4.721	4.514	4.323
30	7.003	6.566	6.177	5.829	5.517	5.235	4.979	4.746	4.534	4.339
35	7.070	6.617	6.215	5.858	5.539	5.251	4.992	4.756	4.541	4.345
40	7.105	6.642	6.234	5.871	5.548	5.258	4.997	4.760	4.544	4.347
45	7.123	6.654	6.242	5.877	5.552	5.261	4.999	4.761	4.545	4.347
50	7.133	6.661	6.246	5.880	5.554	5.262	5.000	4.762	4.545	4.348

n Year	24%	25%	26%	27%	28%	29%	30%	35%	40%
1	0.807	0.800	0.794	0.787	0.781	0.775	0.769	0.741	0.714
2	1.457	1.440	1.424	1.407	1.392	1.376	1.361	1.289	1.224
3	1.981	1.952	1.923	1.896	1.868	1.842	1.816	1.696	1.589
4	2.404	2.362	2.320	2.280	2.241	2.203	2.166	1.997	1.849
5	2.745	2.689	2.635	2.583	2.532	2.483	2.436	2.220	2.035
6	3.021	2.951	2.885	2.821	2.759	2.700	2.643	2.385	2.168
7	3.242	3.161	3.083	3.009	2.937	2.868	2.802	2.508	2.263
8	3.421	3.329	3.241	3.156	3.076	2.999	2.925	2.598	2.331
9	3.566	3.463	3.366	3.273	3.184	3.100	3.019	2.665	2.379
10	3.682	3.571	3.465	3.366	3.269	3.178	3.092	2.715	2.414
11	3.776	3.656	3.544	3.437	3.335	3.239	3.147	2.752	2.438
12	3.851	3.725	3.606	3.493	3.387	3.286	3.190	2.779	2.456
13	3.912	3.780	3.656	3.538	3.427	3.322	3.223	2.799	2.469
14	3.962	3.824	3.695	3.573	3.459	3.351	3.249	2.814	2.478
15	4.001	3.859	3.726	3.601	3.483	3.373	3.268	2.825	2.484
16	4.033	3.887	3.751	3.623	3.503	3.390	3.283	2.834	2.489
17	4.059	3.910	3.771	3.640	3.518	3.403	3.295	2.840	2.492
18	4.080	3.928	3.786	3.654	3.529	3.413	3.304	2.844	2.494
19	4.097	3.942	3.799	3.666	3.539	3.421	3.311	2.848	2.496
20	4.110	3.954	3.808	3.673	3.546	3.427	3.316	2.850	2.497
25	4.147	3.986	3.834	3.694	3.564	3.442	3.329	2.856	2.499
30	4.160	3.995	3.842	3.701	3.569	3.447	3.332	2.857	2.500
35	4.164	3.998	3.845	3.703	3.571	3.448	3.333	2.857	2.500
40	4.166	3.999	3.846	3.703	3.571	3.448	3.333	2.857	2.500
45	4.166	4.000	3.846	3.704	3.571	3.448	3.333	2.875	2.500
50	4.167	4.000	3.846	3.704	3.571	3.448	3.333	2.857	2.500

D Sum of an annuity of £1 for N periods (CVIF$_a$)

Period	1%	2%	3%	24%	5%	6%
1	1.000	1.000	1.000	1.000	1.000	1.000
2	2.010	2.020	2.030	2.040	2.050	2.060
3	3.030	3.060	3.091	3.122	3.152	3.184
4	4.060	4.122	4.184	4.246	4.310	4.375
5	5.101	5.204	5.309	5.416	5.526	5.637
6	6.152	6.308	6.468	6.633	6.802	6.975
7	7.214	7.434	7.662	7.898	8.142	8.394
8	8.286	8.583	8.892	9.214	9.549	9.897
9	9.369	9.755	10.159	10.583	11.027	11.491
10	10.462	10.950	11.464	12.006	12.578	13.181
11	11.567	12.169	12.808	13.486	14.207	14.972
12	12.683	13.412	14.192	15.026	15.917	16.870
13	13.809	14.680	15.618	16.627	17.713	18.882
14	14.947	15.974	17.086	18.292	19.599	21.051
15	16.097	17.293	18.599	20.024	21.579	23.276
16	17.258	18.639	20.157	21.825	23.657	25.673
17	18.430	20.012	21.762	23.698	25.840	28.213
18	19.615	21.412	23.414	25.645	28.132	30.906
19	20.811	22.841	25.117	27.671	30.539	33.760
20	22.019	24.297	26.870	29.778	33.066	36.786
25	28.243	32.030	36.459	41.646	47.727	54.865
30	34.785	40.568	47.575	56.805	66.439	79.058

Period	7%	8%	9%	10%	12%	14%
1	1.000	1.000	1.000	1.000	1.000	1.000
2	2.070	2.080	2.090	2.100	2.210	2.140
3	3.215	3.246	3.278	3.310	3.374	3.440
4	4.440	4.506	4.573	4.641	4.770	4.921
5	5.751	5.867	5.985	6.105	6.353	6.610
6	7.153	7.336	7.523	7.716	8.115	8.536
7	8.654	8.923	9.200	9.487	10.089	10.730
8	10.260	10.637	11.028	11.436	12.300	13.233
9	11.978	12.488	13.021	13.579	14.776	16.085
10	13.816	14.487	15.193	15.937	17.549	19.337
11	15.784	16.645	17.560	18.531	20.655	23.044
12	17.888	18.977	20.141	21.384	24.133	27.271
13	20.141	21.495	22.953	24.523	28.029	32.089
14	22.550	24.215	26.019	27.975	32.393	37.581
15	25.129	27.152	29.361	31.772	37.280	43.842
16	27.888	30.324	33.003	35.950	42.753	50.980
17	30.840	33.750	36.794	40.545	48.884	59.118
18	33.999	37.450	41.301	45.599	55.750	68.394
19	37.379	41.446	46.018	51.159	63.440	78.969
20	40.995	45.762	51.160	57.275	72.052	91.025
25	63.249	73.106	84.701	98.347	133.334	181.871
30	94.461	113.283	136.308	164.494	241.333	356.787

Period	16%	18%	20%	24%	28%	32%
1	1.000	1.000	1.000	1.000	1.000	1.000
2	2.160	2.180	2.200	2.240	2.280	2.320
3	3.506	3.572	3.640	3.778	3.918	4.062
4	5.066	5.215	5.368	5.684	6.016	6.392
5	6.877	7.154	7.442	8.048	8.700	9.398
6	8.977	9.442	9.930	10.980	12.136	13.406
7	11.414	12.142	12.916	14.615	16.534	18.696
8	14.240	15.327	16.499	19.123	22.163	25.678
9	17.518	19.086	20.799	24.712	29.369	34.895
10	21.321	23.521	25.959	31.643	38.592	47.062
11	25.733	28.755	32.150	40.238	50.399	63.122
12	30.850	34.931	39.580	50.985	65.510	84.320
13	36.786	42.219	48.497	64.110	84.853	112.303
14	43.672	50.818	59.196	80.496	109.612	149.240
15	51.660	60.965	72.035	100.815	141.303	197.997
16	60.925	72.939	87.442	126.011	181.870	262.360
17	71.673	87.068	105.931	157.253	233.790	347.310
18	84.141	103.740	128.117	195.994	300.250	459.450
19	98.603	123.414	154.740	244.033	385.320	607.470
20	115.380	146.628	186.688	303.601	494.210	802.860
25	249.214	342.603	471.981	898.092	1706.800	3226.80
30	530.312	790.948	1181.882	2640.916	5873.200	12941.00

Answers to questions

Chapter 1

Questions 1.1

1 **d** maximise the wealth of its owners – in the long term.

2 To provide the community with the most efficient swimming pool service, at lowest cost.

Questions 1.2

1 *F* – to provide additional finance.

2 *I* – will require the allocation of long-term funds.

4 *C* – to safeguard resources.

5 *F* – to provide additional finance.

6 *I* – to allocate finance to the purchase of an asset.

7 *C* – to control resources.

3, 8, 9 – none.

Questions 1.3

3 Assessing how much money is required, and the sources from which it can be obtained.

Questions 1.4

1 Sound investment and financing decisions are certainly prerequisites to attaining long-term objectives, but this is never the end of the story. Invested resources must live up to their promise or give way to more profitable use. In addition, good house-keeping should be practised regarding stock, debtors and cash.

2 Higher sales do not necessarily result in higher profit, if, for example, excessive costs exceed selling prices. Again, if additional investment is necessary to increase sales, then the additional profit should represent an adequate return on the additional investment, bearing in mind any additional risk attaching to the extra sales.

3 **i** *Investment decisions* – concerned with the efficient allocation of finance.
  b *Financing decisions* – relate to the acquisition of finance required to support planned investment.
  g Controlling the resources of the organisation – including monitoring investments to ensure that they continue to be as profitable as planned, and making sure that short-term assets such as cash, debtors and stock are effectively controlled.

Chapter 2

Questions 2.1

1 Let z = the sales to capital employed ratio. Then $0.12 \times z = 0.18$, therefore $z = 1.5$.

2 **i** incorrect; **ii** correct; **iii** correct; **iv** correct; **v** incorrect; **vi** incorrect; **vii** incorrect.

3 **a** A different mix of sales than planned.
  b Selling prices not raised in line with costs.
  c Incorrect stock valuation.
  d Inefficient buying, or production, leading to higher costs.

Questions 2.2

1 This would reduce the sales turnover ratio because of a higher than normal asset ratio. The deterioration would be corrected when the new plant 'comes on stream'.

2 A sales to capital employed measurement may hide deficiencies that would be revealed by examining the relationship between sales and each asset category. Some assets may have performed well, others badly.

Questions 2.3

1 Banks in particular have traditionally favoured a '2 to 1' ratio. They consider that gives them adequate security against default in repayment of debts owing to them.

2 In the case of a retailer, where stock is turned into cash within a relatively short time after purchase of goods, the current ratio is probably as effective as the acid test in measuring liquidity.

3 Current ratio – 600:200 = 3:1
Acid test ratio – 475:200 = 2.4:1.
Stock turnover – 10000 ÷ 125 = 8 times.

Average debt collection period – (250 ÷ 1,500) × 365 = 61 days.

Average creditors' payment period – (200 ÷ 1,000) × 365 = 73 days.

The firm is extremely liquid, probably too much so; in which case it is not controlling its resources effectively.

Over-investment in stock and debtors will divert cash that is needed to pay suppliers; cash which will otherwise have to be borrowed from the bank.

Questions 2.4

1 The twin risks of overborrowing are – the *short-term* risk of not being able to pay interest due, and the *long-term* risk of not being able to repay the loan.

2 **d** Long-term debt related to net assets value.

   a Interest paid divided into profit before tax and interest.

Questions 2.5

1 Essentially, the bank would be concerned with the company's ability to service and repay a loan. *Liquidity* would be uppermost in its mind, and the current and acid test ratios, the average debt collection and creditors' payment periods would help its assessment. Present reliance upon *borrowed* capital is indicated by the total debt to total assets ratio; and because earnings are needed to generate liquidity, the bank would look for a reasonable profit to management's capital ratio.

   All JP's liquidity ratios compare unfavourably with the industry average, although profitability is better. Relatively high investment in all assets points to a condition known as 'overtrading', and the bank will have to consider the loan application with caution.

2 Suppliers take a similar view to that of banks, but are particularly interested in the average creditors' payment period, and total debt to total assets ratios – both worse than the average in the case of JP Tools. They might be wise to insist upon a credit period of no longer than the industry average.

3 All ratios should interest a prospective investor, but particularly profit to investor's capital. In this respect, the *market values* of its shares might be a better denominator to use than the balance sheet figures, as the latter will probably represent historic cost values.

   JP is bettering the industry average on shareholders' return, but future dividends may be at risk because of poor liquidity.

4 Long-term debt to net assets, total debt to total assets, and interest cover are the particular ratios of concern to prospective long-term lenders. Assets mortgaged to cover existing borrowing may leave little asset value as security for new loans. Interest cover is already low, so future profitability is crucial. Comparison with the industry average shows that JP is already borrowing excessively.

Chapter 3

Questions 3.1

1

	£
Loss profit	8,000
less Depreciation	5,000
Net profit	3,000
Average profit	1,000
Accounting rate of return:	
(1,000 ÷ 5,000) 100 =	20%

2　No, it would be the same, because *total* profit is the same.

3　It ignores the *timing* of cash flows.

Questions 3.2

1

Year	Project A £	Project B £
1	5,000	1,000
2	4,000	1,000
3	2,000	1,500
4	1,000	2,500
5	–	4,000
6	–	6,000
	12,000	16,000
less Depreciation	9,000	9,000

a	ARR		3,000/4	7,000/6
			= 750/9,000	= 1,166/9,000
			= 8.3%	= 12.9%
b	Payback		2 years	4.75 years
c	ARR		Project B	
	Payback		Project A	

d　ARR:　　*For:*　　(1) Takes into account *all* the profits of the project.
　　　　　　　　　　(2) Calculated in the same way as the *overall* company ROCE (see Chapter 2).
　　　　Against　(1) Ignores the *timing* of cash flows.
　　Payback:　*For:*　　(1) Calculated using the *cash flow* of the project.
　　　　　　　　　　(2) Emphasises *early* recovery of capital.
　　　　　　　　　　(3) Easy to understand.
　　　　Against　(1) Ignores cash flows *after* the recovery of capital.
　　　　　　　　　　(2) Ignores the *timing* of cash flows.
　　Both　　　　　Do not differentiate between large and small projects.

2 $PV_a = a \times PVIF_a$ (See Appendix C)

$$\therefore a = \frac{PV_a}{PVIF_a} = \frac{50,000}{4,623}$$

$$= \underline{£10,815}$$

3 $PV_a = a \times PVIF_a$ (See Appendix C)

$$\therefore PVIF_a = \frac{PV_a}{a} = \frac{5,000}{2,010} = 2.487$$

∴ Reading along the 3 year row (Appendix C) for the nearest to 2.487 = interest rate of 10%

4 (a) $St = a \times CVIF_a$ (see Appendix D)

$$\therefore a = \frac{St}{CVIFa} = \frac{3,000}{3.152} = \underline{£952}$$

(b) PV = A × PVIF (see Appendix B) = 3,000 × 0.864 = £2,592

Chapter 4

Question 4.1

	DCF Factor @ 15%	Cash flow A	Present value – A	Cash flow B	Present value – B
Year 0	1.000	−11.000	−11.000	−11.000	−11.000
Year 1	0.870	+1,000	+870	+6,000	+5,220
Year 2	0.756	+2,000	+1,512	+5,000	+3,780
Year 3	0.658	+3,000	+1,974	+3,000	+1,974
Year 4	0.572	+5,000	+2,860	+2,000	+1,144
Year 5	0.497	+6,000	+2,982	+1,000	+497
Net present values			−802		+1,615

Note: Year 0 is the beginning of year 1.

A has a *negative* NPV and is not acceptable; B has a *positive* NPV and is acceptable.

Questions 4.2

1 Yield rate – project A:

Year	Cash flow £	PV @ 15% DCF rates*	2nd trial DCF factors @ 10% rates	PV @ 10% DCF rates
0	−11,000	−11,000	1.000	−11,000
1	1,000	+870	0.909	+909
2	2,000	+1,512	0.826	+1.652
3	3,000	+1,974	0.751	+2,253
4	5,000	+2,860	0.683	+3,415
5	6,000	+2,982	0.621	+3,726
Net present value		−802	*Net present value*	+955

*See Question 4.1 (above) for present values at 15%.

By interpolation: $10\% + \left(\dfrac{955}{802 + 955} \times 5\% \right) = 12.7\%$

Yield rate – project B:

Year	Cash flow £	PV @ 15% DCF rates*	2nd trial DCF factors @ 28% rates	PV @ 28% DCF rates
0	−11,000	−11,000	1.000	−11,000
1	6,000	+5,220	0.781	+4,686
2	5,000	+3,780	0.610	+3.050
3	3,000	+1,974	0.477	+1,431
4	2,000	+1,144	0.373	+746
5	1,000	+497	0.291	+291
Net present value		+1,615	Net present value	−796

*See Question 4.1 (above) for present values at 15%.

By interpolation: $15\% + \left(\dfrac{1,615}{1,615 + 796} \times 13\% \right) = 23.7\%$

2 If A and B are considered separately, the yield rate method results in the same decisions as NPV; that is, A is not acceptable because its yield rate of 12.7% is below the required rate of return of 15%; whereas B would be approved because its rate of 23.7% is well above the required rate.

Question 4.3

a Machine A £23,129; machine B £25,230.
b Machine B, as it has a higher NPV.
c NPV, because it reveals that machine B adds more value to the firm than machine A, after paying interest at the appropriate rate, and recovering its capital cost.
d Yes, by calculating the yield rate on the incremental cash flows. This would merely confirm the accept/reject decision already made by using NPV.
e Yes, the NPVs of A and B would be £10,983 and £8,900, respectively, making A the better 'buy' now. The arithmetic of compounding causes B to have a higher NPV at all rates up to approximately 12.5%, after that A is superior under both methods.

Question 4.4

| | Net cash flows | | DCF | Present values | |
Year	2-year completion £	3-year completion £	factors @ 10% £	Two years £	Three years £
0	–50,000	–29,000	1.000	–50,000	–29,000
1	–55,000	–40,000	0.909	–49,995	–36,360
2	145,000	–40,000	0.826	119,770	–33,040
3		160,000	0.751		120,160
Net present values				19,775	21,760

The three-year completion date would be more profitable to Corax Construction, but only marginally so. Earlier recovery of capital costs, less uncertainty and, possibly, taxation advantages might sway the company in favour of the shorter life project.

Note: the yield rates are approximately 24% and 22%, respectively, which is the opposite of the NPV ranking. For reasons already discussed, however, this is not an acceptable method of appraising this mutually exclusive project.

Questions 4.5

1 At the end of two years, because the existing machine is less costly until then. After that, the replacement machine should be purchased for a four-year life.

2 a *B* would be chosen because it adds more value to the business after recovering its capital cost and paying 8% interest on the outstanding capital.

   b The *incremental* capital invested in *B* of £278 generates an incremental cash flow per annum of £44. The yield rate can be calculated by dividing the capital cost by the annual cost flow, i.e. 278 ÷ 44 = £6.32, and then looking along the ten-year row in Appendix B for the discount rate column that contains the nearest to that factor – in this case 9%.

3 Multiple yield rates can occur in a project that has *negative* cash flows later in its life, for example, if large costs are incurred in a year without offsetting revenues. In such a case the NPV method must be used.

4 c.

Chapter 5

Question 5.1

a *No.* Depreciation is merely an accounting method of spreading the prepaid cost of an asset over its estimated useful life.

b *Yes.* These are *incremental* cash flows – they happen because the project is accepted.

c *No.* This is a cost to which the firm is already committed, and it will not be affected by the project.

d *Yes.* These are *incremental* cash flows; but include only the *difference* between selling price and variable costs – *not* the full additional sales value.

e *No.* Unless the amount realised upon sale or trade-in of the old machine coincides with book value.

Question 5.2

	Year				
	0	1	2	3	NPV
Stock outlay	–10,000			9,000	
Shop rental		–500	–500	–500	
Other running costs		–3,000	–3,000	–3,000	
Net cash sales		7,000	8,000	9,000	
Net cash flow	–10,000	3,500	4,500	14,500	
DCF factors @ 18%	1.000	0.847	0.718	0.609	
Present value	–10,000	2,965	3,231	8,831	5,027

The substantial surplus NPV indicates that Paul Schofield should proceed with his venture as long as he has no better alternative in mind.

Note particularly that his stock outlay is substantially recovered by the end of the venture.

Questions 5.3

1 i *Increase* – Capital allowances effectively reduce asset costs and therefore increase net present value.

   ii *Increase* – 'Savings' implies that cash, which would otherwise flow out, does not do so.This is equivalent to an inflow.

   iii *Decrease* – Costs result in cash outflows, and therefore reduce net present value.

2 The statement is not correct. These tax adjustments *are* calculated on the related cash flows, capital or revenue, but are accounted for as cash inflows or outflows in the period in which they affect payment of tax to the Inland Revenue.

3 It would not be correct. The original cost and the salvage value occur in different years, and should be dealt with accordingly. In addition, the cost of the kiln would attract tax capital allowances at (say) 52%, to be treated as a cash *inflow* of £26,000 in year 2. Likewise, its sales value of £5,000 would be taxed and treated as a cash *outflow* of £2,600 in the year following its sale.

4 The cash flow relating to the capital allowance of £26,000 would be delayed until year 5, and then take effect if the whole amount could be absorbed by the *assessable profit* for that year. Any unrelieved balance of capital allowances can be carried forward. The time value of the capital allowance is, of course, reduced by its delayed set-off against profit.

Questions 5.4

1 a Real rate of return = ((1 + money rate) ÷ (1 + inflation rate)) – 1
          = (1.19 ÷ 1.12) – 1 = 6.3%
  b 1 + money rate = (1 + real rate) (1 + inflation rate)
       1 + money rate = (1.04 × 1.10)
                  money rate = (1.04 × 1.10)
                  money rate = 14.4%.

2 The statement is not correct, because the required rate of return includes an estimated weighted element for inflation. Likewise, the project cash flows should also be stated at actual *money* values, that is, adjusted for rising prices. All cash flows may not be adjusted by the same inflation factor.

3

	Year						
	0 £	1 £	2 £	3 £	4 £	5 £	6 £
Working 1							
Machinery	–90,000					6,381	
Software	–50,000						
Capital allowances:							
Machinery			45,000				–3,190
Software			5,000	5,000	5,000	5,000	5,000
Working capital	–20.000					25,535	
Capital cash flows	–160,000	–	50,000	5,000	5,000	36,906	1,810
Working 2							
Sales		160,000	170,000	180,000	190,000	200,000	
Costs		108,150	113,558	119,235	125,197	131,457	
Pre-tax cash flow		51,850	56,442	60,765	64,803	68,543	
less							
Corporation tax			25,925	28,221	30,382	32,401	34,272
Revenue cash flows		51,850	30,517	32,544	34,421	36,142	–34,272
Net cash flows	–160,000	51,850	80,517	37,544	39,421	73,048	–32,462
DCF factors @ 15%	1.000	0.870	0.756	0.658	0.572	0.497	0.432
Present values	–160,000	45,110	60,871	24,704	22,549	36,305	–14,024

Notes:
  1 As the NPV is £15,515 the project should go ahead.
  2 The sale value of the old machine, £10,000, reduces the cost of the new machine to £90,000.
  3 Working capital recovered has been adjusted for inflation.
  4 Cost in year 1 comprises variable £100,000; extra component cost £1,000; supervisory £2,000; plus 5% inflation added; thereafter costs are inflated by 5% in each year.

Chapter 6

Questions 6.1

1 £14,200.

2 b.

3 Number of σ that £16,000 is from the mean = (£16,000 – £8,000) ÷ 4,000 = 2σ. Figure 5.4 shows there to be 50 – 47.5% of values to the right of two standard deviations from the mean. Therefore, there is a 2.5% probability that NPV will be greater than £16,000.

Question 6.2

Sales volume – can be reduced by the number of units valued at £1 contributing, with total value of £689, i.e. 689 – % change: 6.89.
Selling price – can reduce to £2 minus (£689 ÷ 10,000) per unit = £1.9311 – % change: 3.4.
Variable cost – can increase to £1 +(689 ÷ 10,000) a unit = £1.0689 – % change: 6.9.
Fixed cost – can be increased by £689 – % change: 46.0.

Questions 6.3

1 *False.* Profitability begins after payback is achieved. However, payback could be used in assessing alternative projects that are equally profitable.

2 b, c, e, f.

Question 6.4

Such a policy could lead to the acceptance of *high-risk* proposals which might not be viable if a higher, risk-adjusted, discounting rate were used. Conversely, acceptable *low-risk* projects could be rejected if an average rate were used.

Questions 6.5

1 *Positively* – as the cash flows rise and fall together.

2 *False* – as the returns behave in opposite fashion, there will be portfolio risk reduction.

3 Systematic risk is the residual risk after diversification has eliminated operating or unsystematic risk. Investors will therefore expect a return related solely to systematic risk, and will price securities accordingly.

4 The beta of a security measures the sensitivity of a security's returns to those of the market portfolio.

Questions 6.6

1 Both promise an expected value of £5,000; but *B* has a lower utility value than *A*, because more satisfaction would be lost if £2,000 were realised than would be gained from £8,000.

2 $(0.5 \times £8,000) + (0.5 \times £2,000) = £5,000$.

3 It is the statistical measure of dispersion of probable outcomes around their expected (mean) value.

4 $(12,000 - 0) \div 6,000 = 2\sigma = 2.5\%$ probability of a negative return.

5 a 'If the values of any of the forecast variables of a proposed investment change, what difference would each of the changes make to the viability of the project?'

  b i By highlighting sensitive areas for closer examination *before* the investment decision is made.

  ii By spotlighting the factors requiring closest management control during the project implementation stage.

6

i	*ii*	*iii*
Cost of capital 10%	*Payback*	*Cost of capital 7%*
Year 1 4,000 × 0.909 = +3,636	3 years	Year 1 4,000 × 0.935 = +3,740
2 2,000 × 0.826 = +1,652		2 2,000 × 0.873 = +1,746
3 1,000 × 0.751 = +751		3 1,000 × 0.816 = +816
4 1,000 × 0.683 = +683		4 1,000 × 0.763 = +763
+6,722		+7,065
less Capital cost −7,000		−7,000
Net present value −278		*Net present value* +65

i At 10% the project would be rejected because of its negative NPV.

ii The payback period exceeds the maximum of two, therefore reject.

iii At 7% the project would be accepted because it results in a positive NPV.

7 a *Positive correlation* – *X* and *Y*, because changes in the returns of *X* are accompanied by exactly proportionate changes in *Y*.

  b *Negative correlation* – *X* and *Z*, and *Y* and *Z*, because when returns are high in *X* and *Y*, returns in *Z* are low; conversely, if returns are high for *Z*, they are low for *X* and *Y*.

  c Those that have negative correlation, i.e. *X* and *Z*, and *Y* and *Z*.

8 $RS = i + (RM - i)0.9 = 10 + (17 - 10)0.9 = 16.3\%$.

9 The expected return of a portfolio is the weighted average of the returns of the separate securities; portfolio risk is also a weighted average – of the betas of the constituent securities.

Chapter 7

Question 7.1

2, 3, 5, 6, 8.

Question 7.2

1 Capital cost.

2 Load capacity

3 Trade-in values of vehicles

4 Running costs per ton-mile.

5 Maintenance costs.

6 Taxation implications.

7 Estimated life.

8 Flexibility in use, e.g. articulated trailer capability.

9 Information on alternative replacement vehicles.

Questions 7.3

1 c.

2 Because projects cannot be broken down into fractions, the combinations of projects yielding the highest NPV within the capital constraint will not necessarily coincide with the ranking of NPV to capital invested.

Questions 7.4

Your list should include the following:

1 1 The four areas of risk sensitivity noted on the proposal form (Figure 7.2).
  2 Total market size, and the company share.
  3 Capital cost and residual values.
  4 Material, labour and overhead cost variances from standard.
  5 The actual rate of inflation.

2 1 a Sanctioning procedure are guidelines communicated, perhaps through the medium of a capital budgeting manual or software package.
    b Project proposals prepared and submitted on standard documentation.
    c Monitoring the installation of project facilities.
    d Post-audit.

3 b Industrial relations.
  e The budgetary control system.
  g The rate of inflation.

4 *False.* Alternative forecasts based upon different assumptions would point up the sensitive variables, to provide more informed decision-making information.

5 a Improved quality of future investment appraisal.
  b Improved management performance.
  c Early warning of projects not living up to their promise.
  d Strengths and weaknesses in investment appraisal brought to the surface.

Chapter 8

Questions 8.1

1 She will need premises and no doubt these will require decorating and to be tastefully furnished, equipment such as hair-dryers, and special chairs. Stocks of materials and an amount to cover operating expenses should her customers be granted credit.

2 There is a lengthy period between sowing time and receiving payment for harvested crops, during which time wages, operating and living costs have to be paid. Short-term bridging finance is required to cover this period.

Questions 8.2

(a) *Ken Sharpe – Cash forecast months 5–7*

Month		5	6	7
Receipts	A	18,000	24,000	24,000
Cost of sales		16,000	16,000	16,000
Operating expenses		2,000	2,000	2,000
Rent		100	100	100
Total payments	B	18,100	18,100	18,100
Surplus/(Deficit)	A – B	(100)	5,900	5,900
Opening balance		(42,000)	(42,100)	(36,200)
Closing balance		(42,100)	(36,200)	(30,300)

(b) £30,000 ÷ 5,900 = 6 months (approx.)

Questions 8.3

1 George has probably overlooked the operating expenditure he will incur before he receives any cash from customers. Although his suppliers will probably grant him credit, and this will offset some of his expenditure, there will still be a deficit to be financed caused by the time-lag in receiving payments from customers.

2

Long-term cash forecast – Fido Dogfood Ltd		£000
Net cash inflow from operating activities (see below)		25
Returns on investments and servicing of finance:		
Interest payable		(2)
Dividends payable		(1)
Taxation		(2)
Investing activities:		
Purchase of tangible fixed assets		(20)
Net cash flow before financing		–
Financing		
10% Medium-term bank loan		20
Increase in cash		20
Calculation of net cash flow from operating activities		
Increase in retained profit		7
add: Dividend	3	
Tax	3	
Interest	2	
		8
Net operating profit		15
add: Depreciation	12	
Increase in creditors	1	
less: Increase in debtors	(1)	
Increase in stock	(2)	10
Net cash flow from operating activities		25

Notes:

1 Interest *payable* next year (£2,000) is added back to arrive at operating cash flow, but is subsequently deducted as cost of servicing loan finance.

2 Dividend and tax *arising next year* added back in calculating net operating cash inflow. The dividend and tax *payable* next year relate to this year's liabilities.

3 Because 'public' implies that a plc can advertise *publicly* for subscriptions for new share issues it might make.

4 Bridging finance relieves a period of cash shortage. It is needed during a time when cash payments *temporarily* exceed cash receipts, for example, when a new product is launched, and up to the time when the first customers pay for their purchases.

5 A business needs stock of raw materials, work-in-progress, finished goods and debtors, *permanently*. They change into cash and then back into assets frequently, but a continuing business relies just as much on a permanent stock of current assets as it does on fixed assets.

6 c, d, f.

7 *Yes*, it would increase the capital required to £56,500.

8 i The time periods involved – yearly for the long-term forecast, normally monthly for the short-term.

ii The short-term forecast deals with *detailed* receipts and payments; the long-term with larger changes in funds caused by profit or loss in operating, and planned increases or decreases in assets and liabilities.

Chapter 9

Question 9.1

i Owners' funds: **b, c, f, g**.
ii Other sources: **a, d, e, h**.

Questions 9.2

1 A bank *loan* is usually for a fixed amount for a fixed period at a fixed rate of interest; whereas a bank *overdraft*, although having a top limit, may vary in amount from day to day as required by the borrower, and be subject to a variable rate of interest.

2 *No.* Factoring includes such a service if required, but invoice discounting relates solely to the provision of finance.

3 Convertible loan stock possesses all the features of loan stock, but has the additional advantage of giving the holder the option of converting the loan stock into other securities – usually ordinary shares – at a prescribed price, on or between specified dates.

4 *False.* Although it does apply to hire purchase when the last instalment on the hire purchase agreement has been paid. In leasing, the assets do not normally pass into the legal ownership of the lessee.

Questions 9.3

1 Because they accept short-term funds from their depositors, banks tend to keep their lending short, mainly in overdrafts and loans. About an eighth of their money is kept very liquid, however, to meet the possible needs of their depositors who can withdraw their money at short notice.

Insurance companies and pension funds receive a constant stream of premiums and contributions, respectively, but a substantial part of their obligations in respect to these receipts in long-term. Currently maturing insurance policies, insurance claims and pensions can easily be met out of current receipts, the balance being invested in long-term assets such as equity shares and property.

2 *Unit trust* funds are invested in a specified range of securities and the total fund is divided into units allocated to investors. Units can be purchased from, and sold to, the trust managers at any time. The fund is therefore 'open-ended'.

Investment trusts are limited companies which obtain their funds by issuing shares and loan stocks like other companies; and which invest in the stocks and shares of other companies. Trust shares are quoted on the Stock Exchange.

3 1 The ordinary share capital and retained earnings are owners' funds; the remainder has been supplied by other sources.

2 *Short-term*: bank overdraft, trade creditors, bills of exchange.
Medium-term: hire purchase, leasing, 10% loan (repayable 2000).
Long-term: 12% debentures, 14% mortgage loan, share capital and retained earnings.

3 Bank overdraft – a commercial bank.
Trade creditors – suppliers of materials and services.
Bill of exchange – a commercial bank, merchant bank or discount house.
Hire purchase – finance house, merchant bank or a subsidiary of a commercial bank.
Leasing – a specialist independent leasing company, a subsidiary of a commercial bank, merchant bank.
10% loan – commercial bank, merchant bank.
12% debentures – the public, an insurance company or pension fund, investment trust.
14% mortgage loan – insurance company or pension fund.
Share capital and retained earnings – private investors, unit trusts, investment trusts, venture capital provider, insurance company, pension fund.

4 a *Land and buildings* – a second mortgage could raise more funds if and when the property is released from its mortgage; it could also be sold and leased back.

b *Debtors* – could be sold to a factor or invoice discounting company, which may advance up to 80% of the debts offered.

Chapter 10

Questions 10.1

1 Customers who do not pay their accounts as agreed risk damaging their credit rating. Supplies may be cut off, and business brought to an end.

2 d A bill of exchange.

3 a Factoring debts does not affect cash discount allowed to customers who pay their debts promptly.

4 a

$$\text{Cost of taking extended credit: } \frac{2}{98} \times \frac{365}{30} = 24.8\% \text{ p.a.}$$

The amount made available under this option is

$$0.98 \times £52,500 = £51,450$$

Cost of financing:		

Amount made available: Amount sold   £70,000

                   less Fee 2%   1,400

                       75% ×   68,600 = £51,540

Costs: Service fee 2% × £70,000 =   1,400

     Interest 1% per month (12% p.a.)

         × £51,450   =   514

                                      1,914

less Administrative savings, etc.   840

                                  £1,074

$$\text{Finance cost} = \frac{1,074}{51,450} \times 12 \qquad = 25\% \text{ p.a.}$$

b The costs of obtaining the same amount of finance are approximately equal, and both are equally flexible should the full amount not be required; the decision will therefore have to be made on qualitative grounds.

Taking extended credit might affect the company's credit rating if suppliers consider that it has liquidity problems. Using factoring provides finance immediately, and handing sales ledger management over to the factor leaves Simon free to concentrate on production and marketing. In addition, better terms may be negotiated with suppliers. Factoring would thus appear to be more attractive than extending credit in this case.

Question 10.2

False. A medium-term loan is one made for a fixed period of between three and ten years, although its terms can usually be renegotiated during that time.

Questions 10.3

1 *False.* The term 'Eurocurrency' embraces *any currency* deposited with a bank outside the country of the currency's origin. Loans are therefore available in any currency on an international scale, though London dominates the market.

2 A Euronote evidences a medium-term loan of between five and ten years, whereas Eurobonds are issued for longer terms of between ten and fifteen years.

Question 10.4

The legal property in the asset does not pass to the hire purchaser until the final instalment is paid, therefore it cannot be pledged as security for another loan until after that time.

Question 10.5

a Borrow and Buy

Year	Loan £	Tax saving £	PV factor @ 6%	Present value £
0	−100,000		1.000	−100,000
1				
2		+12,500	0.890	+11,125
3		+9,375	0.840	+7,875
4		+7,031	0.792	+5,569
5		+5,273	0.747	+3,939
6		+15,821	0.705	+11,154
NPV cost of borrowing				−60,338

b Hire purchase

Year	Instalments £	Tax saving £	PV factor @ 6%	Present value £
0	−30,000		1.0000	−30,000
1–5	−22,000		4.2123	−92,671
2		+18,500	0.890	+16,466
3		+14,875	0.840	+12,495
4		+11,531	0.792	+9,133
5		+8,273	0.747	+6,180
6		+17,221	0.705	+12,141
NPV cost of hire purchase				−66,256

c Leasing

Year	Rental £	Tax saving £	PV factor @ 6%	Present value £
0	−23,000		1.000	−23,000
1–4	−23,000		3,465	−79,695
2–6		+11,500	3,974	+45,701
NPV cost of hire purchase				−56,994

The leasing alternative has the lowest present value cost, and is therefore preferred on this basis.

Chapter 11

Questions 11.1

1 Any four of these:
   1 Unknown business track record.
   2 Inexperience and lack of knowledge.
   3 High interest rates and lack of security.
   4 Fewer available sources of finance.
   5 Poor financial management
   6 Poor treatment received from large debtors.
   7 Uncertainties of management succession and solvency.

2 1 Designated inner city assistance.
   2 Regional Development Agency assistance.
   3 Regional Development Grants for development areas.
   4 Regional Selective Financial Assistance for all assisted areas.
   5 Enterprise zones.
   6 Regional investment and innovation grants.

Chapter 12

Questions 12.1

1 a A market price for the shares is established; shareholders find it easier to sell shares in a wider market.
   b Access to wider sources of finance; purchase of other companies is made easier by being able to offer shares instead of cash.

2 Because it is relatively easy to purchase the company's shares on the Stock Exchange.

3 Some control may be lost to new shareholders; the company's affairs are more closely scrutinised because more information about it is made public.

Questions 12.2

1 *False. Ordinary* share dividend is not fixed; it is dependent upon there being profit available after all prior rights are satisfied. However, preference share dividend is normally fixed.

2 *False.* Although this may be normally true, it is sometimes the right of preference shareholders to vote if their dividend is in arrears.

3 Preference share issues are now fewer because:
   a unlike interest, dividends cannot be deducted from profit for corporation tax purposes;
   b dividends can be passed over in years of poor profit;
   c inflation reduces the real value of dividends, and the preference capital value.

Questions 12.3

1 The Stock Exchange acts as the medium for new issues of securities, and is the official second-hand market for all industrial, commercial, government, foreign and corporation securities quoted in its daily official listings.

2 A *stockbroker* acts for investment clients, whereas Retail Service Providers (RSPs) are wholesale dealers in certain types of securities, dealing only with other dealers or brokers. When brokers wish to buy or sell shares for a client, they approach the appropriate RSPs who trade in that type of share.

3 The *lower* price is that at which the dealer will *buy*, and the *higher*, that at which s/he will *sell*. The broker does not inform the dealer whether s/he is a buyer or a seller until after s/he be aware of the price 'spread'.

4 *False*. An introduction is a means whereby a large, public company, whose shares are already fairly widely held, obtains a Stock Exchange listing, to improve the marketability of its shares but not to issue further shares.

5 **c** an offer for sale by tender.

6 **a** The Stock Exchange listing agreement must be signed by all companies wishing to obtain a quotation for their shares. It prescribes the information that listed companies are obliged to disclose to the Stock Exchange and to the public.

  b A prospectus is issued by a company to inform and persuade the public to invest in its shares. It specifies the purposes for which the capital to be raised is required, reports on the company's past profit record, discloses the current financial position of the company and its future prospects. Its contents have to comply with the requirements of the Companies Acts and Stock Exchange regulations.

7 *Untrue*. Some preference shares are redeemable, on specified terms; otherwise they do have the characteristics of straight preference shares.

8 **c** Issuing house.

9 AIM (the Alternative Investment Market) is the securities market operated by the Stock Exchange for relatively small companies who do not yet satisfy the conditions for a full quotation.

Chapter 13

Question 13.1

a Theoretical *ex rights* price = $((3 \times £2.80) + £2.00) \div 4 = 10.40 \div 4 = £2.60$.
b Value of the right in each share = $£2.80 - 2.60 = 20$ pence.
c Nil paid value of a right to take up a further share = $£2.60 - 2.00 = 60$ pence.

Question 13.2

a General economic stability and growth.
b Growth in the particular industry.

c Stable and growing, company turnover and profit.

d Current *low* interest rates.

e Forecasts of future high inflation rates, and thus higher interest rates.

f Share prices currently depressed – making debt capital cheaper.

g If the current gearing ratio of a company is low.

h Substantial mortgageable assets available – not already charged.

i The need to convert a present high volume of short-term borrowing into more permanent capital, to avoid the risk to liquidity of having to repay loans at short notice.

j A high corporation tax liability against which to charge debt interest.

k Recognition that borrowing within limits can reduce the cost of capital.

l The desire of existing shareholders to retain control of their company will encourage them to borrow rather than make a public issue of shares.

m Costs of obtaining debt capital are less than for shares.

Questions 13.3

1 a £400,000 ÷ £2 = 200,000 rights shares.

  b ((5 × £2.60) + £2.00) ÷ 6 = £2.50.

  c £2.60 – £2.50 = 10 pence.

  d £2.30 – £2.00 = 30 pence.

  e The rights value is less than its theoretical level mainly because investors consider that the new capital will not yield as high a return as the existing capital. Consequently EPS would be diluted, and dividends may fall. The fall in value could also be attributable to a general fall in share prices or an increase in the risk of the Phoenix Holidays operations.

2 a i Conversion ratio – as stated – 30 shares for each £100 convertible.

    ii Conversion price: £100 ÷ 30 = £3.33 (approx).

    iii Conversion value: 30 × £2.60 = £78.

    iv Conversion premium: £100 – 78 = £22 (or 22 ÷ 78 × 100 = 28%).

  b ▨ As a loan stock, a specific rate of interest is receivable.

    ▨ The risk of capital loss is lessened because of its 'floor' value as loan stock.

    ▨ It is marketable, and because of its equity connection, may sell at a premium over loan stock value.

    ▨ It enables investors to share in the growth of a company after conversion.

    ▨ The conversion right is optional, should the equity prove to be a disappointment.

3 *False.* Convertibles are simply *exchanged* for shares; only warrants require the payment of additional cash.

4 Interest is payable on loans, whereas rent is payable on leases. The rent is normally subject to periodic (about five-yearly) review, and will also vary with the site location and type of property. The interest on mortgage loans will vary according to the quality of the risk associated with the loan.

5

$$Do = \frac{8}{1.06} + \frac{8}{(1.06)^2} + \frac{8}{(1.06)^3} + \frac{100}{(1.06)^3}$$

$$= (8 \times 2.673) + (100 \times 0.840)$$

$$= 21.38 + 84.00$$

$$Do = £105.38$$

Chapter 14

Questions 14.1

1 Long-term debt/net assets: Aqua 20,000 ÷ 220,000 = 1:11 or 9%;
Foam 80,000 ÷ 220,000 = 1:2.75 or 36%.

Interest cover:　　　　　　Aqua 40,000 ÷ 2,000 = 20 times;
Foam 40,000 ÷ 8,000 = 5 times.

2 Foam is the more highly geared because it has more debt to equity capital than Aqua.

3 and **4**

	A	F	A	F	A	F
EBIT	40,000	40,000	120,000	120,000	10,000	10,000
Interest	2,000	8,000	2,000	8,000	2,000	8,000
	38,000	32,000	118,000	112,000	8,000	2,000
less Tax 50%	19,000	16,000	59,000	56,000	4,000	1,000
Shareholders earnings	19,000	16,000	59,000	56,000	4,000	1,000
Numbers of shares	200,000	100,000	200,000	100,000	200,000	100,000
EPS (pence)	9.5	16	29.5	56	2	1

Note that the highly geared Foam produces a better EPS in good profit conditions, but does badly when profits slump.

5

$$\frac{(X - I)(1 - T)}{225,000} = \frac{(X - I)(1 - T)}{200,000}$$

$$\frac{(X - 2,000)}{225,000} = \frac{(X - 7,000)}{200,000}$$

$$200,000X - 400,000,000 = 225,000X - £1,575,000,000$$
$$25,000X = 1,175,000,000$$
$$X = 47,000$$

6 Estimate the prospects for future levels of EBIT being substantially above the indifference point.

Questions 14.2

1 *Benefits of flexibility*:

    ■ cheaper borrowing costs because short-term interest rates are generally lower than long-term, and only the amount of capital required from time to time will be borrowed; even though finance is required for permanent assets, borrowing short-term is more sensible whilst interest rates are falling rapidly.

    Risks of flexibility:

    ■ short-term loans may be called in and perhaps not renewed;

    ■ short-term rates are more volatile than long-term, making cash planning more difficult.

2 *False*. Small firms have more difficulty in obtaining finance than large firms, mainly because of their lack of proven business record, and inexperience of their managers and the operating risks connected with small businesses.

3 If the only place to obtain more capital is the *share* issue market, then some control will have to be sacrificed. This can be obviated by borrowing, as long as this does not increase financial risk inordinately.

Question 14.3

a *Ratios*

Current	98/58	= 1.69:1
Acid test	40/58	= 0.69:1
Stock turnover	240/58	= 4.14 times
Debtors	40/240 × 365	= 61 days
Gearing	70/196	= 0.36:1

The bank would be happier if the current ratio were nearer to 2:1, and the acid test at less than 1:1 could be potentially dangerous for a young, fast-growing business. However, taxation is probably not payable until October next, by which time cash flows resulting from growth should alleviate the liquidity problem (see cash forecast below).

Stock turnover at 4.14 times and debtors outstanding of 61 days' sales compare unfavourably with the industry norms of six times and 45 days respectively. However, most of the over-investment will be absorbed by next year's business expansion.

Debtors ought to be (45/365) × £240,000 = £29,589; and stock £240,000 ÷ 6 = £40,000. The difference of £28,411 between these figures and those in the balance sheet can be released for investment.

Given the fast growth of Rainyday Garment Co., the gearing ratio of 0.36:1 is to be expected, and the existing term loan is adequately secured on property.

b A cash flow forecast for the coming year is shown below:

	£	£
Sales (£240,000 × 1⅓)		320,000
Cost of sales (54% × £320,000) (see Note 1, p. 318)		172,800
Funds generated by operations		147,200
Working capital:		
Debtors 45/365 × £320,000	39,452	
Stock £320,000 ÷ 6	53,333	
	92,785	
less: credit from suppliers 0.26* × 92,785	24,124	
	68,661	
less: current investment in stock, debtors,		
less: creditors	72,000	
Working capital released		3,339
		150,539
less: Taxation	20,000	
Dividend	10,000	
Loan repayment – bank	10,000	
Interest 12% × £70,000	8,400	48,400
Estimated increased in liquidity		102,139

*Percentage of debtors and stock as last year

While the estimated increase in liquidity appears adequate to cover the new £60,000 machine, cash would not be available immediately, and resources would be needed for future replacement of fixed assets and for further expansion.

The bank would probably extend their overdraft to accommodate any temporary loss of liquidity caused by increases in stocks and debtors, but might be unwilling to increase longer-term lending to Rainyday. In any case, it would be advisable to leave the bank facility in reserve in case of need. This would provide more *flexibility* in future financing.

Even if existing shareholders are willing to provide the additional finance (say 20,000 shares at £3 each), it would still appear to be to their advantage to negotiate a further loan on terms similar to the current one, as the EBIT analysis in Note 2 (p. 355) shows. Assuming a tax rate of 50%, EBIT above £117,200 increases their earnings per share with the loan option, and this level of earnings is shown to be attainable in the cash forecast.

A £60,000 term loan repayable over eight years, together with interest at 12% per annum, has therefore been arranged with a bank secured by a floating charge on all the company's assets. This *development* loan immediately worsens the gearing ratio, but the cash flow statement indicates that retained earnings will build-up fairly swiftly to correct that situation, and to provide a broader equity base for future borrowing. The modest dividend policy is evidence of the owner's intention to 'plough-back' the bulk of the earnings available to them.

Alternative arrangements, to lease the machinery or to factor debts could be acceptable but their *costs* would have to compare favourably with the term loan.

Note that Rainyday has reached the stage in its development when types and sources of finance become more *accessible,* although the owners will have to consider going public and giving up some control if growth continues at its present rate.

Note 1: Calculation of cost of sales percentage

£	£	£
Cost of sales last year		150,000
less: Depreciation	12,000	
Interest	9,600	21,600
		128,400
(128,400/240,000)	= 54% (approx.)	

Note 2: EBIT Analysis

Let X = indifference EBIT between loan and equity capital

Then:

<table>
<tr><td align="center">Loan option</td><td align="center">Share option</td></tr>
</table>

$$\frac{(X - \text{interest})\,(1 - \text{tax rate}) - \text{loan repayment}}{\text{No of shares}} = \frac{(X - \text{Interest})\,(1 - \text{tax rate}) - \text{loan repayment}}{\text{No of shares}}$$

$$\frac{(X - 15{,}600)\,(1 - 0.5) - 17{,}500}{60{,}000} = \frac{(X - 8{,}400)\,(1 - 0.5) - 10{,}000}{80{,}000}$$

$$\frac{0.5X - 7{,}800 - 17{,}500}{60{,}000} = \frac{0.5X - 4{,}200 - 10{,}000}{80{,}000}$$

$$8(0.5X - 25{,}300) = 6(0.5X - 14{,}200)$$

$$4X - 202{,}400 = 3X - 85{,}200$$

$$X = 117{,}200$$

Chapter 15

Questions 15.1

1 **c** the investor's cost of capital.

2 The rate of return obtainable on a comparable share of equal risk.

3 *True.* The addition of loan capital reduces the weighted average cost below the cost of equity capital.

4 **a** Loan providers will probably be paid interest out of the 9% yield because they have a prior right to be paid their interest. They will be highly sceptical of present company investment policy, however, of accepting projects below its weighted average cost of capital.

b Ordinary shareholders will only receive satisfactory dividends if investment returns are at least equal to the weighted average cost of capital; they will therefore not be satisfied if present company investment policy continues.

5 a

	Proportion %	Cost %	Weighted average
Shares	⅔	15	10
Loan	⅓	9	3
			13

b The MM view is that the cost of capital is not affected by the way a business is financed, therefore Jerome Ltd's cost of capital will remain at 14%.

Question 15.2

1 Cost of ordinary shares:

$$\frac{D_1}{V_0} + g = \frac{0.10(1.08)}{2.50} + 0.8 = 0.043 + 0.08 = 0.123 \text{ or } 12.3\%$$

Cost of debentures:

$$\frac{I(1-t)}{V_0} = \frac{10(1-0.5)}{90} = 5.5\%$$

Weighted average cost:

	Proportion	Cost %	Weighted cost %
Ordinary shares	⅔	12.3	8.2
Debentures	⅓	5.5	1.8
			10

2 1 *Cost of loan capital*

$$\frac{I(1-t) + (1/n)(V_n - V_0)}{\frac{1}{2}(V_n + V_0)} = \frac{10(1-0.50) + \frac{1}{5}(100 - 83^*)}{\frac{1}{2}(100 + 83)}$$

(*current price *less* accumulated interest)

$$= \frac{5 + 3.4}{91.5} = 9\% \text{ (approx)}.$$

Cost of equity capital

$$r = \frac{D_1}{V_0} + g$$

$$= \frac{10(1 + 0.10)}{220} + 0.10$$

$$= 15\%.$$

Weighted average cost:

	Market value	Proportion	Cost %	Weighted cost %
Ordinary shares	£1,760.00	0.78	15	11.70
Loan stock	498,000	0.22	9	1.98
				13.68
			approx.	14%

2 $RS = RF + (RM - RF)B = 8 + (11 - 8)\ 1.2 = 11.6\%.$

3 The weighted average cost of capital is used in investment appraisal as the minimum required rate of return. A project with a positive NPV, or yielding a return in excess of this rate is deemed to be acceptable. Application of the weighted average cost ensures that both shareholders' and lenders' costs of capital are satisfied.

4 If all the activities of a business are subject to similar risk, then the weighted average cost of capital is appropriate. However, if a company carries on a diversity of operations, with significantly differing risks, as in the case of a conglomerate, then it should apply differential rates of return, according to the risks of each activity. The capital asset pricing model shows us that the return on any asset comprises the risk-free rate plus a premium for risk. The appropriate rate of return to apply to each activity can therefore be approximated by using the return of a company in a similar risk activity.

Chapter 16

Questions 16.1

1 £1,500,000.

2 PE × EPS = 25 × 30 pence = £7.50.

3 (30 ÷ 750) × 100 = 4%.

4 a 2% × £7.50 = 15 pence.

   b EPS/DPS = 30/15 = 2.

5 *Yes.* It has a relatively high PE ratio, although this would have to be confirmed by comparison with other companies in the same industry. The low dividend yield and acceptable dividend cover may also indicate growth.

Questions 16.2

1 a

$$V_0 = \frac{D}{r} = \frac{£0.30}{0.10} = £3.00$$

b

$$V_0 = \frac{D_0(1 + g)}{r - g} = \frac{0.30(1.05)}{0.10 - 0.05} = £6.30$$

2 An efficient capital market is one in which stock prices reflect all publicly available information regarding individual companies and the economy at large, and which *immediately* adjusts to this information.

Question 16.3

Report on the valuation of Alton Engineers Ltd's ordinary shares

To: Director
From: Financial adviser

Overall considerations

1 Small machine tool shares are currently favoured by the market, therefore you should have no difficulty in disposing of your shares.

2 Some companies' articles of association set down a basis for the valuation of shares, but there is no such provision in your articles.

3 Potential investors will be looking for a good profit-to-capital-employed record; will expect the company to have adequate liquidity; and to have an acceptable level of gearing. In all these areas, your company appears to be quite sound.

Bases for valuation

1 Three methods of valuing your shares are illustrated below; implying that valuation is partly subjective and subject to negotiation and compromise between buyer and seller.

2 The bases used are:
  a *Net assets value* – not the most satisfactory method, as balance sheet values are usually stated at historic cost; and net value, particularly in regard to plant, machinery and stocks, is so much dependent upon the accounting valuation bases used by the business.
  b *Price/earnings ratio* – applied to future expected maintainable earnings. This is the basis upon which a person interested in securing a substantial holding of shares would depend, as he would be in a strong position to influence policy and therefore earnings.

c   *Dividend yield* – the basis more applicable to purchasers of small numbers of share, because they are not in a strong enough position to influence earnings. What decision a small investor makes, hangs upon whether he wants income or capital growth from his investment. If the former, a high yield would be expected; if the latter – low yield.

In each case, *asset backing* is important, but the investor looking for capital growth would also expect to see a relatively high *dividend cover*.

Assets valuation

The only information regarding *revaluation* is that concerned with land but further enquiries might reveal the existence of obsolescent machinery or stock, or debtors that may be of doubtful value. Subject to any such further adjustment, asset valuation is:

	£000
Total net assets	1,710
less Term loan	300
	1,410
add Revaluation of land	100
	1,510
Value per share: £1,510,000 ÷ 800,000 =	£1.89 (approx.)

Price/earnings valuation

Similar risk quoted companies have an average PE ratio of 11 but because Alton Engineers is a little-known private company, investors will probably give it a lower rating – perhaps by up to 25%.

Alton Engineers' *earnings per share* for the most recent year are £256,000 ÷ 800,000 = 32 pence. Assuming that this level of earnings will continue, and an appropriate PE ratio is 8, Alton's share value is 8 × 32 pence = £2.56.

Dividend yield valuation

Using the latest dividend paid, Alton Engineers' dividend per share is (101,000 ÷ 800,000) = 12.6 pence. Dividend cover is 256 ÷ 101 = 2.53.

Because Alton Engineers is not known to the financial market, and also because its dividend cover does not match up to its competitors', investors will look for a higher than average yield – say 7% – and its dividend yield valuation would then be 0.126 ÷ 0.07 = £1.80.

Conclusions

The earnings valuation is the highest, therefore, given that £2.56 reflects the future prospects of Alton, this should be the initial asking price for the share, with a 'floor' value of £1.80, the dividend yield valuation.

Chapter 17

Questions 17.1

1 *False*. The residual theory of dividends implies that companies should continue to use profit for reinvestment purposes, as long as the return earned on company projects exceeds its cost of capital. When investment needs are satisfied, the residue of profit can then be distributed as dividends.

2 **b** Modigliani and Miller contend that existing shareholders' wealth is unchanged whatever the choice of finance.

Question 17.2

a *Retained earnings*
Cost of selling shares to make dividends.
Capital gains tax on share sold to make dividends.

b *External finance*
High tax rates on dividends.
Share issue costs.

Questions 17.3

1 Investments financed with *borrowed* capital = ⅓ × £300,000 = £100,000, remaining £200,000 being financed out of retained earnings. Dividend that could be paid = £350,000 – £200,000 = £150,000.

2 **a, c, d, f.**

3 *Alpha* – £4,000: realised profit *less* accumulated realised losses.
Beta – £5,000: realised profit *less* accumulated realised losses – including those of a capital nature.
Gamma – nil: realised accumulated losses exceed realised gains. The revaluation of property is not a realisation (sale) of the property.

4 In the case of a scrip dividend, cash is not paid out by the company, but on a share repurchase, it is.

Chapter 18

Questions 18.1

1 Value of share £3. Exchange ratio 0.625.

2 *False*. The bidder's EPS will be diluted if the pre-merger earnings of the biddee were rated more highly than those of the bidder.

Question 18.2

a Cash, preference shares, loan stock.

b Cash, ordinary shares.

c Cash.

d Convertible loan stock.

Questions 18.3

1 a EPS: Delor – 375,000 ÷ 1,000,000 = 37.5 pence;
    Airpak – 115740 ÷ 450,000 = 25.72 pence.

   b DPS: Delor – 37.5 ÷ 3 = 12.5 pence;
    Airpak – 25.72 ÷ 2 = 12.86 pence.

   c Current Delor share price: 37.5 × 16 = £6.00.
    Value of Airpak share: 25.72 × 14 = £3.60.

   d Share exchange ratio: 3.60 ÷ 6.00 = 0.6 (i.e. 0.6 of a Delor share for each Airpak
    share). Number of Delor shares to be issued: 0.6 × 450,000 = 270,000.

   e

Combined merger earnings			EPS	
	981,480		*Before*	*After*
add 10%	98,148	Delor	37.50	42.50
	1,079,628	Airpak	25.72	25.50*
less tax (50%)	539,814	*0.6 × 42.50		
	539,814			
Number of shares	1,270,000			
EPS	42.50p			

   f Value of Delor share post-merger: 16 × 42.50 = £6.80.

   g Airpak share value: before merger – offer value = £3.60; before merger – asset
    value = £3.77. After merger – 0.6 × £6.80 = £4.08.

   h Delor dividend per share after merger = 42.50 ÷ 3 = 14.17 pence. Effective divi-
    dend per old Airpak share = 14.17 × 0.6 = 8.50 pence.

2 Airpak's shareholders have been offered £3.60 per share against their asset value of
   £3.77 (1,700,000 ÷ 450,000), and although this may not initially appear to be very
   attractive, much will depend upon the expected synergy of the merger. A slowing
   down in the growth prospects of Airpak may have caused the PE rating of 14.

   Further analysis reveals that whilst post-merger Delor EPS improves, that of Airpak
   deteriorates slightly, although this is compensated by a possible increase in share
   value – to £4.08 (see **1g** above). However, if the Delor dividend cover of 3 times is
   maintained, the Airpak dividend per share will effectively fall from 12.86p to 8.50p
   (see **1h** above). In view of this, it is doubtful whether the promise of an increased
   share value will tempt Airpak shareholders to accept the offer. Delor shareholders,
   being better off in every respect after a merger, would have approved the offer.

3 a A 2-for-5 share issue by Delor to Airpak would need $(2 \div 5) \times 450{,}000 = 180{,}000$ shares. At £6 per share this comprises £6 × 180,000 = £1,080,000 of the total consideration of £1,620,000 (£3.60 × 450,000). The balance of £540,000 will be satisfied by the issue of 11% convertible loan stock. Under this offer, the revised post-merger profit and loss account would appear as follows:

	£
Merged earnings – including 10% increase	1,079,628
less Interest on loan stock 11% of £540,000	59,400
	1,020,228
less Corporation tax (50%)	510,114
	510,114
Total shares after the merger	1,180,000
EPS	43.23p
Airpak share of post-merger dividend:	
(510,114 ÷ 3) × (180 ÷ 1,180)	= 25,939
Interest on loan after tax (30%): £59,400 × 0.7	= 41,580
Total net income of Airpak shareholders after merger	£67,518
Total net income of Airpak shareholders before merger:	
DPS × number of shares: 0.1286 × 450,000	= £57,870

b The issue of convertible loan stock as part of the consideration would considerably improve Airpak's shareholders' income as shown above, whilst their capital value would be little changed from the first offer, i.e.

$$\text{Share value} = 0.4323 \times 2/5 \times 16 = £2.76 \text{ (assuming PE of 16)}$$

$$\text{Loan stock per share}$$
$$= 540{,}000 \div 450{,}000 \qquad = \underline{\;1.20\;}$$
$$\underline{£3.96}\text{ (see \textbf{1g} above)}$$

The capital and revenue advantages ought to be sufficient to compensate for shareholders losing some part of their equity voting control – at least until the conversion date.

Given a compound growth rate of 10% during the next four years, shareholders' net income would be approximately £800,000 by the assumed conversion date. If the conversion price of each share is £7, then the stock would convert into 540,000 ÷ 7 = 77,143 shares; making 1,257,143 shares in issue at that time.

Earnings per share would then be 63.64 pence with a possible share price of 16 × 0.6364 = £10.18, showing considerable growth despite the additional capital gearing. If the Delor dividend cover of 3 times is maintained, the dividend income of Airpak four years hence would be (800,000 ÷ 3) × (257,143 ÷ 1,257,143) = £54,545. Although this is lower than their total income before the conversion date, the capital appreciation on their shares and continuing evidence of future growth, would probably make this second offer acceptable to them.

Chapter 19

Questions 19.1

1 a Current ratio 1:1   Stock days outstanding 49.
   Acid test 0.5:1   Creditors' days outstanding 36.
   Debtors' days outstanding 49.
   Cash as a % of current assets nil.
   Sales to capital employed 1.9:1.

   b The *trading* results of Base appear to be very satisfactory. Turnover has doubled over the two years, and the return on capital employed has increased from 10½% to 11¼%, largely as a result of a more effective use of capital evidenced by an improved sales to capital employed ratio. Stock, debtors and creditors appear to be well managed. Unfortunately this success has been bought at the risk of insolvency, as the current and acid test ratios testify.

   All current assets are financed by short-term capital and if the overdraft cannot be renewed, permanent current – and perhaps fixed – assets may have to be sold to repay the debt. The company could be *technically insolvent* if unable to meet current obligations. Base is *undercapitalised* (i.e. overtrading) because it is financing long-term assets with short-term finance.

2

	£
1 *Working 1*	
Closing stock of raw materials = (80 ÷ 365) × 130,031 =	£28,500
Working 2 Opening stock raw materials	20,000
add purchases	130,031
	150,031
less Closing stock of raw materials	28,500
Cost of sales	£121,531
Working 3 Gross profit	78,469
add Cost of sales	121,531
Sales	£200,000
Working 4 **Value of net current assets at the year end:**	
Stock of raw material (see working 1)	28,500
Stock of finished goods (45 ÷ 365) × 121,531	14,983
Debtors (60 ÷ 365) × 200,000	32,877
	76.360
less Creditors (40 ÷ 365) × 130,031	14,250
	£62,110
2 *Net current asset value should have been:*	
Stock of raw materials (65 ÷ 365) × 130,031	23,156
Stock of finished goods (35 ÷ 365) × 121,531	11,654
Debtors (50 ÷ 365) × 200,000	27,397
	62,207
less Creditors (50 ÷ 365) × 130,031	17,812
	£44,395

Chapter 20

Question 20.1

£

Currently interest is being lost on 25,000 (¼ × 100,000) for 3 weeks
25.000   for 2 weeks
25.000   for 1 week
6

Interest lost per 4-weekly period: £25,000 for 6 weeks @ 0.25%* per week = £375
Lost interest per annum £375 × 13 = £4,875
*Interest rate per week = 13 ÷ 52 = 0.25%.

Questions 20.2

1 This implies that management have to assess the degree of insolvency risk they are prepared to tolerate, and balance this against lower profitability resulting from paying interest on cash held.

2 a iii; b ii; c iv; d i.

Question 20.3

a

Cash forecast January to June			£000			
	Jan.	Feb.	Mar.	Apr.	May	Jun.
Sales receipts:						
75% end of 1st month	210	120	120	150	180	240
20% end of 2nd month	32	56	32	32	40	48
5% end of 3rd month	6	8	14	8	8	10
Grant						30
	248	184	166	190	228	328
Materials	48	60	72	96	108	96
Labour	64	64	80	96	128	144
Expenses	28	16	16	20	24	32
Capital expenditure			90			
Dividend				40		
	140	140	258	252	260	272
Net cash flow	108	44	(92)	(62)	(32)	56
Balance brought forward	30	138	182	90	28	(4)
Balance carried forward	138	182	90	28	(4)	52

b i Short-term investments could be employed to 'soak up' the surplus cash of £118 at the end of January, and a further amount added through February. Some withdrawal from investments would occur in March, but a balance of short-term investments could be held until mid-April.

ii If the capital payment of £90,000 could be deferred until later in the year, this would solve the expected liquidity problem in May; but failing that, the accountant should ensure that an overdraft facility is arranged and available should the worst occur in May.

Questions 20.4

1 a Daily banking of receipts; centralised banking; direct debit to current accounts; express clearance of cheques; collect large payments from customers; electronic funds transfer.

b There is an opportunity interest cost in delaying the banking of receipts.

2 a A cash forecast looks to the future, a profit and loss account reports on the past.

b All cash received and paid in a period is included in a cash forecast; a profit and loss account is prepared to measure *profit*, which embraces all revenue and expenditure relevant to a period, regardless of whether cash has been received or paid.

c Non-cash items such as depreciation are included in a profit and loss account.

3 a Investment interest lost, as well as opportunities for capital gains on investments.

b The difference between the necessary cost of borrowing to cover the cash shortfall and the investment interest earned. Also a possible loss of credit rating.

Chapter 21

Questions 21.1

1

Number of orders placed	1	2	4	5	8	10	25	50
Quantity ordered	10,000	5,000	2,500	2,000	1,250	1,000	400	200
Average stock	5,000	2,500	1,250	1,000	625	500	200	100
	£	£	£	£	£	£	£	£
Annual holding cost @ 8 pence per fitting	400	200	100	80	50	40	16	8
Annual order cost @ £4 per order	4	8	16	20	32	40	100	200
Total annual cost	404	208	116	100	82	80	116	208

The economic order quantity (EOQ) is 1,000 fittings, because at this level total holding and ordering cost is minimal.

You will observe that holding and ordering costs are equal at the EOQ point. Thus $(Q \div 2) \times H = (A \div Q) \times C$, and after cross-multiplying, $Q^2 H = 2AC$, and $Q^2 = (2AC) \div H$ and finally $Q = \sqrt{((2AC) \div H)}$, which is the well-known EOQ model.

2 $Q = \sqrt{((2 \times 10,000 \times 4) \div 0.08)} = \sqrt{(80,000 \div 0.08} = \sqrt{1,000,000} = 1,000$

Questions 21.2

1 a 150 units, i.e. when holding and out-of-stock costs are at a minium of £80 (£60 + £20).

b 550 units, i.e. re-order level of 400 calculated in the previous activity, plus 150 safety stock (see **a** above).

2 i b Stocks tend to follow the trend of sales.

ii a Too high a stock of low-shelf life products would lead to wastage.

iii b Additional safety stock will be needed to meet the uncertainty.

iv a Such a policy effectively transfers stock to customers.

v a 'Made to order' products are not carried in stock as finished goods.

3 a $Q = \sqrt{(2AC \div H)} = \sqrt{(2 \times 80,000 \times 3 \div 0.01)} = \sqrt{48,000,000} = 6,928$

b
$$\left(\frac{Q}{2} \times H\right) + \left(\frac{AC}{Q}\right) = \left(\frac{6,928 \times 0.01}{2}\right) + \left(\frac{80,000 \times 3}{6,928}\right)$$

$$= 34.64 \qquad + 34.64 \qquad = £69.28$$

c Total quantity discount – (additional holding cost – reduction in ordering cost).

Total quantity discount = 80,000 × £0.001 = 80.00

Additional holding cost $= \dfrac{15,000 - 6,928}{2} \times 0.01 = 40.36$

less

Reduction in ordering cost $= 34.64 - \left(\dfrac{80,000}{15,000} \times 3\right) = \underline{18.64} \quad \underline{21.72}$

Net saving from taking quantity discount: £58.28

Chapter 22

Question 22.1

An increase in sales caused by changing credit policy does not automatically add to profit. Such a change is justified only if the increased profit is greater than the consequent increased costs of carrying higher levels of debtors and stocks.

Question 22.2

b, c, e, f, h, i, k.

Question 22.3

False. Such information is restricted to that already obtainable from published accounts. Further reassurance might be necessary in the form of special agency reports, direct enquiries to the customer, and bank and trade references.

Question 22.4

1 a The customer's credit rating and the potential value of each customer's debts.
   b Custom in the industry, competition, customer's cash flow performance.

2

$$\left(\frac{2}{98} \times \frac{365}{23}\right) \times 100 = 32\%$$

Questions 22.5

1 Because payment of existing customers' debts is extended by one month, the whole invoiced value, i.e. including profit, is counted as increased investment, whereas the investment in new debtors takes account only of *variable* cost, i.e. the incremental outlay.

2 The cost of the next-best alternative use of the additional capital invested in debtors. This would normally be the company's marginal cost of capital, unless the additional debtors are to be permanently financed by bank overdraft or loan, when the cost of bank finance would apply.

3 Extension of the credit period delays the payment of debts, and the longer this delay the higher the bad debts. In addition, sales will be made to new, riskier, customers, a higher percentage of whom will probably default on their debts.

4 a decrease; b decrease; c increase; d decrease; e increase; f decrease.

Questions 22.6

1

	£	£
Reduction in bad debts (1%–0.5%) × £2 million		10,000
Reduction in opportunity cost of debtors:		
Investment now (45 ÷ 356) × £2 million	= 246,575	
Reduced investment (35 ÷ 365) × £2 million	= 191,781	
20% of	= 54,794	= 10,959
		20,959
less Marginal cost of debt collection	15,000	
Net benefit from increasing collection cost		**£5,959**

Therefore the additional expenditure is justified, and more especially so if future turnover is expected to increase.

2

			£
Increased contribution	10% × £300.000		= 30,000
less			
Increased bad debts	X 5% × £200,000	= 10,000	
	Y 10% × £100,000	= 10,000	20,000
Investment opportunity cost	$\dfrac{£300,000}{6} \times 0.12$		= 6,000
Increased costs			26,000
			£4,000

The surplus of £4,000 indicates that the new policy would be a viable proposition, but sensitivity analysis should first be applied to assess the risk of the proposal.

Chapter 23

Question 23.1

The use of *documentary letters of credit* enables an overseas buyer to arrange with his bank for a credit to be opened to a bank in the exporter's country in favour of the exporter. The latter will be paid by the bank using the credit, upon receipt of all the shipping documents and a bill of exchange.

Questions 23.2

1 The issue of guarantees; to be used by the exporter to obtain finance from his bank.

2 Exporters receive supplier credits; overseas buyers receive buyer credits.

Question 23.3

If the export invoice is priced in the buyer's currency, and the exporter simply waits for receipt of the currency and converts it into sterling at the then prevailing spot rate, he will be accepting the risk of loss.

Question 23.4

a $1.5510

b $1.5510 + 0.0030 = $1.5540.

c In this case the importer has to buy dollars at 1.5540 – the dealer's three-month forward selling rate, therefore his sterling cost would be: 40,000 ÷ 1,5540 = £25,740.

Questions 23.5

1 When business is conducted on 'open account'. The overseas buyer pays the exporter on short credit terms similar to those offered on the home market, and settles by cheque, bankers' draft, mail payment order or telegraphic transfer.

2 Factoring; leasing; bank overdrafts.

3 *False* – the exporter may also:

- borrow the invoiced amount of foreign currency at the date of shipment, and sell it spot for sterling, repaying the foreign currency loan when the invoiced proceeds are received;
- open a foreign currency account in which receipts and payments of the same currency can be offset;
- invoice the overseas customer in the home currency;
- accept a 'lead' or 'lagged' payment;
- buy an option to sell the expected currency at an agreed rate in the future.

4 a *False.* Such payments should be advanced, because the current relatively high exchange rate will yield more sterling now than when the rate falls in the future.

 b *False.* 1,000 Deutschmarks repaid now would cost $500, but $400 in six months' time. Repayment should therefore be delayed until the dollar is stronger against the Deutschmark.

Index